An Introduction to Engaged Buddhism

ALSO AVAILABLE FROM BLOOMSBURY

Buddhism in America, Scott A. Mitchell
Cultural Approaches to Studying Religion, edited by Sarah J. Bloesch and Meredith Minister
The Body in Religion, Yudit Kornberg Greenberg

An Introduction to Engaged Buddhism

PAUL FULLER

BLOOMSBURY ACADEMIC
LONDON · NEW YORK · OXFORD · NEW DELHI · SYDNEY

BLOOMSBURY ACADEMIC
Bloomsbury Publishing Plc
50 Bedford Square, London, WC1B 3DP, UK
1385 Broadway, New York, NY 10018, USA
29 Earlsfort Terrace, Dublin 2, Ireland

BLOOMSBURY, BLOOMSBURY ACADEMIC and the Diana logo are trademarks of
Bloomsbury Publishing Plc

First published in Great Britain 2022

A catalogue record for this book is available from the British Library.

Library of Congress Cataloging-in-Publication Data
Names: Fuller, Paul, 1968- author.
Title: An introduction to engaged Buddhism / Paul Fuller.
Description: New York: Bloomsbury Academic, 2021. | Includes bibliographical
references and index.
Identifiers: LCCN 2021006962 (print) | LCCN 2021006963 (ebook) | ISBN 9781350129061
(paperback) | ISBN 9781350129078 (hardback) | ISBN 9781350129092 (epub) |
ISBN 9781350129085 (pdf)
Subjects: LCSH: Buddhism–Social aspects.
Classification: LCC BQ270 .F85 2021 (print) | LCC BQ270 (ebook) | DDC 294.3/37–dc23
LC record available at https://lccn.loc.gov/2021006962
LC ebook record available at https://lccn.loc.gov/2021006963

ISBN: HB: 978-1-3501-2907-8
PB: 978-1-3501-2906-1
ePDF: 978-1-3501-2908-5
eBook: 978-1-3501-2909-2

Typeset by Deanta Global Publishing Services, Chennai, India
Printed and bound in Great Britain

To find out more about our authors and books visit www.bloomsbury.com and
sign up for our newsletters

For May Oo Lwin

Contents

Figures

Acknowledgements

I am very thankful for all the help over many years from friends, students and colleagues. Some have read through chapters, others have offered guidance and support. An amazing group of students have attended my lectures in the UK, Asia and Australia and listened as I worked out the ideas contained in this book. I am incredibly honoured to have spent time with you all.

A special mention for Ziggy, Haymun, Kyaw and Zaw. This book has followed us around for many years. It has greatly benefitted from the lack of attention you have all shown towards it. I could not have written a single sentence without all your love and support.

This book is dedicated to May Oo Lwin with profound love and gratitude.

A final thanks to all at Bloomsbury.

Abbreviations

A	Aṅguttara-nikāya
D	Dīgha-nikāya
DHP	Dhammapada
J	Jātaka
KHP	Khuddakapāṭha
KVU	Kathāvatthu
M	Majjhima-nikāya
MIL	Milindapañha
MMK	Mūlamadhyamakakārikā
NETT	Nettippakaraṇa
P	Pāli
PAṬIS	Paṭisambhidāmagga
PTS	Pāli Text Society
S	Saṃyutta-nikāya
SKT	Sanskrit
SN	Suttanipāta
VIN	Vinayapiṭaka

1

Introduction

Engaged Buddhism

Engaged Buddhism is a term used to describe a form of Buddhism that focuses on politics, society and the environment. In engaged Buddhism there is an emphasis upon both personal and social transformation. It is involved with a wide range of social and political issues that have arguably not formed the basis of Buddhist thinking in the past. It forms part of the Buddhist encounter with race, ethnicity and identity. It is also a Buddhist conversation with ideas about human rights, sexuality, gender and politics. It proposes that the causes of suffering are not only found within the mind but can also be found in society, in political oppression and in social inequality. A political ideology, an ecological strategy or an ethnic identity might enforce greed, hatred and delusion. Therefore, engaged Buddhist traditions strive to tackle these issues and alleviate suffering. One of the defining features of engaged Buddhism is that it addresses a wide range of social, political, economic and environmental issues.[1] The reason for this is where it locates suffering.

The idea of suffering is central to Buddhism. In one understanding of suffering, the causes are internal – that is, they are in the mind. Suffering is caused by craving things that can never bring satisfaction, because they are impermanent. In the second understanding, the causes of suffering can be found in the world – in a corrupt and uncaring government, in an oppressive political ideology, in a society that does not allow for individual sexual identity, in one that destroys the natural environment, or one that does not protect one's religious and cultural identity (Bodhi, 2009: 2). This book is concerned with describing the latter, but its ideas originate in the former.

Many studies of engaged Buddhism use the term as a moral category. Engaged Buddhism is based upon the ethically sound principles of Buddhism.

The term is applied to those Buddhist groups with a moral or ethical message. In describing engaged Buddhism this is often the case. Engaged Buddhists campaign against social inequality, racial discrimination, the climate crises and gender discrimination. They create strategies based upon Buddhist principles to fight addiction; they visit prisons to act as Buddhist chaplains; and they form grass roots organizations around Asia to help those orphaned and in need. They use Buddhist teachings in a constructive way, and engaged Buddhism means those Buddhist groups that we approve of. These are all essential aspects of engaged Buddhism.

However, I would like to briefly explain why I think we need to widen our understanding of precisely what constitutes engaged Buddhism. Buddhism usually follows a universal message which goes beyond local, cultural and sectarian ideas related to politics and identity. As I will describe, there are also local and ethnic expressions of Buddhism, and these can give rise to distinct expressions of engaged Buddhism. There can sometimes be a tendency in descriptions of Buddhism to reject Buddhist culture when it tends towards sectarianism, becomes violent and is chauvinistic. Although I argue that engaged Buddhism is primarily passive, I will not ignore more local and aggressive expressions of it.[2] I intend to use the category of engaged Buddhism to analyse Buddhist groups, movements and individuals who apply Buddhist ideas to tackle inequalities, problems, injustices, political and social structures in ways that might not meet with general approval. These are still Buddhists who are engaged Buddhists: they are using Buddhist ideas, doctrines, identities and methods to overcome suffering in the modern world.[3] I am therefore widening the vocabulary of engaged Buddhism to include Buddhist groups with a passive message and those based upon local ethnic identities.

In this book I will argue, as I have indicated, that engaged Buddhism is not necessarily liberal, progressive and non-violent. One of my key points is that in studying engaged Buddhism we are analysing the activities of Buddhist communities who are reacting to suffering in ways that they might not have done in the past. There are two reasons for this. Either the causes of suffering in the twenty-first century were not apparent in the ancient history of Buddhism, or, put quite simply, engaged Buddhists are interpreting Buddhist teachings in new and innovative ways. I accept scholarly critiques of engaged Buddhism – for example, Temprano (2013) and Lele (2019) offer valid and often brilliant critiques of engaged Buddhism. However, I also think that some Buddhists, at various points in history and in different geographical locations, have practised Buddhism in ways that I describe in this book.

This book is not intended to be a history of engaged Buddhism, exhaustive in discussing Buddhism from different cultures, schools or groups, or to offer case studies of engaged Buddhism (though I do occasionally discuss the latter). Rather, I am more concerned with furthering our understanding of engaged Buddhism by considering the theories and philosophies which form its basis. It is, then a theology of engaged Buddhism. More precisely one could term the approach a critical, constructive Buddhist theology. By this I mean that I am myself engaging with the material; my selections made of what I discuss are made, in part, because I think that they are important themes, ideas, conceptual categories, doctrines, and Buddhists who taught them. Different writers could and indeed would have chosen differently. I also want to make sense of engaged Buddhist movements and to offer a conceptual map of the field so that students can become familiar with the conceptual terrain and be enabled to also constructively engage with engaged Buddhism. I offer in this book some of the skills to become literate in the understanding of engaged Buddhism. Other books offer more case studies and history, and I have suggested these studies in the further reading section and in the extensive bibliography. In taking this critical and constructive approach I am instigating a conversation on which we can make different conclusions, but the debate – to be engaged in the debate and, in fact, to be able to do so – is the important thing.

In this book I am covering a large number of ideas. This has led me to a certain bias in my selection of material. It also means that I have emphasized locations where engaged Buddhism is practised. There could be much more debate on race and racism, which I clearly talk about from a particular perspective in Chapter 8, particularly related to Buddhist participation in Black Lives Matter. Material has been appearing throughout the summer of 2020 on both Buddhist responses to BLM and to Covid-19. The former will likely have a large body of material over the coming years, while early discussions of the latter can be found on Pierce Salguero's excellent Jivaka.net, which involves a number of exceptional scholars discussing Buddhist responses to the global pandemic.

The origins of the term 'engaged Buddhism'

The term 'engaged Buddhism' is usually attributed to the Vietnamese Buddhist monk Thich Nhat Hanh. It has become standard to suggest that he coined the term somewhere around 1963.[4] Its specific occurrence, however, is not clear.

The term appears to have first been used in a book, published in Vietnamese, called *Dao Phat Di Vao Cuoc Doi* (1964), which translates as 'Buddhism entering into society' or 'Buddhism entering into life'.[5] A list of Thich Nhat Hanh's books I have received from Plum Village (Thich Nhat Hanh's community is France) states that *Dao Phat Di Vao Cuoc Doi*[6] was published in 1964 by La Boi press (Nhat Hanh, 1964). The list states that the title of the book literally

FIGURE 1 *Thich Nhat Hanh and Martin Luther King Jr, 31 May 1966, Chicago Sheraton Hotel. Credit: Provenance unknown.*

means 'Buddhism entering into society', and that Thich Nhat Hanh translated this title as 'Engaged Buddhism'.

There is an English translation of *Dao Phat Di Vao Cuoc Doi* (or a version of it) made by Trinh Van Du dated 1965 called *Engaged Buddhism (with Other Essays)*. This would, of course, suggest that Trinh Van Du's English translation contains the first occurrence of the term engaged Buddhism. The following offers some context:

> The phrase engaged Buddhism itself is not satisfactory, because if we analyse it, we will have the feeling that Buddhism is something which is outside life and therefore we need to bring it into life. In reality, it is not so. Buddhism was born right in the lap of life, it has been nourished by it and restored by life. If Buddhism is present in life, is it necessary to bring it into life? [. . .]
>
> Therefore, to engage Buddhism into life means to realize Buddhist principles in life, by methods which are suitable to real situations of life to transform it into a good and beautiful one. Only when Buddhist energies are clearly seen in every form of life, can we be able to say that Buddhism is really present in life. (Nhat Hanh, 1965a: 2)[7]

In the translation Thich Nhat Hanh also speaks of rebuilding Buddhism, and applying Buddhist principles to spiritual, cultural, economic, artistic and social activities (Nhat Hanh, 1965a: 93).

The first occurrence of the English term 'engaged Buddhism' is in Trinh Van Du's translation, in the form of the title of the book and in its opening pages, published in 1965. However, it is not clear who Trinh Van Du is or was; it is also not known if he coined the term himself, or if it was done in collaboration with Thich Nhat Hanh, or if it was suggested by the latter. What is clear is that Thich Nhat Hanh has favoured the term 'engaged Buddhism' as a translation of *Dao Phat Di Vao Cuoc Doi* in the later years.[8]

A reasonable timeline for the occurrence of the term engaged Buddhism is the following:

- The concept of 'Buddhism entering into society' (*Dao Phat Di Vao Cuoc Doi*), which is the title of the Vietnamese book published in 1964;

- 'Engaged Buddhism' which is the translation of the book written by Trinh Van Du in 1965 that I have just been discussing;

- Thich Nhat Hanh uses the term engaged Buddhism in 1967 (Nhat Hanh, 1967: 52), which is the first time he uses the term in English. (Main and Lai, 2013: 16)

Thich Nhat Hanh spoke about the original Vietnamese book in a public talk in Vietnam in 2008. He first explains how he formulated the idea of engaged Buddhism in a series of ten articles in the 1950s, giving them the title 'A Fresh Look at Buddhism'. He states that the idea of engaged Buddhism originated in 1954: 'It is in this series of ten articles that I proposed the idea of Engaged Buddhism—Buddhism in the realm of education, economics, politics, and so on. So Engaged Buddhism dates from 1954' (Nhat Hanh, 2008a: 30) He describes how, after lecturing in Buddhist studies at Columbia University in 1963–4, he returned home to Vietnam:

> So I went home. I founded the Van Hanh University, and I published a book called *Engaged Buddhism*, a collection of my articles I had written before. [. . .] This is the beginning of 1964. I had written these articles before that, but I put them together and published under the title *Engaged Buddhism*, or *Dao society. Di vao cuoc doi. Cuoc doi* here is 'life' or 'society'. *Di vao* means 'to enter'. So these were the words that were used for Engaged Buddhism in Vietnam: *di vao cuoc doi*, 'entering into life, social life'. (Nhat Hanh, 2008a: 30–1)

The term is also explained by Thich Nhat Hanh:

> In Vietnamese we use the phrase *Đạo phật đi vào cuộc đời* [*Dao Phat Di Vao Cuoc Doi*] literally meaning Buddhism entering into life, entering into society. We have translated that term into English as 'engaged' giving the phrase 'Engaged Buddhism'. (Parallax Press, 2019: 297)

The term translated as engaged Buddhism originally had the meaning of Buddhism being involved in life. I would like to take this as the starting point to describe two understandings of engaged Buddhism. First, there is the accepted or prevailing use that engaged Buddhism is a form of Buddhist activism which uses Buddhist ideas to tackle contemporary problems. Often, in this use, there is an assumption about engaged Buddhism, which is that it promotes ethically sound principles. To classify a Buddhist movement as engaged is then to suggest that it is in line with the moral norms of modern Western culture. The second understanding is that engaged Buddhism can be a compassionate or divisive influence in society, politics and culture. If we allow for the second meaning, as is suggested by the term, 'Buddhism entering into life' then it simply means Buddhism that is involved in society, and the concept loses some of its prevailing meaning of being an overt form of Buddhist activism.

The term socially engaged Buddhism is often given as an alternative to engaged Buddhism (Henry, 2013; King, 2009; Main and Lai, 2013; Ladwig, 2006; Pistono, 2019; Tsomo, 2009). Engaged Buddhism is a type of Buddhism which is socially engaged. Buddhism can be involved in the world, can be engaged Buddhism, in compassionate and divisive ways. This is Buddhism in life. This is the Buddhism of engagement with social and political issues. Engaged Buddhism in this sense can get messy, because it is involved, because it is a Buddhism which has a social, political, ecological and even an ethnic voice. It can tackle issues of identity, whether national or sexual, and can lend its voice to support liberal and conservative political agendas. Engaged Buddhists can be on the wrong side of history, supporting genocidal regimes, or standing in the way of social progress.

The primary focus of engaged Buddhist movements is that they understand social action as a primary feature of religious practice. To put this more directly, social action constitutes religious practice for engaged Buddhism (Main and Lai, 2013: 17–18). Engaged Buddhism can be political, nationalistic, socialist, sectarian, local and cultural. It can be used as a vehicle to promote the ideas of particular ethnic groups. Engaged Buddhists can support blasphemy laws and political institutions that are racist, and be part of violent uprisings. This understanding of engaged Buddhism allows for a larger debate about how modern Buddhists, ethnic Buddhists, white Buddhists, Asian Buddhists, gay Buddhists, queer Buddhists, trans-Buddhists, straight Buddhists, genocidal Buddhists, racist Buddhists and Buddhists fighting racism, eco-Buddhists, new-age Buddhists, punk Buddhists, Buddhist politicians, Buddhists fighting addictions, Buddhist monks and Buddhist nuns – in fact, anyone professing Buddhist identities – interact with society. This is the engaged Buddhism described in this book.

There is one more important factor which I take as fundamental to engaged Buddhism. This is that engaged Buddhism, like all forms of Buddhism, takes suffering as its starting point. In the opening discourse of the Buddha suffering (*dukkha*) is described:

> This is the noble truth of suffering: birth is suffering, aging is suffering, illness is suffering, death is suffering; union with what is displeasing is suffering; separation from what is pleasing is suffering; not to get what one wants is suffering . . . . (S V 421)

Buddhism is in many ways a dialogue about suffering. Its description of suffering, from the textual traditions to the present day, has been central. Because suffering has been explained as originating in the mind, solitary and introspective meditation has been central.[9] However, if we accept that Buddhist teachings are valid and given authenticity when they tackle suffering, such as the forms of suffering caused by the modern ecological crises, by religious diversity, by racism, by political oppression and by sexual identity, then engaged Buddhism is simply a form of Buddhism with a wider discourse about suffering, the causes of suffering and the origins of suffering, and with overcoming and eradicating suffering. Engaged Buddhism is a Buddhist path to eradicate suffering. This is the approach to engaged Buddhism taken in this book.

Engaged Buddhist movements

The great Indian ruler Aśoka (ruled: 268–232 BCE), often referred to as Emperor Aśoka, is regarded as an early example of engaged Buddhism due to his efforts to improve the welfare of his subjects (Queen, 2013: 527). The towering figure of Śāntideva (685–763), an Indian Buddhist monk, also looms large in the history of engaged Buddhism, reflecting ways that engaged Buddhism is configured from the earlier Buddhist traditions. His 'Guide to Bodhisattva Practice' (*Bodhicaryāvatāra*) is taken by engaged Buddhists to be a precursor of some of its themes (Clayton, 2018). Other figures in Asian Buddhist history like the Japanese reformers Hōnen (1133–1212 CE), Shinran (1173–1263), Dōgen (1200–53) and Nichiren (1222–82) are often mentioned as precursors of engaged Buddhism. These figures are used to suggest that Buddhism has historically had a social and political message (Queen, 1996: 40–1; Henry, 2013: 2). In the twentieth century, aside from Thich Nhat Hanh, other notable figures that have formed part of the engaged Buddhist movement include Bhimrao Ramji Ambedkar (1891–1956), whose conversion to Buddhism led to the conversion of Indian Dalits or outcastes (Queen, 1996a; Rinker, 2018), Buddhadasa (1906–93. Santikaro, 1996; Jackson,

2003) and A. T. Ariyaratne and his Sarvodaya Shramadana movement (Bond, 1996). In Thailand, Sulak Sivaraksa, who founded the International Network of Engaged Buddhists in 1989, is at the forefront of engaged Buddhism (Pistono, 2019). They produce a tri-yearly journal, *Seeds of Peace*. Their focus includes peacebuilding and reconciliation, human rights and social justice, gender and women's empowerment, Buddhist economics, environment and climate change, reform and revival of Buddhist institutions and interfaith dialogue and collaboration.[10] In 2020 they formed a Covid-19 relief fund under the heading of mindful action. This was to relieve the suffering caused by the Coronavirus in South and Southeast Asia.[11]

There are a number of engaged Buddhist groups in Taiwan following Humanistic Buddhism (*rénjiān fójiào*). They focus on this life, rather than the next life – that is, they focus on the human rather than the supernatural elements of Buddhism. These groups follow the principles of Buddhism in life. They often emphasize social welfare and seek to improve the lives of the laity. These groups include the Buddhist Compassion Merit Society (Tzu Chi. Yao, 2012), Dharma Drum Mountain (Fagushan; Schak and Hsin-Huang, 2005) and Buddha Light Mountain (Fo Guang Shan; see Hsin Yun, 2016).[12]

There are also Nichiren inspired groups of Japan. Nichiren was a thirteenth-century Japanese Buddhist reformer. During an age when the Buddha's

FIGURE 2 *Followers of Fo Guang Shan donate stationery and school bags to children in India. Credit: London Fo Guang Shan Buddhist temple.*

FIGURE 3 *Buddhist nuns from the Jogye Order of Korean Buddhism. Credit:*
Venerable Bon-gak.

teachings were in decline, he taught a distinctive way – involving the recitation
of the title of a renowned Buddhist text – to achieve liberation, based upon
the need to overcome suffering. These modern groups include Soka Gakkai
(Metraux, 1996), Rissho Kosei-kai and Nipponzan Myohoji (Queen, 1996a:
40–1, note 69: Henry, 2013: 2; see also Stone, 2003). There are also engaged
Buddhist groups found in contemporary Lao (Ladwig, 2006) and in Korea
(Yoon and Jones, 2014). In Korea, the National Bhikṣuṇī Association of the
Jogye Order of Korean Buddhism tackles social problems using Buddhist
solutions. They also use Buddhism to tackle the environmental crisis and
gender discrimination. There has been an annual Buddhist peace walk in
Cambodia (Poethig, 2002).[13] This peace walk is known as Dhammayietra. It
was originally undertaken by the revered Cambodian monk Maha Ghosananda
(1913–2007). Its aim is to promote peace and to heal the wounds caused by
decades of conflict in Cambodia.

There are also a number of broader engaged Buddhist movements; these
include Buddhist Global Relief (founded by Bhikkhu Bodhi); the Buddhist
Peace Fellowship (Baroni, 2017)[14] and Zen Peace Makers. One Earth Sangha
(oneearthsangha.org) has a particular emphasis on eco-Buddhism and
training eco-sattvas, who are engaged Buddhist individuals who use Buddhist
ideas to save the planet from environmental disaster. The topic of gender,
with a particular focus on female monastics, is led by the 'Daughters of the
Buddha' (*Sakyadhītā*).[15] There are also individual Buddhist women, such as
the Thai activist Ouyporn Khuankaew who leads the International Women's
Partnership for Peace and Justice and uses Buddhist ideas to campaign for

gender equality and to end violence against women (Khuankaew, 2009; King, 2009: 162). Of particular concern is the Buddhist culture's concept of karma being weaponized to justify social inequality given that suffering is caused by social structures that cause harm to women (King, 2009: 162). For example, violence against women is justified in terms of the karma of the victim and the male aggressor.

A number of Buddhist groups support engaged Buddhist issues related to gender and sexuality. These include *Rainbodhi*, an LGBTQIA+ Buddhist community in Sydney, Australia, *Rainbow Sangha Network* in Europe, the *Gay Buddhist Fellowship*, in London, UK. Groups with a trans-Buddhist identity include *TransBuddhists* (transbuddhists.org) and the *International Trans Buddhist Sangha*.

A small number of movements have challenged nationalist Buddhist groups in Asia. The Burmese punk band *Rebel Riot* challenge the authority of Buddhist ideology based on ethnicity and privilege. Their film *My Buddha is Punk* argues that there must be a reassertion of fundamental Buddhist principles of compassion and loving-kindness to counter the current Burmese Buddhist ideological culture of racism and discrimination.[16] A comprehensive survey of the field of engaged Buddhism is given by Ann Gleig (2021). Her article contains the most concise and comprehensive analysis of engaged Buddhism available.

Christopher Queen (1996a: 25) suggests that three key texts are central in the formulation of engaged Buddhism. These are Henry Steel Olcott's *A Buddhist Catechism* (1881); Anagarika Dharmapala's *Gihi Vinaya*, 'The Daily Code for Laity' (1898); and Bhimrao Ramji Ambedkar's *The Buddha and his Dharma* (1957). These texts would then be the canon of what Christopher Queen has described as a new yāna, a new vehicle, to liberation, or a modern turning of the wheel of Dharma (2000: 17–26).[17]

Added to these could be Walpola Rahula's *The Heritage of the Bhikkhu* (1946; Queen, 1996a: 14). Rahula's work, according to Grant (2009: 83), encouraged Buddhist monks to become involved in politics. In this sense it can be understood as a manifesto for monastic involvement in politics. Thch Nhat Hanh's *Fourteen Precepts of Engaged Buddhism*, which I will discuss in detail in Chapter 1, could also form part of this engaged Buddhis canon. Mention should also be made of Donald Lopez's *A Modern Buddhist Bible*, which remains a useful resource for some of the key texts of the historical rise of both engaged and modern Buddhism (Lopez, 2002).

Scholarly studies of engaged Buddhism

Academic scholarship on engaged Buddhism came of age in 1996 with the publication of *Engaged Buddhism: Buddhist Liberation Movements in Asia.*

This collection of articles edited by Christopher S. Queen and Sallie B. King contains a seminal introduction to engaged Buddhism by Christopher Queen. The book covers material such as Ambedkar, the Sarvodaya Shramadana movement in Sri Lanka, Buddhadasa and Sulak Sivaraksa in Thailand, Thich Nhat Hanh in Vietnam, and the Soka Gakkai in Japan.[18]

It was followed in 2000 by Christopher S. Queen's edited volume *Engaged Buddhism in the West*. This book covered themes and movements that included Buddhist environmentalism, the Free Tibet movement, the Gay Buddhist Fellowship and Buddhist prison ministries.

In 2003 Charles Prebish and Damien Keown published *Action Dharma: New Studies in Engaged Buddhism*. It includes important historical articles on the Bodhisattva as an engaged Buddhist pioneer along with studies of Dōgen and Nichiren's legacy to engaged Buddhism. The book includes critiques of engaged Buddhism, with Thomas Yarnall's 'Engaged Buddhism: New and Improved!(?) Made in the U. S. A. of Asian Materials' making an important and lasting contribution to the field of engaged Buddhism.

Other notable studies include Kenneth Kraft's edited *Inner Peace, World Peace: Essays on Buddhism and Nonviolence* (1992) and his *The Wheel of Engaged Buddhism: A New Map of the Path* (1999), Ken Jones, *The New Social Face of Buddhism: A Call to Action* (2003), Sallie B. King's *Socially Engaged Buddhism* (2009) and Phil Henry's *Adaptation and Developments in Western Buddhism: Socially Engaged Buddhism in the UK* (2013).

Engaged Buddhism: Traditional or modern?

An ongoing debate in engaged Buddhist circles is the debate over whether Buddhism has always been socially engaged or if it is a modern phenomenon; in other words, is it traditional or modern (Temprano, 2013)?[19] Traditionalists would hold that the Buddha was, to some extent, a social reformer who had very real concerns with the politics of his day. They would argue that Buddhism has always had a social and political message. As Thich Nhat Hanh has argued:

> Buddhism means to be awake – mindful of what is happening in one's body, feelings, mind and in the world. If you are awake you cannot do otherwise than act compassionately to help relieve suffering you see around you. So Buddhism must be engaged in the world. If it is not engaged, it is not Buddhism. (Jones, 2003: 179)[20]

This discussion centres around the idea that Buddhism has always been socially engaged, and that any form of Buddhism that does not adhere to this idea is not a true form of Buddhism.[21] Engaged Buddhism is simply socially practised Buddhism (Kraft, 1992: 18; Yarnall, 2000: 7). In a more recent publication, Thich Nhat Hanh states:

> If Buddhism is not engaged, it is not real Buddhism. This is the attitude of the *bodhisattvas*, beings whose whole intention and actions are to relieve suffering. (Thich Nhat Hanh in Parallax Press, 2019: 297)

This is a line of argument Thich Nhat Hanh has followed since as early as 1967, when in *Vietnam: The Lotus in the Sea of Fire* he argued that disengaged Buddhism was the result of colonialism and that Buddhism has always been actively engaged in society (Nhat Hanh, 1967; Main and Lai, 2013: 14). In other words, a passive and non-reactionary form of Buddhism suited colonial powers who wanted to control local Buddhist populations. The argument is somewhat circular, in that colonial scholarship could argue that true Buddhism is one without a social and political message and that Buddhists who are socially engaged are not practising the authentic message of the Buddha. Therefore, Buddhists in parts of Asia under colonial rule should preserve the true spirit of Buddhism by being passive in the face of colonial aggression. Of course, and this is the point, there were always local Buddhist groups, who rebelled against the colonial powers. In a talk given in 2010, Thich Nhat Hanh clearly makes the case that in his understanding, Buddhism has always been practised in society:

> What we talk about as Engaged Buddhism is not easy to practice. It's been there for a very long time. It's not just from 1930; it's been in our tradition for hundreds of years, millennia. We are the continuation; we are not a new movement. We are only a continuation. And we have books like Buddhism Today, Updating Buddhism, Bringing Buddhism into the World.[22]

Modernists would disagree and suggest that engaged Buddhism is a modern phenomenon. They would argue that until modern times Buddhism had little or no concern with society, politics or the environment. Richard Gombrich, a modernist, has stated:

> My interpretation puts me at odds with those who see the Buddha as a social reformer. Certainly, in consenting to preach and then in establishing an Order of monks to do likewise, he showed his great compassion and concern for mankind. Moreover, he was supremely kind and understanding towards everyone, so far as we can tell. But his concern was to reform individuals and help them to leave society forever, not to reform the world. Life in the world he regarded as suffering, and the problem to which he

offered a solution was the otherwise inevitable rebirth into the world. Though it could well be argued that the Buddha made life in the world more worth living, that surely was an unintended consequence of his teaching. To present him as a sort of socialist is a serious anachronism. He never preached against social inequality, only declared its irrelevance to salvation. He neither tried to abolish the caste system nor to do away with slavery. (Gombrich, 2006: 30)[23]

These scholars would hold that to argue that Buddhism is socially and politically engaged is wishful thinking. The Buddha, as preserved in the Buddhist textual tradition, had very little to say about social change, had few arguments about social inequality and had little in the way of a political message.[24]

It has also been argued that Buddhist social and political engagement is the result of a Western influence on Buddhism. It is suggested that this happened during the colonial period, under the influence of Western philosophy and religion. I have already suggested that the colonial image of Buddhism is problematic. However, a slightly different argument is being made in this context. This way of understanding engaged Buddhism has principally been argued for by Christopher Queen who talks about 'European and American religious and political thought' being the 'hidden ingredient' in the origins of engaged Buddhism (Queen, 1996a: 21). As he argues:

While nineteenth-century Asian-Americans (Chinese and Japanese Americans) were occupied in the ritual observance of their imported faiths and twentieth-century Caucasian readers of D.T. Suzuki, Alan Watts, and the Beats were increasingly attracted to the aesthetic and psychological ethos of Zen Buddhism, it has been mainstream Protestant Buddhist sympathizers and adherents who forged the conception of an activist, socially engaged Buddhism.

And it was this amalgam of Eastern and Western elements – nontheistic, ethical, contemplative, reformist, communitarian, utopian – that was transmitted back to Asia by figures such as Olcott. (Queen, 1996a: 31)

The general argument in this reading of engaged Buddhism, and of much of modern Buddhism, is that Asian Buddhism was passive until the intervention of Western philosophy and religion. In Buddhist studies this movement has been termed Protestant Buddhism (Gombrich, 2006: 171–95). The Buddhism of the Western imagination is often passive, ascetic and world renouncing. Buddhism is caricatured as uninvolved in society and culture, in the affairs of the state, and in the politics of villages, towns and nations.

Our idea that Buddhism is not engaged and that there is a historically pure form of Buddhism that had no social message and no cultural contact could well be due to the legacy of the Western encounter with Buddhism in the eighteenth and nineteenth centuries. In this encounter Buddhism was often contrasted with other religions and made distinct from them by stressing those aspects of Buddhism which are ascetic and removed from society. It is clear, as I have suggested, that this caricature of Buddhism would have suited Western colonial powers, as a passive Buddhist population made the job of exploiting Asian countries much easier. However, as any historian of Asian history will point out, Buddhism has always been involved with all the people and institutions that make up culture and society – from kings, queens, emperors and rulers to urban and village education, rituals and commerce. Buddhism has never existed in an ideological vacuum.

Buddhism, as it thrives in Asia, is central to communities and imbued with local cultures. One could say that the West invented non-engaged Buddhism, and, in turn, there was the need for the category of 'engaged Buddhism'. The argument would follow that engaged Buddhism is simply Buddhism in culture, society and politics. Centrally, some of the leading figures in engaged Buddhism, such as A. T. Ariyaratne, who founded the Sarvodaya Shramadana ('awakening of all through shared labour') in Sri Lanka, would hold that the social and political position of Buddhist monks has been played down in Buddhist history (Ariyaratne, 1980: 588). By focusing upon the ascetic ideals of the monastic, the close symmetry between monks and society has not been made clear. Engaged Buddhism revives this historical alliance.

Another factor could be a fundamental difference between modern Western (or perhaps urban) forms of Buddhism and Buddhism as it exists in traditional Asian cultures. In the former, to be a practising Buddhist is to meditate. The problems encountered are in the mind – whereas to be a Buddhist in Asia, and I am clearly simplifying these ideas, is to offer various types of social service, such as making offerings to monks or donations to orphanages (Kawanami, 2020). Buddhism in Asia is civic, social and charitable. The monastics are involved in education, in dealing with issues in the local community. Thus, in modern Western Buddhism there is a culture of the mind, while in traditional Asian Buddhism there is a culture of giving. This helps to explain the different nature of engaged Buddhism in the two settings. The point could be made that engaged Buddhist movements in Asia can adhere to their institutional roots, or operate away from the monastic setting. This could contribute to the differences in their outlooks and practices.

In Western Buddhism, with established Buddhist institutions often absent, the form of Buddhism practised is fundamentally removed from its cultural setting. Buddhism in Asia is often conservative, whereas in the West it is often progressive and liberal. In more general terms there are two forms of Buddhist practice. Traditional Buddhist practice is mostly based upon generating merit in order to attain a good rebirth; on the other hand, the focus of modern Buddhists is meditation and philosophy. In this description we are close to a distinction that is made between ethnic Buddhists and convert Buddhists. The term used by Anna Gleig to describe the latter is 'liberal convert Buddhism' (Gleig, 2012: 201). A possible and substantive problem is that there is a hierarchy, and even an inherent racism, in these distinctions, with the Western convert Buddhist practising a modern and 'better' form of Buddhism (Hickey, 2010 discusses this problem). All of these categories are important to engaged Buddhism.

The original question posed in this section asked if engaged Buddhism is a modern phenomenon or if Buddhism has always had a social and political message. Did engaged Buddhism emerge in the twentieth century or can its antecedents be found in the ancient Buddhist traditions? I am suggesting that the answer to this question, and the arguments that we make in support of our position on the question, depends on how we understand the fundamental nature of Buddhism. There are ascetic Buddhist traditions and there are those that are more political in nature; similarly, there are Buddhist traditions that could be described as world renouncing, while others take an interest in society. Some Buddhist traditions have had contact with colonial powers and have been influenced by a Christian or Muslim social message, while others have put forward a political and ecological message prompted by a reflection on the key doctrines of Buddhism. Buddhists can be engaged with or without the need for external influence. Encounters with colonial powers could influence the nature of Buddhism. In simple terms, we should be careful that the categories of traditional and modern do not distort the complexities of Buddhist doctrinal, political and social history.

Models of engaged Buddhism

There are a number of key themes which form the basis of engaged Buddhism – for example, war and violence, ecological degradation, race, human rights, ethnicity, healthcare, prisons, schools, sexual orientation, gender relations and the workplace (Henry, 2013: 42).

Sallie B. King has discussed six shared principles of engaged Buddhism and a number of controversial issues. The shared principles are (1) causation; (2) the four noble truths; (3) interdependence; (4) engaged spirituality; (5) non-violence; (6) non-adversariality. The controversial issues are (1) Westernization; (2) karma; and (3) gender (King, 2012: 195–213).

Christopher Queen suggests that there are three characteristics of engaged Buddhism. These are (1) awareness or mindfulness (*sati*) – that is, seeing the interdependence of self and other; (2) identification of self and the world – 'a

sense of oneness, nondualism, interdependence and empathy for all beings';
(3) the imperative of action – once there is awareness of suffering there must
be action (Queen, 2000: 6–7; Henry, 2013: 42). He has also described 'three
marks of engaged Buddhist philosophy'. These are suffering (*dukkha*), action-
rebirth (*karma*-saṃsāra) and the five precepts *(pañcasīla*; Queen, 2013: 524–
35). Finally, he considers three central themes: agnosticism, interdependence
and globalization (Queen, 2002).

Kenneth Kraft has attempted to give a comprehensive description of
engaged Buddhism. He describes ten paths of engaged Buddhist practice,
symbolized by a wheel, which is a common way to represent the Buddha's
teachings: (1) cultivating awareness in daily life; (2) embracing family; (3)
working with others; (4) participating in politics; (5) caring for the earth; (6)
moving into the world; (7) extending compassionate action; (8) exploring new
terrain: Buddhism adapting to different cultures and circumstances; (9) at
ease amid activity; and (10) spreading joy in the ten directions (Kraft, 1999: 18).

Ken Jones has described seven 'distinguishing characteristics of Engaged
Buddhism'. These can be summarized as follows: (1) engaged Buddhism is
based on the Dharma, what he describes as the 'core tenets' of Buddhism –
'compassion', 'interdependence', 'selflessness' and 'the practice of morality
and mindfulness'. Jones describes these as 'the inner work of radical personal
change'; (2) Jones next describes a type of humanism called 'Buddhist
humanism' explained as a type of 'Buddha nature' that exists in all humans; (3)
interdependence, using the analogy of Indra's net which prompts an evaluation
of the environment; (4) a form of non-violence that 'recognises the common
humanity of the adversary'; (5) a striving for the equal rights of genders and
ethnic groups; (6) engaged Buddhists adopt a form of 'internationalism' with
positive relationships between affluent and economically poor people; (7)
engaged Buddhism is pluralistic and 'non-sectarian' (See Jones, 2003: 181–2;
Henry, 2013: 30).

In all of these models, a number of key ideas become clear: action,
interdependence and compassion. These ideas will be considered in this book.

Engaged Buddhism in practice

Finally, we must briefly consider the urgency of engaged Buddhism. Bhikkhu
Bodhi has argued that modern engaged Buddhists must become actively
involved in politics (Bodhi, 2007 and 2018). This political involvement should
be one based upon Buddhist principles, with the aim of alleviating suffering.
Bodhi suggests that Buddhist ideas should be used to fight racism, the
poor treatment of immigrant communities, the environmental crisis and

the growing militarism in international politics (Bodhi, 2018).[25] Buddhists need to be vocal in the fight against social injustices and the aggressive attitudes of governments. This action should be based upon the Buddhist principles of loving-kindness and compassion. Bodhi argues that engaged Buddhism should become central to Buddhism in the modern world (Bodhi, 2008). Bhikkhu Bodhi founded Buddhist Global Relief in 2007. Its engaged Buddhist agenda acts as a useful model of engaged Buddhism. Buddhist Global Relief describes three core beliefs and nine values. I will concentrate here on the core beliefs: (1) to extend loving-kindness (mettā), to the entire world, regarding each person as a member of one's own family; (2) the idea of interdependence. In Buddhist Global Relief this idea is explained by emphasizing the high standards of the geographical and social West being dependant on the East for the cheap manufacture of goods. Interdependence, as shall be shown, is often regarded as the central teaching of Buddhism when considering engaged Buddhism (McMahan, 2008: 149–82; Queen, 2002); (3) to establish a just social and political order. Buddhist Global Belief suggests that the duty of a government is to 'guard and protect' its residents, 'eliminating poverty through state-sponsored deeds of charity'. This should be extended by affluent nations to the global community.[26] In these core beliefs we have a key to understanding engaged Buddhism. Its practice is loving-kindness, its philosophy is interdependence, and its governance is one of charity and protection. In Buddhist Global Relief we have a model of an active engaged Buddhist organization. It can be used as an example of strategies used by engaged Buddhists to tackle suffering within the world.

A note on material used in this book

It will become abundantly clear throughout this book that I use texts from the Pāli Canon far more than material from other Buddhist traditions. I acknowledge that this is a shortcoming in the textual, geographical and historical data used.[27] On the plus side, I hope to give an account of the material I use with some degree of competence. I do not consider the material in the Pāli Canon to be more original, earlier or any more or less historically accurate than other Buddhist textual traditions. In fact, it is as problematic as any other textual tradition, perhaps more so. One of my difficulties is to assume that these texts are known by Buddhists whose ideas I am suggesting are influenced by the texts. I cannot claim this. I can suggest that engaged Buddhist ideas are anticipated by the Pāli Canon. However, the Pāli Canon suggests a normative and idealized version of Buddhist culture, society and politics. Just because the Pāli Canon (and other Buddhist textual canons) does not give evidence of political ideas, it does not mean that Buddhism in Asia was not political. It seems highly likely that the monks and nuns portrayed in Buddhist texts are an ideal, suggesting what an ideal version of what might have been or might be – not concrete historical actors in a realistic version of Buddhist culture. There is likely to have always been Buddhists, or individuals influenced by Buddhist ways of thinking, interacting with society, culture and politics in various ways – some a lot, some very little. There is likely to have always been Buddhist ideas and practices concerned with making this life and the next life better, without a focus upon escaping from *saṃsāra*. Buddhism has had views on gender, class, ethnicity and race; it has been involved in the generation of wealth and the protection of power; it has had allegiances with compassionate rulers and supported massacres and corruption. Our discussion of engaged Buddhism, I would hold, is profoundly useful, but only if it is used to tease out our assumptions about how Buddhism as a historical phenomenon has interacted with Buddhist and non-Buddhist cultures from its beginning to modern times.

This book also has a focus on Southeast Asia. This is not because this geographical area is especially relevant for engaged Buddhism. The reason for the focus is that my own research expertise is in this area. I do feel that conclusions reached from this area can be applied to South and East Asia, and to Western encounters with engaged Buddhism.

Discussion questions

1. What did Thich Nhat Hanh mean by the term 'engaged Buddhism'?
2. How does engaged Buddhism differ from other forms of Buddhism?
3. Which questions does engaged Buddhism tackle that are not addressed by earlier forms of Buddhism?

Suggestions for further reading

DeVido, Elise A. 2009. 'The Influence of Chinese Master Taixu on Buddhism in Vietnam'. *Journal of Global Buddhism* 10: 413–58.

Gleig, Ann. 2021. 'Engaged Buddhism'. In *Oxford Research Encyclopedia of Religion*. New York: Oxford University Press. Full details unavailable at the time of publication.

King, Sallie B. 2012. 'Socially Engaged Buddhism'. In *Buddhism in the Modern World,* ed. David L. McMahan, 195–214. New York: Routledge.

Lele, Amod. 2019. 'Disengaged Buddhism'. *Journal of Buddhist Ethics* 26: 239–89.

Main, Jessica L and Rongdao Lai. 2013. 'Introduction: Reformulating "Socially Engaged Buddhism" as an Analytical Category'. *The Eastern Buddhist* 44 (2): 1–34.

Queen, Christopher S. 1996a. 'Introduction: The Shapes and Sources of Engaged Buddhism'. In *Engaged Buddhism: Buddhist Liberation Movements in Asia*, ed. Christopher S. Queen and Sallie B. King, 1–44. Albany: State University of New York Press.

Temprano, Victor Gerard. 2013. 'Defining Engaged Buddhism: Traditionists, Modernists, and Scholastic Power'. *Buddhist Studies Review* 30 (2): 261–74.

2

The foundations of engaged Buddhism

The aim of this chapter is to describe how engaged Buddhism adapts several fundamental Buddhist ideas so that they can be used to tackle, among other things, social, economic, ecological and political problems. To begin with I will briefly consider some of the relevant ideas of the Buddhist path. In this chapter I will begin to explain how some key Buddhist ideas are used in engaged Buddhism, not to escape from the cycle of suffering, but in order to change the world and to make it a better place. A fundamental idea of engaged Buddhism is that *saṃsāra* can be fixed. Buddhism is involved in the process of alleviating suffering within the world. One could suggest that traditional Buddhism is preoccupied with death and the afterlife, whereas engaged Buddhism focuses upon the current life and has little interest in rebirth. In turn, there is a re-evaluation of suffering. In traditional Buddhism suffering originates in the mind and meditation is practised to alleviate ignorance. In engaged Buddhism suffering originates in the world, and peaceful protest and activism are used to change the world. Finally, in traditional Buddhism the causes of suffering are usually craving and ignorance. In engaged Buddhism, too, suffering is caused by craving and ignorance, but it is also supposed to originate in various types of discrimination, exploitation, political oppression and inequality.

Buddhism teaches that there is suffering, that suffering is caused by craving (and in a different context, by ignorance) and that suffering can be eradicated by practising the Buddhist path. The Sanskrit term for suffering is *duḥkha*, the Pāli term is *dukkha*. In this book, due to the material I will consider I will more often favour the Pāli terms. In many respects, Buddhism teaches that there is nothing wrong with the world; what is wrong is how we perceive the world, with craving and attachment. We make the world a certain way, and we need to transform the mind to escape from suffering.

For a general understanding of the Buddhist path, three categories are useful. These are shared by all Indian ascetic traditions to a greater or lesser extent. An ascetic (or renouncer) is someone who leaves society to seek liberation or salvation. The term being translated as ascetic is *śramaṇa* in Sanskrit, or *samaṇa* in Pāli. Sanskrit and Pāli terms will be found throughout this book. They are two of the ancient languages of Indian religions, and Buddhist textual canons were composed in both languages. Ascetic traditions became widespread in ancient India before the time of the Buddha. The three categories central to the Indian ascetic traditions are (1) *saṃsāra*: the idea that people, gods and animals are involved in an endless cycle of rebirths. This cycle is where we are now, where we have been, and where we will be for an extremely long period of time; (2) *karma*: this term means 'action'. It is the theory that all the actions we perform as individuals have consequences. Our good or wholesome actions have positive consequences, and our bad or unwholesome actions have negative consequences – on a basic level karma will cause a good or bad rebirth; and (3) liberation: the notion that the purpose of the religious life is to find a way to escape from the endless cycle of rebirths. This has been variously described as *mokṣa*, literally, an 'escape' in Hindu traditions, *kaivalya* or 'isolation' (from 'action' or karma) in Jain traditions, and *nirvāṇa*, literally 'blowing out', of greed, hatred and delusion in Buddhism. Indian religions can be understood as soteriological – they are paths to salvation.

As we shall see in our study of engaged Buddhism, some fundamental elements of this soteriological model need to be adapted, reinterpreted, changed or even abandoned. For example, the idea of an endless cycle of existences is often downplayed in engaged Buddhism in which there is a focus on this life. The idea of karma, that actions have consequences, is frequently adapted. This is due to some of the conclusions made about the nature of individuals based upon this idea. For example, different genders and sexualities could be attributed to the negative workings of karma. Finally, liberation, as an end point in the sense of escaping from the cycle of rebirths, is often adapted in engaged Buddhism to suggest that awakening can be experienced in the present life.

Redefining the causes of 'suffering' (*dukkha*)

Central to all forms of Buddhism is suffering. Suffering is explained in the following terms:

Now this [. . .] is the noble truth of suffering: birth is suffering (*dukkha*), ageing is suffering, illness is suffering, death is suffering, union with what is displeasing is suffering; separation from what is pleasing is suffering; not to get what one wants is suffering; in brief, the five aggregates of grasping (or attachment) are suffering. (S V 421)[1]

Suffering is copious in the Buddhist description of the world and reality. It pervades human experience and forms the basis for the Buddhist analysis of experience in all Buddhist traditions.

Buddhism uses three ideas to expand upon its description of suffering. First, there is physical suffering; second, there is the suffering of conditions; and third, there is the suffering of change. This is all described in the aptly named 'Discourse on Suffering' (Dukkha-sutta):

Friend [. . .] it is said, 'suffering, suffering.' What now is suffering? 'There are, friend, these three kinds of suffering: the suffering due to pain (dukkhadhukkhatā), the suffering due to conditions (sankhāradukkhatā), the suffering due to change (vipariṇāmadukkhatā). These are the three kinds of suffering.' (S IV 259)

Physical pain is the pain we feel when we touch something hot, stub our toe, or have a toothache. Second, there is the suffering of conditions. In Buddhist philosophy all physical and mental phenomena are conditioned. By this is meant that they are put together – they are a collection of processes that are in constant change; events and experiences and ideas and concepts, including our idea and experience of a 'self', are not stable. They are subject to fall apart, adapt and become something else. Finally, the suffering of change refers to the impermanence of all physical and mental phenomena in the Buddhi's understanding of existence. Nothing lasts forever; everything is subject to change.

I would suggest that pivotal to engaged Buddhism, and the idea that distinguishes it from traditional and philosophical forms of Buddhism, is its interpretation of suffering. The textual tradition rarely, if ever, describes suffering as being caused by a political system, a sexual orientation, an entrenched form of ethnic identity, or by the destruction of the natural environment. Its focus was elsewhere. Its audience was a group of religious wanderers, travelling alone and in groups and attempting to alleviate suffering in order to escape the endless cycle of rebirths. Engaged Buddhism reinterprets the nature of suffering and how to eradicate it. Added to physical suffering, the suffering of conditions and the suffering of change is social suffering, political suffering, economic suffering and ecological suffering (see Darlington, 2012: 6). Social suffering can include gender, sexual orientation, class and caste, ethnicity, colour, race, religious beliefs and education; political suffering can include political views, political oppression, political infringement on other freedoms, a lack of political control, and political rights. Economic suffering includes a lack of economic freedom, an unfair economic culture, a lack of basic income and economic exploitation for underprivileged members of society, notably, slavery and sexual exploitation. Finally, ecological suffering is suffering grounded in climate change, deforestation, pollution and overpopulation.[2]

How engaged Buddhism adapts Buddhist ideas

Engaged Buddhists often focus upon particular Buddhist doctrines which can be used as an outlet for engaged Buddhist activism. For example, the notion of impermanence is fundamental to Buddhist philosophy. It is often used to express a fundamental outlook about the nature of reality. It is stated that all things are impermanent (*aniccā*), suffering (*dukkha*) and not-self (*anattā*). In meditation the practice would involve the perception of all reality as impermanent, suffering and not-self. In engaged Buddhism the idea of impermanence is put into the service of social and political activism. It can express the idea that social, political, class-driven and ethnic identities are fluid. Prevailing political, social and economic narratives cause suffering and are conditioned. Identities which give rise to suffering are not-self. In this context activists are using Buddhism to rebel against political and social norms. There is clearly something of a gap that needs to be traversed in different uses of Buddhist ideas. On the one hand it is a simple fact that engaged Buddhists are focusing on problems that were either not a concern for traditional Buddhists or simply did not exist. The ecological crises is a modern problem, and we obviously find no comment on it in the Buddhist textual traditions. Similarly, discussions of sexuality, identity, ethnicity and racial difference rarely appear in Buddhist canonical history. If these questions did occur, then they were considered to be part of the mundane world and therefore not part of the Buddhist path, which attempted to escape from the world of attachment and suffering. Buddhism is part of the spiritual world, removed from everyday reality. Issues of gender, sexuality, ecology and politics were simply not issues that Buddhism tackled. In engaged Buddhism there is a mending of this dichotomy, and it is this that I will now move on to discuss.

Treading the sacred and profane paths: Lessening the tension between the 'mundane' and 'supramundane' realms of activity

A key idea of engaged Buddhism is its mending of a perceived dichotomy between worldly and religious activity.[3] Engaged Buddhism needs to address this issue for it to tackle the issues fundamental to its Buddhist practice. There is a valid argument that engaged Buddhism is addressing issues that are not the concern of genuine forms of Buddhism. Part of this argument is based upon the ideas which I will consider in this section.[4]

Historically, Buddhism has described the realms of social and religious activity. According to this description, there are two realms of human activity: this world, which is the one we are likely to be experiencing now and which is the mundane world of unenlightened activity; and a supramundane world, which we are not likely to be experiencing while reading this book and which is a world or realm of awakened experience. Behaviourally, prior to awakening, a person exists and experiences the mundane world; after awakening, they experience the supramundane world. Socially, there is a mundane world which is not the concern of Buddhist teachings and practice and a supramundane world which is the concern of Buddhist preaching, practice and rituals. Clearly, these distinctions do not relate to definite, completely distinct areas of existence, but, as general ways of describing the world, they serve a useful purpose for Buddhism.

In the technical vocabulary of Buddhism, this phenomenon is described as the mundane (*lokiya*) and supramundane (*lokuttara*) worlds. The term mundane is described as 'belonging to the worlds' (Ñāṇamoli, 1962: 302). The term supramundane is described as 'dissociated from the worlds' (Ñāṇamoli, 1962: 302).

The mundane world is sometimes described as having eight worldly ideas associated with it: gain, non-gain, fame, ill-fame, blame, praise, pleasure and pain (A IV 157, Nett: 863). Whereas the supramundane world has five supramundane faculties associated with it: the faith faculty, the energy faculty, the mindfulness faculty, the concentration faculty and the understanding faculty (S V 193, Nett 865). From these descriptions it is immediately clear that their intention is to describe two distinct realms of human activity. In simple language, we might describe these as the non-religious and religious worlds. The former is characterized by non-religious pursuits, the latter with the path to the overcoming of suffering. The textual tradition stresses that these two worlds cannot be mixed – they are distinct (Nett 58). The doctrine of dependent-origination is sometimes used to make this point. This idea is central to Buddhist thought. The doctrine of dependent-origination contains a number of the central teachings of Buddhism. It states that all of our experiences are conditioned. By this is meant that they are put together and are the product of a number of factors. For example, if an individual is ignorant that attachment causes suffering, then they will undertake an unwholesome course of activity, one based on greed, hatred and delusion, and this will result in a life filled with suffering. If, however, they cultivate wisdom, this will lead to non-attachment, a wholesome course of action based on generosity, friendliness and wisdom.

That person will be free from suffering. One of the essential points made by dependent-origination is that because of ignorance, which is not knowing things as they really are, a process of conditionality leads us to become attached to things, for our craving to increase and for individuals to experience endless births, rebirths and suffering. This is the mundane world. However, in the absence of ignorance there is no conditioned process, and suffering is alleviated. This is the supramundane world (Nett 388). The idea of these two realms is widely accepted in the Buddhist textual traditions, and it has important consequences for engaged Buddhism.

In the textual tradition the distinction between the mundane and supramundane worlds is essential in maintaining the integrity of the path. This need to preserve the sanctity of Buddhism is often reflected in modern Buddhist societies in which the monastic is considered to be removed from society and should not, therefore, be involved in politics. Their political disenfranchisement is often constitutionally enshrined in Buddhist Asia. It is a line of Buddhist monastic integrity which should not be crossed. I will return to these arguments in the chapter on Buddhism and politics.

Phil Henry (2013: 10–11) has taken up a part of this discussion and gives it an interesting perspective by considering what he describes as a 'this-worldly' Buddhism linked to modernity (what I have termed mundane/*lokiya*), located and a product of the modern world, and an 'other-worldly' Buddhism having its roots in the ancient Buddhist traditions (what I have termed supramundane/*lokuttara*). Using this idea, it could be suggested that modern Buddhism is concerned with this world, whereas the ancient Buddhist traditions were more other-worldly and were not so concerned with everyday suffering. I have already alluded to this idea by suggesting that traditional forms of Buddhism were concerned with death and the afterlife while modern Buddhism focuses upon the here-and-now and the current life. Clearly, these ideas are related to the distinctions between the mundane and supramundane worlds.

A key idea of engaged Buddhism is its mending of this perceived dichotomy between worldly and religious activity. In attempting this, engaged Buddhism moves away from a Buddhism with a focus on meditation and escaping the world to one that tackles the issues of the world. Valid arguments could be made that tackling political and social issues and fighting poverty and inequality have not formed part of traditional Buddhist practice. Decisively, engaged Buddhists propose a new vision of the issues that are part of the Buddhist path. It is an innovative move, and this innovation needs to be stressed. The engaged Buddhist realignment of the Buddhist path radically alters Buddhist practice. In doing so, a political and social Buddhism becomes possible. In terms of engaged Buddhism, these distinctions are pivotal to its validity in Buddhism. If the everyday world remains entirely distinct from a religious world, if there is a realm of non-Buddhist activity, and one of Buddhist activity, then engaged Buddhism loses much of its legitimacy. However, in engaged Buddhism the political involvement of the monastic is allowed. The monk is political, there is a discussion of gender and Buddhist environmental movements emerge.

Reimagining the causes of suffering

Historically the origins of suffering are said to be two: craving (*taṇhā*), characterized as greed (*lobha*), hatred (*dosa*) and delusion (*moha*), often referred to as the three unwholesome roots (*tīni akusalamūlāni*; D III 214, 275), and ignorance (*avijjā*), characterized as a lack of 'knowledge and vision of the way things really are' (*yathābhūtañāṇadassanaṃ*, A III 19, 200; IV 99, 336, etc). Craving and ignorance are the causes of suffering. By extension, there is nothing wrong with the world but with the way we perceive it. The problem is with the mind and its propensity for attachment and craving. We perceive the world with greed, hatred and delusion. Social structures are, in a way, part of the problem: they enforce craving and ignorance. This understanding of Buddhism might suggest that, to adapt Sallie B. King's useful phrase, *saṃsāra* cannot be fixed.[5] In a sense, the entire world is found within the individual's body. This idea is found in the *Paṭhamarohitassasutta-sutta* (A II 47–9):

> I say, friend, that by traveling one cannot know, see, or reach that end of the world where one is not born, does not grow old and die, does not pass away and get reborn: Yet I say that without having reached the end of the world there is no making an end of suffering. It is in this fathom-long body endowed with perception and mind that I proclaim (1) the world, (2) the origin of the world, (3) the cessation of the world, and (4) the way leading to the cessation of the world.[6]

Suffering originates within the mind, and meditation is used to analyse and control the mind and therefore eradicate suffering. Engaged Buddhists would disagree with this, and argue that *saṃsāra* can be fixed. Engaged Buddhism analyses social structures and adopts the view that suffering may originate from them. It identifies certain political, economic and social institutions as manifestations of greed, hatred and delusion. Greed, hatred and delusion need to be tackled socially, politically and environmentally. The Buddhist is compelled to strive for social liberation through engaging with the external causes of suffering. It might therefore be suggested that both personal and social transformation are important in engaged Buddhism. For example, personal and social transformation are important in the Buddhist approach to human rights abuses (Kittel, 2011: 907). It could be said that engaged Buddhism takes a holistic view of suffering, while traditional forms of Buddhism are atomistic in their analysis. By this I mean that the latter breaks phenomena down into its parts, with the aim of eradicating craving and attachment, while engaged Buddhism analyses the interconnected nature of the world and focuses on the wider causes of suffering.

The adaptation of meditation and the precepts

Buddhist practices, such as meditation and the adoption of the five precepts, can be used in several contexts in engaged Buddhism. As we shall see in Chapter 4, mindfulness has a part to play in the interaction of Buddhism and politics. These basic Buddhist ideas are used, for example, in the treatment of addiction recovery. The engaged Buddhist organization Recovery Dharma (recoverydharma.org) uses Buddhist principles and practices to help individuals overcome addiction. There is a long history of mindfulness being used for addiction recovery (Johnson, 2019). The Buddhist prison chaplaincy organization Angulimala (angulimala.org.uk) uses basic Buddhist ideas to help in the rehabilitation of prison inmates (Parkum and Stultz, 2000). Finally, Anālayo (2019) offers an analysis of how mindfulness can be used in eco-Buddhism and how the four noble truths can be used as a Buddhist response to climate change.

There is also an abundance of evidence from groups like the Sri Lankan engaged Buddhist movement Sarvodaya Shramadana, founded by A. T. Ariyaratne, that traditional Buddhist practices, particularly forms of meditation, can be adapted so that they can be applied by practitioners in their daily lives.[7] Meditation can become a this-worldly path, not an activity performed in solitude away from society. Its aim can be the betterment of society, and its central principle can be the building of communities (Bond, 1996: 126–7).

It is clear that engaged Buddhism retains the importance of meditation in Buddhist practice but there is an adaptation of it to include reflection upon the world. As I have already suggested, a basic idea of engaged Buddhism is that the causes of suffering are found in the world. Therefore, it is to be expected that the focus of engaged Buddhist meditation highlights this idea. A notable practice is to combine meditation and the five precepts (*pañcasīla*). The five precepts are listed in what follows:

1. I undertake the training-precept (*sikkhā-padaṃ*) to abstain from onslaught on breathing beings: To refrain from harming living creatures.

2. I undertake the training-precept to abstain from taking what is not given: To refrain from taking what is not given.

3. I undertake the training-precept to abstain from misconduct concerning sense-pleasures: To refrain from sexual misconduct.

4. I undertake the training-precept to abstain from false speech: To refrain from false speech.

5. I undertake the training-precept to abstain from alcoholic drink or drugs that are an opportunity for heedlessness: To refrain from intoxicants that cause heedlessness (Harvey, 2000: 67. See A III 203; A IV 324. In a different form see S II 68–9).

The precepts mean that the Buddhist who adopts them refrains from harming living creatures, refrains from taking what is not given, refrains from sexual misconduct, refrains from false speech and refrains from intoxicants that cause heedlessness (Gethin, 1998: 170). We also found them given in the following form, along with taking refuge. This is a good summary of the practices adopted in order to be a Buddhist:

In whatever village or town a man or a woman has gone for refuge to the Buddha, the Dhamma (the teachings of the Buddha), and the Saṅgha (the community of monks and nuns); he or she is virtuous and of good character, abstaining from the destruction of life, taking what is not given, sexual misconduct, false speech, and liquor, wine, and intoxicants, the basis for heedlessness. (A I 226)[8]

Before moving on to consider Thich Nhat Hanh's synthesis of the precepts and meditation, I would like to describe some basic meditation practices which are used throughout engaged Buddhism. A very common form of meditation found in the early Buddhist texts is called the four foundations of mindfulness (satipaṭṭhāna). They are practised in order to eliminate suffering. The four foundations of mindfulness are (1) mindfulness of the body (kāya); (2) mindfulness of feelings (vedanā); (3) mindfulness of the mind (citta); and (4) mindfulness of mental-objects (dhammas, M I 56). A useful resource is the 'Discourse on the Foundations of Mindfulness' (Satipaṭṭhāna-sutta, M I 55–63).

Thich Naht Hanh has combined the five precepts and the four foundations of mindfulness to create a distinctively innovative form of engaged Buddhist practice. They are called the five mindfulness trainings. These deserve our attention as they adapt traditional Buddhist practices in order to tackle contemporary problems. There is a theme in engaged Buddhism in which meditation is not a solitary discipline. For example, as Christopher Queen reports, Sulak Sivaraksa, the Thai Buddhist activist and scholar, compares the mindful writing of protest letters to political figures and the press as a form of meditation (Queen, 1996: 36, note 25).

There are two extensive descriptions of the five mindfulness trainings (Nhat Hanh, 2009: 35–8; 2014: 27–32). The latter version of the mindfulness trainings are significantly expanded, and I use them in the following. The language changes over the years from being simply explained as the 'first mindfulness training', etc., to include more descriptive headings, 'reverence for life', etc. As shall be shown, each mindfulness training matches one of the precepts. I have given the precept in its basic form after the heading for each mindfulness training.

1. *Reverence for Life* (to refrain from harming living creatures)

    Aware of the suffering caused by the destruction of life, I am committed to cultivating the insight of interbeing [a term used for interdependence or dependent-origination] and compassion and learning ways to protect the lives of people, animals, plants, and minerals. I am determined not to kill, not to let others kill, and not to support any act of killing in the world, in my thinking, or in my way of life. Seeing that harmful actions arise from anger, fear, greed, and intolerance, which in turn come from dualistic and discriminative thinking, I will cultivate openness, non-discrimination, and non-attachment to views in order to transform violence, fanaticism, and dogmatism in myself and in the world.

2. *True Happiness* (to refrain from taking what is not given)

    Aware of the suffering caused by exploitation, social injustice, stealing, and oppression, I am committed to practicing generosity in my thinking, speaking, and acting. I am determined not to steal and not to possess anything that should belong to others; and I will share my time, energy, and material resources with those who are in need. I will practice looking deeply to see that the happiness and suffering of others are not separate from my own happiness and suffering; that true happiness is not possible without understanding and compassion; and that running after wealth, fame, power and sensual pleasures can bring much suffering and despair. I am aware that happiness depends on my mental attitude and not on external conditions, and that I can live happily in the present moment simply by remembering that I already have more than enough conditions to be happy. I am committed to practicing Right Livelihood so that I can help reduce the suffering of living beings on Earth and stop contributing to climate change.

3. *True Love* (to refrain from sexual misconduct)

    Aware of the suffering caused by sexual misconduct, I am committed
    to cultivating responsibility and learning ways to protect the safety
    and integrity of individuals, couples, families, and society. Knowing
    that sexual desire is not love, and that sexual activity motivated by
    craving always harms myself as well as others, I am determined not
    to engage in sexual relations without true love and a deep, long-
    term commitment made known to my family and friends. I will do
    everything in my power to protect children from sexual abuse and to
    prevent couples and families from being broken by sexual misconduct.
    Seeing that body and mind are one, I am committed to learning
    appropriate ways to take care of my sexual energy and cultivating
    loving kindness, compassion, joy and inclusiveness – which are the
    four basic elements of true love – for my greater happiness and the
    greater happiness of others. Practicing true love, we know that we will
    continue beautifully into the future.

4. Loving Speech and Deep Listening (to refrain from false speech)

    Aware of the suffering caused by unmindful speech and the inability
    to listen to others, I am committed to cultivating loving speech and
    compassionate listening in order to relieve suffering and to promote
    reconciliation and peace in myself and among other people, ethnic
    and religious groups, and nations. Knowing that words can create
    happiness or suffering, I am committed to speaking truthfully
    using words that inspire confidence, joy, and hope. When anger
    is manifesting in me, I am determined not to speak. I will practice
    mindful breathing and walking in order to recognize and to look
    deeply into my anger. I know that the roots of anger can be found in
    my wrong perceptions and lack of understanding of the suffering in
    myself and in the other person. I will speak and listen in a way that
    can help myself and the other person to transform suffering and see
    the way out of difficult situations. I am determined not to spread
    news that I do not know to be certain and not to utter words that can
    cause division or discord. I will practice Right Diligence to nourish my
    capacity for understanding, love, joy, and inclusiveness, and gradually
    transform anger, violence, and fear that lie deep in my consciousness.

5. Nourishment and Healing (to refrain from intoxicants that cause
    heedlessness)

    Aware of the suffering caused by unmindful consumption, I am
    committed to cultivating good health, both physical and mental,

for myself, my family, and my society by practicing mindful eating, drinking, and consuming. I will practice looking deeply into how I consume the Four Kinds of Nutriments, namely edible foods, sense impressions, volition, and consciousness. I am determined not to gamble, or to use alcohol, drugs, or any other products which contain toxins, such as certain websites, electronic games, TV programs, films, magazines, books, and conversations. I will practice coming back to the present moment to be in touch with the refreshing, healing and nourishing elements in me and around me, not letting regrets and sorrow drag me back into the past nor letting anxieties, fear, or craving pull me out of the present moment. I am determined not to try to cover up loneliness, anxiety, or other suffering by losing myself in consumption. I will contemplate interbeing and consume in a way that preserves peace, joy, and well-being in my body and consciousness, and in the collective body and consciousness of my family, my society, and the Earth. (Nhat Hanh, 2014: 27–32)

I have given these precepts in full as they illustrate some very important points. They suggest what engaged Buddhist practices look like, and they combine different parts of the Buddhist path to show how engaged Buddhism encounters suffering in ways that earlier Buddhist practice did not. They are clearly intended to counter problems faced by laypeople and monastics alike. They suggest how engaged Buddhism is not focused upon an escape from the cycle of rebirths, but on a more sustainable Buddhist practice that brings clarity to a Buddhist life, which clears away impediments to a meaningful life. In considering engaged Buddhism we encounter familiar Buddhist ideas. There are descriptions of suffering, given along with the remainder of the Four Noble Truths. Ideas like not-self and dependent-origination also appear. Ethical practices like the five precepts remain important as does meditation. However, in many of these ideas and practices their place on the Buddhist path is challenged. They are used in ways that the non-specialist can understand. They do not require the mediation of a monk or nun. In many ways, this is the innovative message of engaged Buddhism and, arguably, marks a return to a simpler form of Buddhist teachings.

Conclusion

In this chapter I have explained that suffering is central to Buddhism and that it is usually said to originate in the mind. This is not remarkable. However, engaged Buddhism (and I am aware that engaged Buddhism is not a homogenous phenomenon, but am speaking in general terms) explains that suffering can also originate in society, that it can be caused by discrimination, racism, inequality, the destruction of the natural environment and political oppression.

This leads engaged Buddhists to question the validity of the distinction between the mundane and supramundane realms of experience. Although these two ideas might appear to be abstract, I feel that they are of some importance in analysing engaged Buddhism. There is not a sacred space which is the location of Buddhist practice and the focus of the Buddha's teaching contrasted with a material realm untouched by Buddhism. With the collapsing of the mundane and supramundane, engaged Buddhism open the entire world to Buddhist practices.

Once this has been accomplished, Buddhist practices like meditation and the five precepts are combined to eradicate worldly suffering. Buddhists have always taught that suffering is all-pervasive in life, but less attention has been given to the suffering caused by the structural violence of politics, gender, identity and sexuality. This, it appears to me, is where engaged Buddhism departs from traditional Buddhist practices.

Discussion questions

1. How is suffering described in traditional forms of Buddhism and how does this differ from engaged Buddhism?

2. What is the importance of the ideas of the mundane and supramundane realms of existence to engaged Buddhism?

3. How does the standard practice of meditation and the five precepts change in engaged Buddhism?

Suggestions for further reading

Anālayo, Bhikkhu. 2020. 'Confronting Racism with Mindfulness'. *Mindfulness*: 1–15.
Khuankaew, Ouyporn. 2009. 'Buddhism and Domestic Violence: Using the Four Noble Truths to Deconstruct and Liberate Women's Karma'. In *Rethinking Karma: The Dharma of Social Justice*, ed Jonathan S. Watts, 199–226. Chiang Mai: Silkworm Books.
King, Sallie B. 2017. 'Right Speech Is Not Always Gentle: The Buddha's Authorization of Sharp Criticism, Its Rationale, Limits, and Possible Applications'. *Journal of Buddhist Ethics* 24: 347–67.

King, Sallie B. 2018. 'The Ethics of Engaged Buddhism in Asia'. In *The Oxford Handbook of Buddhist Ethics,* ed. Daniel Cozort and James Mark Shield, 479–500. New York: Oxford University Press.

Queen, Christopher S. 2013. 'Socially Engaged Buddhism: Emerging Patterns of Theory and Practice'. In *A Companion to Buddhist Philosophy,* ed. Steven M. Emmanuel, 524–35. Chichester: Wiley-Blackwell.

Slott, Michael. 2015. 'Secular, Radically Engaged Buddhism: At the Crossroads of Individual and Social Transformation'. *Contemporary Buddhism* 16 (2): 278–98.

3

Beyond belief

The danger of attachment to views in engaged Buddhism

Daṇḍapāṇi the philosopher

In ancient India there was once a young man named Daṇḍapāṇi. According to tradition he was round-shouldered, spending all his time debating with others. He walked around, leaning on his stick, looking somewhat arrogant. His name appears to suggest this, literally meaning 'stick in hand'. Daṇḍapāṇi heard reports about the great teacher, who people called a 'buddha', an awakened being, who taught a doctrine that could liberate all humans from suffering. Daṇḍapāṇi decided he would like to meet this Buddha, to find out more about his teaching, the nature of his arguments, and engage him in debate. Daṇḍapāṇi approached the Buddha and asked him, 'what is the doctrine of the recluse, what does he proclaim?' The reply he received from the Buddha is probably not what he had expected:

> I assert and proclaim such a doctrine that one does not quarrel with anyone in the world with its gods, its Māras, and its Brahmās [great gods, one malevolent, one good], in this generation with its recluses and brahmins [priests], its princes and its people; such a doctrine that apperceptions [or ideas] no more underlie that brahmin, who abides detached from sense pleasures, without perplexity, remorse cut off, free from craving for any kind of being. (M I 108)

Daṇḍapāṇi, not a little confused, shook his head, raised his eyebrows, grimaced three times and walked away, leaning on his stick. He wanted an answer he could argue with, one he could analyse and dissect. The Buddha replied that his teaching has the aim of eradicating all arguments and disputes. How can one proclaim a doctrine that cannot become an object of attachment? This story appears in a Buddhist text called a *Sutta* (also known as *Sūtras*). *Suttas* are discourses, of various length, in which the Buddha often appears. This discourse is from a collection which are neither short or long and are then collected together in The Middle Length Collection, the *Majjhima-nikāya*. It is given the title the *Madhupiṇḍika-sutta*, the 'honey-ball discourse', comparing the Buddha's teachings to a delicious sweet cake. The sweet cake of the Buddha's doctrine has a calming effect on those who hear the teachings, and the teaching itself points to the abandoning of all views, opinions and beliefs. This idea forms one of the central themes of engaged Buddhism. So, in this chapter I am describing one of the foundational philosophical ideas of engaged Buddhism.

The engaged Buddhist focus on non-attachment to views and opinions

The idea of non-attachment has always been very influential. Even the liberating truth of the Buddha cannot be an object of attachment. The idea of non-attachment to views has been significant to various philosophical schools of Buddhism, and this significance can be traced to an early point in Buddhist history (Fuller, 2004: 3). It is also a central idea of engaged Buddhism. Thich Nhat Hanh, the Vietnamese Zen Buddhist monk who we have already mentioned as being one of the founders of engaged Buddhism, proposed fourteen precepts of engaged Buddhism. These focus upon the idea that attachment to views, opinions and beliefs needs to be eradicated in order to practice engaged Buddhism.[1]

The idea that there is a danger in attachment to views is clear throughout the philosophical history of Buddhism (Fuller and Webster, 2008). Notable sections of the *Sutta-nipāta* (which most scholars regard as early in the textual history of Buddhism) continuously stress that any view is a potential object of cognitive attachment. The so-called 'unanswered questions' were left unanswered for similar reasons. These questions, usually in a group of ten, are most famously described in the 'Shorter Discourse to Mālunkyāputta' (*Cūḷamālunkya-sutta*, M I 426–32). In this text the Buddha refuses to answer whether the world is eternal or not, whether the soul and the body are the same or different, or whether or not the Buddha exists after death. Any answer to these questions would simply give the mind something to be attached to, rather than eradicate suffering. The Buddha famously compared his teachings to a raft which should not become an object of attachment (M I 134–5). A famous Mahāyāna philosopher, Nāgārjuna, expressed similar ideas, and this teaching became very important as Buddhism migrated through East Asia. His philosophical school, Madhyamaka, became very influential in Tibet and East Asia. I also think that the teachings about views are a key to understanding engaged Buddhism. The idea of the danger of views is central to many of Thich Nhat Hanh's ideas, particularly the fourteen precepts of engaged Buddhism. It also appears as a central theme in the thinking of Sulak Sivaraksa and his idea of Buddhism with a small 'b'. The reasons for the centrality of views in Buddhist teachings are described by Charles Muller:

> The problem of views is one of significantly greater importance in Buddhism as compared to other religious and philosophical traditions, as the most fundamental problem confronting unenlightened sentient beings in Buddhism is an epistemological one – our distorted way of knowing the world. (Muller, 2018: 363)

Views distort the true nature of reality and become an object of attachment. A key concept in Buddhist ideas about liberation is that the follower of the Buddha should strive to 'see things as they are'. To eradicate suffering, we should know and experience the world, not according to a set of beliefs, but as it really is. Such an insight will, according to Buddhist teachings, alleviate all

FIGURE 4 *Sulak Sivaraksa, one of the founders of the International Network of Engaged Buddhists. Credit: Jirasak Paisalkul.*

suffering. In an important sense, views embody both craving and ignorance, the two primary causes of suffering (keeping in mind the departure from this basic idea I introduced in the previous chapter). Importantly, they also express many of the impediments to liberation in engaged Buddhism. They can be used to express, for example, the rigid attitude to race, the environment, gender and political bias.

The fourteen precepts of engaged Buddhism

The fourteen precepts of engaged Buddhism offer an idea of the philosophical principles of engaged Buddhism. They were formulated for the founding of the Order of Interbeing (*Tiep Hien*) in February 1966, when six people, three men and three women, were ordained into the order (Nhat Hanh, 1993a: VII). There were originally four guiding principles of the Order of Interbeing, which act as an introduction to the fourteen precepts of engaged Buddhism:

1. Non-attachment from views: To be attached means to be caught in dogmas, prejudices, habits, and what we consider to be the Truth. The first aim of the practice is to be free of all attachments, especially attachment to views. This is the most important teaching of Buddhism.

2. Direct experimentation: Buddhism emphasizes the direct experience of reality, not speculative philosophy. Direct practice-realization, not intellectual research, brings about insight. Our own life in the instrument through which we experiment with the truth.

3. Appropriateness: a teaching, in order to bring about understanding and compassion must reflect the needs of people and the realities of society. To do this, it must meet two criteria: it must conform with the basic tenets of Buddhism and it must be truly helpful and relevant. It is said that there are 84.000 Dharma doors through which one can enter Buddhism. For Buddhism to continue and a living source of wisdom and peace, even more doors should be opened.

4. Skilful means (*upaya*): Skilful means consist of images and methods created by intelligent teachers to show the Buddha's way and guide people in their efforts to practice the way in their own particular circumstances. These means are called Dharma doors (Nhat Hanh, 1993a: 8–9; King, 1996: 323; Emmanuel, 2012: 38–9).

These principles form the basis of Thich Nhat Hanh's engaged Buddhism. They pinpoint ideas that he considered essential to its practice. These are views, experience, adaptation of the teachings, and making the teachings available to all sentient beings through the notable Buddhist idea of skilful means. Skilful means is the way in which a great teacher adapts her teaching to the abilities of her audience. The first principle clearly states that non-attachment to views is the central idea of Buddhism. It appears to me that there are a number of reasons that Thich Nhat Hanh placed views and opinions at the centre of Buddhism, and these will be explored in this chapter. Primarily, Thich Nhat Hanh proposed that attachment to truth claims, ideologies, political opinions, and religious and political doctrines are detrimental to the practice of engaged Buddhism.

Originally described as the Fourteen Precepts (*sila*) of the Order of Interbeing, from 1996 they were termed the Fourteen Mindfulness Trainings.[2] They are also known as the Fourteen Guidelines for Engaged Buddhism.[3] I am using the original term.

The Fourteen Precepts of Engaged Buddhism

The first precept, the lion's roar: Do not be idolatrous about or bound to any doctrine, theory, or ideology, even Buddhist ones. Buddhist systems of thought are guiding means; they are not absolute truth.

The second precept, truth is found in life: Do not think the knowledge you presently possess is changeless, absolute truth. Avoid being narrow-minded and bound to present views. Learn and practice nonattachment from views in order to be open to receive others' viewpoints. Truth is found in life and not merely in conceptual knowledge. Be ready to learn throughout your entire life and to observe reality in yourself and in the world at all times.

The third precept, freedom of thought: Do not force others, including children, by any means whatsoever, to adopt your views, whether by authority, threat, money, propaganda, or even education. However, through compassionate dialogue, help others renounce fanaticism and narrowness.

The fourth precept, awareness of suffering: Do not avoid contact with suffering or close your eyes before suffering [. . .]

The fifth precept, living simply: Do not accumulate wealth while millions are hungry [. . .]

The sixth precept, compassion is understanding: Do not maintain anger or hatred. [. . .]

The seventh precept, mindful and joyful living: Do not lose yourself in dispersion and in your surroundings. Practice mindful breathing [. . .] in the present moment [. . .]

The eighth precept, harmony in the community: Do not utter words that can create discord and cause the community to break [. . .]

The ninth precept, mindful speech: Do not say untruthful things for the sake of personal interest or to impress people. [. . .]

The tenth precept, standing up to injustice: Do not use the Buddhist community for personal gain or profit, or transform your community into a political party [. . .]

The eleventh precept, right livelihood: Do not live with a vocation that is harmful to humans and nature [. . .]

The twelfth precept, protecting life: Do not kill. Do not let others kill. Find whatever means possible to protect life and prevent war.

The thirteenth precept, social justice: Possess nothing that should belong to others. Respect the property of others [. . .]

The fourteenth precept, three sources of energy: Do not mistreat your body. Learn to handle it with respect [. . .] Be fully aware of the responsibility of bringing new lives into the world [. . .] (Summarized from Nhat Hanh, 1998).

Thich Nhat Hanh arranges the fourteen precepts according to their origination in body, speech and mind, which is a familiar arrangement in Buddhism. He explains that precepts one to seven deal with the mind, eight and nine, speech, while the remaining precepts, ten to fourteen, deal with the body (Nhat Hanh, 1993a: 11). The precepts are to be practised, with the devotee affirming that they have adhered to each precept during a recitation ceremony once every two weeks (Nhat Hanh, 1993a: 12–13). This is similar to the use of precepts in the monastic setting.

Though all the precepts are important to engaged Buddhism, I would like to concentrate on the first three in this chapter. The commentary accompanying their description mentions a number of ideas for each precept. For the first precept, it explains that the Buddha's teachings are like a raft, to take us from suffering to freedom from suffering. They have this specific purpose. They should not become an object of attachment as they are not absolute truths. This echoes the teaching found in an early Buddhist text known as the *Alagaddūpama-sutta* (M I 134–5), where the teachings of the Buddha are compared to a raft, 'for the purpose of crossing over, not for the purpose of grasping'. Thich Nhat Hanh suggests that 'ideological inflexibility is responsible for much of the conflict and violence in the modern world' (Nhat Hanh, 1993a: 14). He is explaining a common theme in the Buddhist description of views and opinions. This is that dogmatically clinging to the truth, or truths, causes arguments with those who adhere to other truths, and this causes conflict and violence in the world. As discussed in the opening of this chapter, the Buddha's teachings are meant to lessen disputes, arguments and quarrels. The point could be made that this open attitude to religious truth gives Buddhism its tolerant attitude. In engaged Buddhism, one must base one's political and social activism on the conviction that Buddhist doctrines should be used as guiding principles, not strict doctrines which can become an object of attachment, a set of beliefs.

The second precept prompts the practice of seeing things clearly, as they really are, not with a preconceived idea of how things are. Thich Nhat Han proposes that our minds must gain the flexibility to see that the world is based on 'interbeing and dependent-co-arising', alluding to the Order of Interbeing (Nhat Hanh, 1993a: 24). This is his way of describing interdependence and dependent-origination. The world is a conditioned phenomena with no fixed entities that can become an object of attachment. This is a central theme, that we have already encountered, and will explain in detail in Chapter 3 and Chapter 6.

The third precept entails respecting other people's viewpoints. A flexibility with one's own views, opinions and beliefs leads to a similar open attitude to other people's views and beliefs.[4] Thich Nhat Hanh suggests that this will lead to 'compassionate dialogue' which is the basis of non-violence (Nhat Hanh, 1993a: 25).

In the first three precepts of engaged Buddhism, we have a description which sets parameters of how engaged Buddhism should be practised. It is in some ways an agenda of engaged Buddhism, described by the person who coined the very term. Thich Nhat Hanh places views, opinions and beliefs at the centre of engaged Buddhism, and it is this topic that I will explore in more detail.

A certain point of view: What are views and opinions?

As we have seen, a central idea of Buddhism considers how views influence actions and how actions influence views. Wrong-views, indeed all views, can cause craving and attachment.

The term we are translating as 'views', 'opinions' or beliefs is *diṭṭhi* in Pāli (Sanskrit *dṛṣṭi*). The term *diṭṭhi* is most easily translated as 'views', though it embraces the wider notions of opinions and beliefs. The first distinction made in the early Buddhist texts are between views that are 'wrong' (*micchā*) and 'right' (*sammā*). Any view that does not agree with Buddhist doctrine is a wrong-view. Any view that agrees with Buddhist doctrine is a right-view. The aim of the path is the cultivation of 'right-view' (sammā-diṭṭhi) and the abandoning of 'wrong-views' (micchā-diṭṭhi). I refer to this as the opposition understanding of views – right-view stands in opposition to, or corrects, wrong-view. This is the most simple and basic explanation of views in the early Buddhist canon and is by far the most usual understanding found in early Buddhism.[5]

However, there is also a tradition of Buddhist thought that equates 'right-view' with 'no-view' at all. I shall refer to this as the no-views understanding of views. The aim of the Buddhist path is here seen as the overcoming of all views, even right-views (Fuller, 2004: 1–4; Collins, 1982: 87–155). Views, if held with attachment, are wrong-views. Just as objects of the senses are a hindrance, so all views and opinions, both 'wrong' and 'right' and even 'knowledge', are rejected as the means towards the goal of complete non-attachment. The aim of the path is not the cultivation of right-views and the abandoning of wrong-views but the relinquishment of all views, wrong or right. It is this type of understanding which is more in line with Thich Nhat Hanh's fourteen precepts of engaged Buddhism.

I have used the term views a number of times, and this has been adequate for the discussion so far, but how is the term precisely understood in Buddhism? What are wrong-views, and what are right-views?

There are two explanations of wrong-views. First, wrong-views are those that deny that actions have consequences; they deny the law of karma (in so doing they lead to what is unwholesome). Second, wrong-views are views about the Self (ātman/attā). They take what is not the Self, our bodies, feelings and experiences, to be the self and become attached to them.

What is right-view? These can be summarized in the following four ways. First, right-view is knowing that our 'actions have consequences'. It is acceptance of the law of karma. Second, right-view is knowing what is wholesome and unwholesome, which actions will lead to a good future state of existence, which will lead to a bad state of existence, either in this life or the next. Third, right-view is knowledge of the four noble truths, to know suffering, its cause, its overcoming and the path to overcoming suffering. This is the Noble Eightfold Path: right-view; right-intention; right-speech; right-action; right-livelihood; right-effort; right-mindfulness; and right-concentration. Fourth, right-view is knowledge of dependent-origination (paṭicca-samuppāda), what is often termed interdependence in engaged Buddhism, or in Thich Nhat Hanh's writing, interbeing. It is the knowledge that all of our experiences are conditioned – they depend on other experiences and situations, which are themselves conditioned and impermanent. Our happiness and sadness, our relationships, what we care for, and what we have hatred for are all unstable and will not last. This includes the truths by which we live, including religious truths.

This leads to the idea that views and beliefs are not an incorrect form of knowledge, or a factual or doctrinal error, but a form of attachment. It's not what they propose which makes them wrong, but what they do. Views are a problem because they become reified. When they are reified they cause suffering because they are prone to become an object of attachment. There is a fundamental idea in Buddhism that even the Buddha's teachings should not become an object of attachment. The aim of the teachings of the Buddha is to alleviate suffering, not for the teachings to become another view, opinion or belief.

To put this another way, the problem with views is their rigidity rather than their falsity. I think this is the key to their centrality in Buddhism. To rid oneself of views is not to abide in a state of blankness, but one of mental fluidity. For engaged Buddhist thinkers this mental state is an essential component of the engaged Buddhist path – Buddhist social engagement requires a state of mind in which the mind is freed from views, from mental rigidity and reification of ideas, particularly Buddhist ideas (which have the potential to become an object of attachment).

The problem with views is what they do to the individual who grasps them and is attached to them. They are an obstacle to the solitary path to awakening and the social path to Buddhist engagement. A standard way to describe them is as follows:

> The thicket of view, a wilderness of view, the contrariness of view, the turmoil of view, the fetter of views, holding, fixity, adherence, clinging, a bad path, a false way, falsity, the hold of the perverted views. (*Dhammasaṅgaṇi*, 78; Fuller, 2004: 79)

Views are sticky, clingy, a form of attachment. Right-views are the opposite. Right-views are not essentially a form of correct knowledge, but a form of non-attachment: they signify the cessation of craving (Gethin, 1997). If wrong-views are a form of attachment, not essentially a form of ignorance, then it follows that right-view is not essentially a form of knowledge, but a way of seeing the world without attachment or craving. They are a form of insight. So, although there are two ways that Buddhism describes wrong- and right-views, what I have termed the opposition and no-views understandings, the two approaches can be interpreted as proposing the same understandings of views.[6] In fact, their separation could suggest a historical tension in Buddhist philosophy. These are religious and philosophical truths which, ultimately, must be abandoned, if their purpose is to be fulfilled. Right-views are 'correct' because of the non-attachment that they achieve. One is reminded of the Mahāyāna philosopher Nāgārjuna who made the famous statement that 'emptiness is a remedy for all views, but those who take emptiness to be a view are incurable' (Burton, 1999: 37). No 'Truth' can be an object of attachment, even those that guide the Buddhist to liberation. However, a path is needed, a Buddhist teaching, that leads the Buddhist to realize this.

These ideas are central to engaged Buddhism because engaged Buddhists focus on how views affect actions and actions affect views. Wrong-views, indeed all views, can cause craving and attachment, but Buddhism does propose a right-view. However, this view is not essentially a correction of wrong-views, but a different order of seeing, one that is free from craving and attachment. Importantly for engaged Buddhism, right-view can be interpreted as forcing the individual to undertake a course of action, to be engaged – right-view then becomes an embodiment, a leading principle, of engaged Buddhism.

A Buddhist call to social activism: The Pāṭali-sutta

Certain texts in the early Buddhist canon could be understood as offering agendas for Buddhist social activism. One such text is the *Pāṭali-sutta* (S IV 340–58) from the *Saṃyutta-nikāya* (Fuller, 2004: 124–6). This *sutta* is significant because it does not support right-views which are usually prescribed. I think this points to the correct understanding of right-view. Right-view is not assent to a proposition, but a way of seeing that goes beyond doubt, calms the mind and leads to wholesome action. This has important implications for engaged Buddhism. Wholesome action, so central to the teachings of Buddhism, clearly forms the basis of engaged Buddhism. Action Dharma is a term that has been used to describe engaged Buddhism (Queen, Prebish and Keown, 2003). As I shall suggest, the ten wholesome courses of action which are the focus of the *Pāṭali-sutta* could clearly be taken as the central idea of engaged Buddhism. Indeed, in this text we have the doctrine of karma brought into the service of engaged Buddhism. Karma, in this context, is not a justification for inequalities in society, as it can be in matters of gender and sexuality which will be key to our discussions in Chapter 5. Right-action (*sammā-kammanta*), usually understood as refraining from harming living creatures, from taking what is not given and sexual misconduct (Gethin, 1998: 81), shapes involvement in the world. It illustrates how karma is a central theme of engaged Buddhism.[7]

The second half of this *sutta* follows a conversation between Pāṭali and the Buddha. Pāṭali owns a guesthouse (or an ancient Indian variety of one) where various people come to stay. Pāṭali informs the Buddha that, on certain occasions, ascetics and brahmins stay there. He recalls one particular occasion when 'four teachers holding different views (*diṭṭhi*) following different systems' came to stay. Pāṭali then recounts how each teacher taught their own religious and philosophical ideas.

The first teacher held the view of nihilism (*natthika-diṭṭhi*, S IV 348), the wrong-view that actions do not have consequences. We already know that it is a wrong-view, because to deny the law of karma is the primary type of wrong-view in the Pāli Canon. The second teacher held the view of affirmation (*atthika-diṭṭhi*, S IV 348–9), the right-view that actions do have consequences. This view affirms the existence of karma, that all actions have a consequence. Therefore it is a right-view. The third teacher held the view of non-doing (*akiriya-diṭṭhi*, S IV 349), the wrong-view that if we act in an unwholesome way, for example kill living beings, no wrong is done by the performer of these actions. Clearly, this is another wrong-view. The fourth teacher held the view that there is doing (*kiriya-diṭṭhi*, S IV 349–50), the right-view that if we act in an unwholesome way, for example kill living beings, wrong is done by the performer of these actions. Again, this is a right-view.

All of these views are to do with actions (karma) and describe wholesome and unwholesome actions. Two of them are wrong-views, denying the law of karma and that unwholesome actions will have consequences. Two of them are right-views, those that affirm that actions have consequences, and that propose that unwholesome actions will have consequences.

Wrong-views	Right-views
The view of nihilism	The view of affirmation
The view of non-doing	The view that there is doing

On hearing these different views, Pāṭali explains to the Buddha that he has doubt and uncertainty not knowing which of the recluses and brahmins were speaking truth and which were speaking falsehood (S IV 350). He wants the Buddha to simply explain which views are wrong and which are right. This should be simple for the Buddha to answer. The Buddha should respond that two of the ascetics and brahmins are speaking the truth – those who explain the right-views upholding karma and the idea that performing wholesome and unwholesome actions will lead to verifiable results, in this life or the next. A Buddha would want to help Pāṭali, and their conversation should come to a conclusion at this point. However, the Buddha explains that one of his followers should change their state of mind, and then act. In many ways he is proposing an inner and outer transformation. The Buddha explains to Pāṭali precisely what he should do:

(1) Abandoning the killing of living beings; abstaining therefrom; (2) abandoning the taking of what is not given, abstaining therefrom; (3)

abandoning misconduct in sensual pleasure [. . .] (4) abandoning false speech [. . .] (5) malicious speech [. . .] (6) harsh speech [. . .] (7) gossip, abstaining therefrom; (8) abandoning covetousness, he is no more covetous; (9) abandoning malevolence and hatred, his heart becomes free from ill will; (10) abandoning wrong-view, he becomes one of right-view. (S IV 350–2)

The Buddha has replied to Pāṭali by offering a path of action as an antidote to doubt and uncertainty. Don't bother with intellectual propositions, he seems to be saying; do something, act, be engaged, and the Buddhist path will give you answers. Technically, in the language of early Buddhism, the Buddha has suggested to Pāṭali that he abandons the ten unwholesome courses of action and adopts the ten wholesome courses of action. The follower of the Buddha knows what is unwholesome, what will lead to a negative mental state, what is wholesome and what will lead to a positive mental state. By practising in this way the follower of the Buddha is freed from covetousness, malevolence, not bewildered, but attentive and concentrated, with a mind full of loving-kindness (mettā). That person then abides (or meditates), suffusing the whole world with a mind possessed of loving-kindness (SIV 351). The idea of loving-kindness is essential to engaged Buddhism. In many of its movements, from eco-Buddhism described in Chapter 6 to trans-Buddhism described in Chapter 7 (where the full text on mettā will be given), it is a practice used to positively fight ecological disaster and gender discrimination. In the present discussion, it overcomes intellectual doubt and promotes a positive course of action. It is a call to social activism.

I consider this teaching about views to be essential to engaged Buddhism. We have seen how Thich Nhat Hanh makes these ideas the key to both the fourteen precepts of engaged Buddhism, and how they are described as the most important teachings in Buddhism. They suggest how, in order to be engaged, the Buddhist must follow some of the basic principles of the Buddhist path. Most importantly, teachings about views are emphasizing that mental stubbornness, fixations, or subjective attachment will hinder the engaged Buddhist.

Buddhism with a small 'b'

Sulak Sivaraksa is a Thai Buddhist activist who founded the International Network of Engaged Buddhists in 1989, as I mentioned in Chapter 1. His central idea is Buddhism with a small 'b'. The basic premise of this is that Buddhist ideas should not be reified. If they are reified, they are likely to become something that needs to be protected and defended. His ideas are very much in line with the danger of attachment to views and beliefs. Sivaraksa outlines what he means by Buddhism with a small 'b' (which I will summarize):

- Buddhism is a religion focused upon suffering, and this teaching is given in the four noble truths.

- To argue that Buddhism is primarily an ascetic religion, uninvolved in society, is a mistake.

- Buddhism from the outset had concepts promoting both inner and outer harmony: personal and social transformation are central to Buddhism.

- Buddhist ideas should not be reified; they should not be used to legitimate power, but to promote tolerance. It is not 'Buddhism' but 'buddhism'.

Sivaraksa begins his description of Buddhism with a small 'b' in a familiar fashion, by arguing that the Buddha himself was an ordinary man. This is a recurrent theme in both modern Buddhism and engaged Buddhism (Lopez, 2012). The supernatural character of the Buddha is downplayed. Sivaraksa's Buddha is a Buddha for normal people, who acts as a guide in how to live an ethical and worthwhile life in the modern world. The Buddha that Sivaraksa wishes to promote has a message which is universal (Sivaraksa, 1992: 62). His involvement in the world is gentle and persuasive. He is compared to a doctor, who lives for the benefit of all sentient beings. Humans require a rational and skilled physician to diagnose and help cure our suffering. We place rational faith in their skill and knowledge. This is Sivaraksa's engaged Buddhist Buddha.

Sivaraksa maintains that to understand Buddhism as a religion removed from society is a mistake. Buddhism is not, according to Sivaraksa, a religion of 'deep meditation and personal transformation' (Sivaraksa, 1992: 65). He attributes this understanding to the nineteenth-century German Sociologist Max Weber, who will be discussed in Chapter 5. For Sivaraksa, the Buddhism of South and Southeast Asia has always been concerned with personal transformation and social order. In his analysis, the Buddhist community of monastics, the Saṅgha, should act as awakened representatives of Buddhism, who have a harmonizing influence on society through their ethical deeds and virtuous lives. This, for Sivaraksa, is in contrast to contemporary Buddhism, in which the Saṅgha simply legitimizes power:

Buddhism, as practiced in most Asian countries today, serves mainly to legitimize dictatorial regimes and multinational corporations. If we

Buddhists want to redirect our energies towards enlightenment and universal love, we should begin by spelling Buddhism with a small 'b.' Buddhism with a small 'b' means concentrating on the message of the Buddha and paying less attention to myth, culture, and ceremony. We must refrain from focusing on the limiting, egocentric elements of our tradition. Instead, we should follow the original teachings of the Buddha in ways that promote tolerance and real wisdom. It is not a Buddhist approach to say that if everyone practiced Buddhism, the world would be a better place. Wars and oppression begin from this kind of thinking. (Sivaraksa, 1992: 68)

Sivaraksa's 'vision for renewing society' (Sivaraksa, 1992) is one based upon a thorough reading of Buddhist history. He suggests that the ideal of Buddhism that he has outlined has been lost, and in its place, Buddhism has become a tool of power, rather than a vehicle of a harmonious society. Sivaraksa's small 'b' Buddhism follows many historically important ideas. It evokes the simile of the raft from the *Alagaddūpama-sutta* (MI 130–42), according to which Buddhism should not become an object of attachment:

Bhikkhus, I shall show you how the Dhamma is similar to a, for the purpose of crossing over (to awakening), not for the purpose of grasping. (M I 134)

One should not regard Buddhism as maintaining set and irrefutable truths. The phrase used in early Buddhism for this attitude is to regard the teachings of the Buddha as 'only this is truth, anything else is falsehood' (M II 170–1). This leads to arguments and disputes, and, as was shown at the beginning of this chapter, the Buddha maintained that his teachings lead away from quarrels and disputes. Sivaraksa's vision of Buddhism fits well with expressions of Buddhism in which non-attachment to views is central.

Conclusion: Views and engaged Buddhism

There is a psychological problem involved in holding and obstinately clinging to views. This is a hindrance not only in more passive and ascetic forms of Buddhist practice. It is also emphasized in engaged Buddhism. For example, in the study of Buddhism it has often been noted that the teachings do not point to the changing of the world, but to the changing of our perception of it – there is nothing wrong with the world, but with the way we perceive the world. The problem of 'suffering' (*dukkha*) is not ultimately to do with the world, but with the fact that people tend to grasp and become attached to all sorts of things. The world is seen with greed, hatred and delusion. This aspect of Buddhist teaching suggests that Buddhist doctrines should not be used to change the world, but to change the way we view the world. They should be used to lessen greed, hatred and delusion and, in so doing, solve the problem of *dukkha*. What is needed is a way of 'seeing' that eradicates craving. The danger for the engaged Buddhist is that political conviction is often betrayed by rigid opinions leading to suffering.

However, as has been shown, the attitude of the holder of right-view is indicative of a course of action that leads to the abandonment of *all* views – precisely this is right-view. But to achieve right-view it is essential to act in accordance with the insight which it describes: by abandoning greed, hatred and delusion. The problem of attachment to views is central to Buddhist political and social engagement. Rather than advocating a set agenda in its political engagement, it seems to me that the distinctiveness of Buddhism is precisely to do with seeing danger in strict and immovable standpoints. On closer analysis it is action, as is often the case in Indian and Buddhist philosophy, which should be the object of religious contemplation. Views focus upon cognitive actions, the correct and incorrect grasping of Buddhist doctrines, and in turn they are the means by which philosophically complex issues are seen in their correct context.

Many issues, both in the wider Buddhist context and in the more specific study of engaged Buddhism, are brought into sharp focus with our consideration of views and their problematic nature in Buddhism. Right-view is suggestive of a mindful and non-attached attitude which is taken into the world to encounter issues in politics, ecology, gender and identity. It is often our greed for specific views, and our hatred of our opponents' opinions, that lead to conflict and delusion. Therefore, a mindful reflection on our views and opinions is essential for the practice of engaged Buddhism (Kabat-Zinn, 2005: 508–9; Moore, 2016b: 278). Views inhibit both personal and social transformation. From the most pervasive view, which proposes that there is an individual, unconditioned and permanent self (Fuller, 2004: 26–8), to views which propose a particular truth, ideology, gender or race, Buddhist teachings on views is one of the philosophical foundations of engaged Buddhism.

Discussion questions

1. What does the Buddha's reply to Daṇḍapāṇi tell us about the nature of Buddhism?

2. How are Thich Nhat Hanh's fourteen precepts of engaged Buddhism a summary of the Buddha's teachings?

3. Are all views problematic on the Buddhist path, or are some views more or less harmful than others?

Suggestions for further reading

Collins, Steven. 1982. *Selfless Persons: Imagery and Thought in Theravāda Buddhism,* 116–44. Cambridge: Cambridge University Press.

Edelglass, William. 2009a. 'Thich Nhat Hanh's Interbeing: Fourteen Guidelines for Engaged Buddhism'. In *Buddhist Philosophy: Essential Readings*, ed. Jay Garfield and William Edelgass, 419–27. Oxford: Oxford University Press.

Fuller, Paul and David Webster. 2008. 'A View from the Crossroads: A Dialogue.' *Buddhist Studies Review* 25 (1): 106–12.

Gethin, Rupert. 1997. 'Wrong View (miccha-ditthi) and Right View (samma-ditthi) in the Theravada Abhidhamma'. In *Recent Researches in Buddhist Studies: Essays in Honour of Professor Y. Karunadasa*, ed. Bhikkhu Kuala Lumpur Dhammajoti, Asanga Tilakaratne and Kapila Abhayawansa, 211–29. Hong Kong: Y.Karunadasa Felicitation Committee, Colombo, Chi Ying Foundation.

Muller, Charles A. 2018. 'An Inquiry into Views, Beliefs and Faith: Lessons from Buddhism, Behavioural Psychology and Constructivist Epistemology'. *Contemporary Buddhism* 19 (2): 362–81.

Sivaraksa, Sulak. 1992. *Seeds of Peace: A Buddhist Vision for Renewing Society,* 62–72. Berkeley: Parallax Press.

4

Dismantling metaphysics
Nirvāna, rebirth and interdependence

In this chapter I would like to consider how metaphysical ideas are described in engaged Buddhism. Engaged Buddhists offer innovative explanations on such ideas as rebirth and liberation. New interpretations doctrines, such as interdependence, are also formulated, and there are also encounters with science and modernity. There is, to an extent, a partial dismantling of metaphysics. By this I am suggesting that engaged Buddhism has less emphasis on teachings that describe the nature of reality and a focus on those with more practical aims.

Modern Buddhism

Buddhism, like other religions, began to change and adapt with new discoveries in science from the seventeenth century. New scientific discoveries, the separation of church and state (and in turn the formation of modern nation states) and the promotion of reason and empirical observation had a profound influence on religious thought, including Buddhism (Mitchell, 2016: 35–8). This period is referred to as the Enlightenment. During the nineteenth century European knowledge of Buddhism was profoundly influenced by the new focus on reason, empiricism, egalitarianism and tolerance.[1] Added to this was, from as early as the mid-fifteenth century, the shaping of the concepts of 'East' and 'West' that became concrete and profoundly influential, particularly during the colonial period, when Western powers controlled large parts of Asia, thus making the ideas of East and West geographically visible (Mitchell,

2016: 33). This period has irrevocably shaped the Western understanding of what constitutes Buddhism (Lopez, 1995).[2]

Natalie Quli has usefully summarized some of the key themes and features of modern Buddhism. In the following I will use many of her ideas, but also adapt and change her description. The key factors of modern Buddhism are:

> (1) reason and rationality are given a privileged position; (2) the tendency to define Buddhism as a philosophy rather than a religion; (3) increased status of women; (4) the laity is given a prominent position; (5) meditation is a central practice and widely practiced by lay people; (7) an optimistic view of Nirvāna in which it is realised in the present life; (8) interest in social engagement; (9) there is a rejection of ritual, 'superstition' and cosmology; (10) also a rejection of 'spirit' or 'folk' religion as mere cultural accretions (introduced through the process of decay) to be separated from the rational core of Buddhism; (11) an understanding that doctrines and texts are more authentically Buddhist than such practices such as relic veneration or chanting of Buddhist texts; (12) democracy and democratic principles are central; (13) a return to the 'original' teachings of the Buddha, particularly as ascribed to the Pāli canon; (14) a focus on texts. (See Quli, 2009: 11–12)[3]

This summary is not intended to be conclusive but indicates some of the key themes of modern Buddhism. In many ways, the Western idea of Buddhism was profoundly shaped by the ideas of the period when the West encountered it. For example, in the nineteenth century Buddhism has been portrayed as rational and scientific (Lopez, 2012) and sometimes nihilistic (Droit, 2003), while in the second half of the twentieth century it has been described as liberal and part of popular culture (Lopez, 1998a). Developments in science and a reorientation of philosophy clearly impacted on the religious conception of the universe, which not only influenced religious ideas but also had a profound influence on religious practices. Buddhism was particularly influenced during the eighteenth and nineteenth centuries through the interaction of Buddhist cultures with colonial powers. The idea that Buddhism is rational and scientific owes much to the context in which Buddhism was first encountered by the West and to colonial discourses. The idea that Buddhism is inherently apolitical should be viewed in the same way.

In the past, many of the features of modern Buddhism have been termed 'Protestant Buddhism' (Gombrich, 2006: 171–95; Mellor, 1991). Protestant Buddhism was a concept used to describe the interaction and influence of Protestant Christianity and Buddhism. The key feature of Protestant Buddhism is the importance of the laity in modern Buddhism. The idea is that this is a phenomenon in Buddhist history influenced by Protestant Christianity. This idea could have important consequences, such as the downplaying of the importance of the Saṅgha for Buddhism. It would further affect ideas regarding the spiritual capacities of laypeople and even the notion that Nirvāna can be attained by laypeople, or simply that laypeople have advanced spiritual capacities which was not necessarily the case in Buddhist history.

Those criticizing the idea of Protestant Buddhism would suggest that developments in modern Buddhism have a number of causal factors, and the interaction with Christian missionaries is one of these factors. To interpret Buddhism through the lens of Protestant Buddhism is to suggest that Buddhism needs outside influences to develop and to realize its potential. It also proposes that Asian Buddhist history has been static for much of the last fifteen hundred years (Quli, 2009: 13: Blackburn, 2002: 12; 2010).

These issues are particularly important when we consider engaged Buddhism. There might be a tendency to view Buddhist engagement as the result of Buddhism's interaction with the West during the colonial period. Buddhism was historically passive needing the influence of Christianity to find its social and political voice. Buddhism has always been dynamic; it has always contained dissenting voices, opposing political ideas, conflicting identities and unorthodox practices.

This is not to suggest that modern Buddhism, as a category, is not useful. It gives an overview of a number of assumptions about Buddhism which have shaped our understanding of what constitutes Buddhism in the modern world, and this includes engaged Buddhism. Engaged Buddhism, from its inception in the 1960s, clearly shared many of the concepts of modern Buddhism, and it is both a part of modern Buddhism and a continuation of it. Engaged Buddhism is moving beyond these confines and, in so doing, I would suggest, is embracing some of the dynamism that has always been important to Buddhism as a living religion. Many ideas of engaged Buddhism, while originating in modern Buddhism, might better be described as postmodern Buddhism. Postmodern Buddhism, in the sense I am using it, is the process by which Buddhism becomes the vibrant living tradition it is likely to have been throughout its history. Engaged Buddhism needs to dismantle some of the traditional metaphysics of Buddhism, not to mimic Western ideas and become a secular or scientific Buddhism, but in order to confront suffering. As I have explained, engaged Buddhism has a wider definition of suffering and its causes. Engaged Buddhism removes some of the metaphysical impediments to the practice of Buddhism in the modern world. I will now focus directly on some of these issues.

Nirvāna in this life

Engaged Buddhists often re-evaluate the description of Nirvāna, the soteriological goal of the Buddhist path. The term Nirvāna literally means the 'blowing out' of greed, hatred and delusion, in the individual, not in society. It is the realization of a state which is free from the endless cycle of rebirth and free from suffering. The concept of Nirvāna is central to Buddhism. When an individual achieves Nirvāna, this is the central accomplishment that makes him a Buddha. The achievement of Nirvāna is often regarded as a distant goal. The idea of the Buddhist path consisting of various stages suggests this. Some Buddhist traditions describe four 'noble-persons' (ariya-puggala):

1. The stream-attainer (sotāpatti) who is assured of awakening (nirvāna) within a maximum of seven rebirths;

2. The 'once returner' (sokadāgāmin), will be reborn as a human no more than once and is assured of awakening;

3. The 'non-returner' (anāgāmin) will, at death, be reborn in a 'pure abode' (suddhāvāsa) and gain awakening there;

4. The Arahant, who achieves Nirvāna and will never be reborn again.[4]

Christopher Queen describes a 'profound change in Buddhist soteriology' (the concepts of salvation) expressed by engaged Buddhist liberation movements in Asia, which move 'from a highly personal and other-worldly notion of liberation to a social, economic, this-worldly liberation' (Queen, 1996: 10). A key feature of engaged Buddhism is that awakening is available to laypeople as well as monastics, and this is something of an innovation in Buddhism (Gombrich and Obeyesekere, 1988: 216). In characterizing the idea that salvation is a universal goal Buddhadāsa states:

> This is a nibbāna in which everyone should be interested. It is a natural matter, something that everyone can understand and do. It is of many kinds and many levels of calm and we can attain it according to our own ability. (Cited by Jackson, 2003: 142)[5]

Buddhadāsa has also expressed the need to demystify Nirvāna and make it an achievable goal in the present life:

> Nibbāna (Nirvāna) has become a secret that no one cares about. We've turned it into something barren and silent, buried away in the scriptures, to be paid occasional lip service in sermons while no one really knows what it is. (Buddhadāsa, 2016: 2)

The engaged Buddhist Sarvodaya Sharmadana movement originated in Sri Lanka in 1958 (Ariyaratne, 1980: 588). The term Sarvodaya means 'awakening for all' (Bond, 1996: 129), while the term Shramadana has the meaning of the 'sharing of labour'. Awakening does not simply apply to the individual but an awakening of society (Bond, 1996: 130), hence the term 'awakening for all' (Bond, 1996: 2, 129).[6] The movement stresses this-worldly activity and the idea that the eightfold path should be practiced in one's daily life (Bond, 1996: 126). There are six levels of awakening in the Sarvodaya model: personality awakening, family awakening, village/community awakening, urban awakening, national awakening and global awakening (Bond, 1996: 130). Both the individual and society are liberated, awakened and overcome suffering. There is the idea of constructing a Dharmic society, which is the result of the awakening of individuals and communities – this results in a non-violent revolution. In turn this eradicates the suffering caused by colonialism and the inequalities of the contemporary social order (Bond, 2004: 3). The aim of the

FIGURE 5 *Venerable Bodhirak, founder of the Thai Santi Asoke Buddhist movement in Thailand. Credit: Samana Porbudh Chantasetdho.*

Sarvodaya movement is the awakening of society, or what can be termed a social Nirvāna – a Buddhist utopia based on truth, non-violence and self-denial. The aim is a middle way between the extremes of poverty and affluence (Bond, 2004: 3).

Santi Asoke is a Thai engaged Buddhist movement, originating in the 1970s. The meaning of their name has two interpretations. According to Keyes (1989: 137, note 1), the term Santi Asoke can be translated as 'peace transcending sorrow' (Pāli: *santi*, 'tranquillity', 'peace' and *asoka*, 'free from sorrow'). Their name also evokes the related third century BCE Indian Buddhist ruler Aśoka. Santi Asoke also offers a radical departure from traditional interpretations of Nirvāna. It gives an economic, environmental and social vision of it. In the understanding of Santi Asoke followers, Nirvāna is a state of mind achievable in this life (Heikkilä-Horn, 1997: 117).

This differs from its widely accepted interpretation in Thai Buddhism in which it is a distant goal open only to monks. The central aspiration of Thai Buddhist laypeople is to generate merit, which will afford a fortunate rebirth in a future life when one might be ordained and therefore achieve Nirvāna. However, the founder of Santi Asoke, Bodhirak (b. 1934), teaches that Nirvāna is a state of mind, and it can be achieved in this life (Heikkilä-Horn, 1997: 118). It is described as a state of calm and tranquillity, and the overcoming of the idea of a self (MacKenzie, 2007: 174). Defilements of body, speech and mind that are usually

FIGURE 6 *Monks from the Thai Dhammakāya movement. Credit: Samana Porbudh Chantasetdho.*

FIGURE 7 *A. T. Ariyaratne, founder of the Sarvodaya Shramadana Movement, pictured in 2018. Credit: Sarvodaya Shramadana Movement.*

eradicated over several lifetimes (as in the model of four holy persons given earlier) are removed in the present lifetime (MacKenzie, 2007: 181–4). This adaptation of practice radically impacts on ideas about the ultimate goals of Buddhism. The ideal of breaking an endless cycle of rebirths is replaced by the idea of freeing the mind from its cravings and attachments. As in other forms of engaged Buddhism, distant goals are adapted and made accessible to the laity.

Engaged Buddhism and rebirth

Engaged Buddhists problematize the classical Buddhist doctrines of karma and rebirth. This is necessary because both ideas can be used to enforce discrimination and to justify social inequalities. In Chapter 5 it shall be shown how the doctrine of karma is adapted in debates about gender and sexuality. In this section I would like to focus on rebirth (though karma and rebirth are clearly often related).

Let me begin with a brief example of the centrality of rebirth to Buddhism. In accounts of the Buddha's awakening, there are descriptions of three special knowledges (*tevijja*). According to the first of these, the Buddha could remember his previous lives over a vast period of time. His second knowledge related to how humans are reborn according to their actions (karma). Finally, he had knowledge of the destruction of his 'corruptions' (*āsavas*). These are fundamental types of craving and ignorance (M I 22–3, M I 247–9, D I 81–4). Rebirth and karma are central to the experience of becoming a Buddha and, indeed, to the Buddha's teachings (Fuller, 2004: 42–4).

Given this example, it is surprising that engaged Buddhists often deny that rebirth is a central teaching of the Buddha (Jackson, 2003: 113).[7] One of the most influential thinkers on engaged Buddhism has been Buddhadāsa (1906–93). He stressed throughout his teachings that rebirth should be reinterpreted (Jackson, 2003: 101–27). Buddhadāsa suggests that rebirth is not a central teaching of Buddhism:

> With ultimate understanding, one knows that, because there is no one born, there is no one who dies and is reborn. Therefore, the whole question of rebirth is quite foolish and has nothing to do with Buddhism at all. (Buddhadāsa, 1994: 4)

Logically, if there is no 'self' then there can be no rebirth. Buddhadāsa's Buddhism is logical and rational (Jackson, 2003: 114–16). This is in line with much of modern Buddhism, as we have seen. The key doctrine of not-self is, for Buddhadāsa, inconsistent with the idea of rebirth. To preserve the centrality of not-self, the notion of rebirth needs to be abandoned. The doctrine of not-self is more important than rebirth to Buddhadāsa.

Buddhadāsa also maintained that rebirth was not originally taught by the Buddha and that it was introduced into Buddhism in the first few centuries of its history (Jackson, 2003: 109). The problem with Buddhist practice is that it is based on future rebirths. As I suggested in the preceding paragraphs, because attention is directed to achieving a fortunate rebirth, religious activities are focused upon the means to achieve this. The basic way to gain a good rebirth in the future is to generate what is known as 'merit' (*puñña*). Merit is an idea closely related to karma and is understood as one's accumulation of beneficial actions that will determine the nature of an individual's rebirth. The Buddhist needs to generate merit in order for their rebirth to be prosperous and happy. Merit can be generated through meditation, adhering to the five precepts and making offerings (primarily to monks). However, with the attention focused upon future rebirths, these practices are corrupted.[8]

Buddhadāsa explains how there is a need to realign Buddhism with ethical behaviour that will benefit the individual in the here and now. By denying that rebirth is a basic Buddhist teaching, he hopes that Buddhist practice will be focused on the present life and on alleviating suffering:

> The Buddha refused to deal with those things that don't lead to the extinction of *dukkha*. He didn't discuss them. Take the question of whether or not

there is rebirth after death. What is reborn? How is it reborn? What is its 'karmic inheritance'? These questions don't aim at the extinction of *dukkha*. That being so, they are not the Buddha's teaching nor are they connected with it. They don't lie within the range of Buddhism. Also, the one who asks about such matters has no choice but to believe indiscriminately any answer that's given, because the one who answers won't be able to produce any proofs and will just speak according to his own memory and feeling. The listener can't see for herself and consequently must blindly believe the other's words. Little by little the subject strays from Dhamma until it becomes something else altogether, unconnected with the extinction of *dukkha*. (Buddhadāsa, 1994: 4)

Buddhadāsa adapts the idea of rebirth to suggest that its original use in Buddhism was to point to the (re)-birth of a selfish individual from moment to moment (Jackson, 2003: 108, 116). When the Buddhist texts talk about birth (and rebirth), they are referring to the false idea of the arising of 'I', or the self (Jackson, 2003: 116). Rebirth happens from moment to moment, with the arising of the sense of a self. From the arising of the sense of 'me' and 'mine', there are unethical actions. From the ending of this process the rebirth of the sense of me and mine is stopped. Suffering is overcome by eliminating this process of self-centredness. This cycle of birth of the sense of 'I', of the self, is the cycle of *saṃsāra* in Buddhadāsa's interpretation of Buddhism (Jackson, 2003: 117). To relinquish the ideas of a self is to experience liberation in this life. His ideas fit into an engaged Buddhist critique of the metaphysical trappings of Buddhism.

Finally, B. R. Ambedkar (1891–1956) was an Indian 'untouchable', who campaigned for the rights of outcastes, or those without a caste, in India. India has traditionally held to strict caste distinctions, which are based upon preserving the purity of each social group. Ambedkar was born into the lowest part of this system, the Mahar caste, which is a Dalit group, often referred to as untouchable. He converted to Buddhism in an attempt to escape from the Hindu caste system. His was a self-proclaimed neo-Buddhism, a new vehicle or Navayāna, mimicking the Mahāyāna or Vajrayāna of Buddhist history. He campaigned that Buddhism offered an alternative to those in the lower sections of the Hindu system. In his most famous book, *The Buddha and His Dhamma*, he made many innovative claims about the purpose of Buddhist doctrines. Notable is that the conventional doctrines of karma and rebirth are not in line with the compassionate message of the Buddha. The reason for this is that both ideas tend to subordinate and entrap individuals in an unfair system of reward and punishment. The lowly status of individuals can be justified by karma and rebirth. Ambedkar criticizes the idea because it implies that the Buddha taught a doctrine that punishes individuals for their lowly

FIGURE 8 *Venerable Bhikkhu Buddhadāsa. Credit: Buddhadāsa Indapanno Archives BW-07-073_028.*

rebirth and is used by the state to explain away inequalities in society without tackling the real cause:

> The doctrine of past karma is a purely Brahminic doctrine. Past karma taking effect in the present life is quite consistent with the Brahminic doctrine of soul, the effect of karma on soul. But it is quite inconsistent with the Buddhist doctrine of non-soul. It has been bodily introduced into Buddhism by someone who wanted to make Buddhism akin to Hinduism, or who did not know what the Buddhist doctrine was. This is one reason why it must be held that the Buddha could not have preached such a doctrine. There is another and a more general reason why it must be held

that the Buddha could not have preached such a doctrine. The basis of the Hindu doctrine of past karma as the regulator of future life is an iniquitous doctrine. What could have been the purpose of inventing such a doctrine? The only purpose one can think of is to enable the state or the society to escape responsibility for the condition of the poor and the lowly. Otherwise, such an inhuman and absurd doctrine could never have been invented. It is impossible to imagine that the Buddha, who was known as the Maha Karunika [the compassionate one], could have supported such a doctrine. (Rathore and Verma, 2011: 182. See Queen, 2013: 531)

Ambedkar argued that the Buddha did not teach that past karma influences our current life – in other words, Ambedkar argued that karma cannot be inherited. Ambedkar held that pleasure and pain experienced in the current life is the result of other factors, such as the environment, not the actions in a previous life. The idea of karma, as a controlling force that justifies lowly forms of rebirth, and the wider idea of rebirth were edited into the Buddhist traditions by Buddhist monastics wishing to align Buddhism with Hinduism (Ambedkar, Rathore and Verma, 2011: 182), which is similar to Buddhadāsa's arguments:

If a man is born in a poor family, it is because of his past bad karma. If a man is born in a rich family, it is because of his past good karma. If a man is born with a congenital defect, it is because of his past bad karma. This is a very pernicious doctrine. For in this interpretation of karma there is no room left for human effort. Everything is predetermined for him by his past karma. This extended doctrine is often found to be attributed to the Buddha. (Ambedkar, Rathore and Verma, 2011: 179)

Ambedkar clearly has in mind here the *Cūḷakammavibanga-sutta* at M III 202–6 in which this idea is found: 'It is action that distinguishes beings as inferior and superior' (M III 203). It is due to people's actions that they are inferior or superior, live long lives or short, are sickly or healthy, ugly or beautiful, uninfluential or influential, poor or wealthy, low-born or high-born, stupid or wise (M III 202–3). Ambedkar distinguishes the Buddhist doctrine of karma from the Hindu idea quite unequivocally on the grounds that the Buddhist does not believe in a transmigrating self. Ambedkar argues that the Buddhist idea of karma applies only to the present life (Ambedkar, Rathore and Verma, 2011: 178–9) and is aligned to a scientific idea of inherited traits – he argues even that the Buddhist idea is close to a modern genetic model (Ambedkar, Rathore and Verma, 2011: 179, 181).

These are similar arguments with these ideas that we find problematized in discussions of gender and sexuality which I will discuss in Chapter 5. As shall be suggested in Chapter 5, a number of issues relating to the low status of women in Buddhism and to do with alternative sexualities are justified by a strict and literal interpretation of the doctrines of karma and rebirth. Ambedkar and Buddhadāsa, in their different ways, are raising issues about some of the fundamental doctrines of Buddhism which can be used to foster prejudice and inequalities in society.[9]

Interdependence: A hybrid Buddhist doctrine

The idea of interdependence forms the philosophical basis of engaged Buddhism (King, 2009: 13–14; Loy, 1993). It is a pivotal idea throughout the history of engaged Buddhism and is central to the justification for social action (Poethig, 2002: 20). It is thought not only to be central to engaged Buddhism but a key doctrine of Buddhism (Ives, 2009a: 166–8; Bodhi, 1987: Vii). In this section I will suggest that the idea of interdependence is best understood as a hybrid of Buddhist ideas.[10]

A fundamental difference between traditional accounts of dependent-origination and interdependence is its account of the nature of the world. In traditional accounts dependent-origination describes a world of conditionality which is precarious and impermanent and pervaded by suffering. It was also used to describe rebirth over a number of lifetimes. It is a process that binds individuals to the cycle of rebirths. The modern accounts of interdependence are often imbued with a sense of wonder. They are a description of how everything is connected, a sense of natural togetherness, how nature, humans, animals and the ecological environment are dependent on each other for their existence. There is a focus upon this life or, much wider, the well-being of the planet over vast periods of time. One could say that the former is pessimistic and the latter optimistic; the former has no interest in involvement in the world, while the latter's involvement in the world, particularly the natural environment is essential. The former is focussed upon the mind, the latter on the world; the former on solitary meditation, the latter widens the analysis to the world, politics, society and ecology. There is a fundamental difference between the two outlooks, which share an essential idea – the dependent nature of phenomena. This is very much in line with the basic principles of engaged Buddhism. Interdependence needs to be formulated to give engaged Buddhism its foundational doctrine. It is the basic principle of engaged Buddhism.

In discussions of interdependence the image of Indra's net is often used (McMahan, 2008: 148; Hu, 2011: 92). Indra's net is taken from a school of Chinese Buddhism known as Huayan Buddhism, the so-called 'Flower

Garland tradition' (Williams, 2009: 129–48). The name perhaps implies that it is the pinnacle of the Buddha's teaching, a garland of flowers. A key text of this school is the *Avataṃsaka Sūtra* (the term Huayan is a Chinese translation of *Avataṃsaka*).[11] It is in this text that the image of Indra's net is said to originate. Indra's net, which is described in a separate section of the *Avataṃsaka Sūtra* called the *Gaṇḍavyūha* (Williams, 2009: 130–40) is a visionary description of the truth of the emptiness of all phenomenon. It consists of a vast net of jewels, with each jewel reflecting and being reflected in the other jewels. Everything is contained in everything else. Interdependence suggests the interconnected nature of the world and experience. It is a view of the world from the experience of a Buddha (Williams, 2009: 133). He sees the world as lacking concrete differences, because all things are empty. To use the language of Buddhist philosophy, they lack intrinsic existence (*svabhāva*).

The world is seen in its true nature. It is not the one that we perceive, but one of flow and intermingling – of interdependence. It is a world, as Paul Williams' puts it, without hard edges and one of interpenetration. It is a correct version of reality (Williams, 2009: 135). All phenomena in the universe are interconnected and woven together in an intricate net of interdependence:

> Far away in the heavenly abode of the great god Indra, there is a wonderful net that has been hung by some cunning artificer in such a manner that it stretches out infinitely in all directions. In accordance with the extravagant tastes of deities, the artificer has hung a single glittering jewel in each 'eye' of the net, and since the net itself is infinite in all dimensions, the jewels are infinite in number. There hang the jewels, glittering like stars of the first magnitude, a wonderful sight to behold. If we now arbitrarily select one of these jewels for inspection and look closely at it, we will discover that in its polished surface there are reflected all the other jewels in the net, infinite in number. Not only that, but each of the jewels reflected in this one jewel is also reflecting all the other jewels, so that there is an infinite reflecting process occurring. (Cook, 1977: 2; Loy 1993: 481)

This is the source for much of the imagery of interdependence (McMahan, 2009: 158). The idea has been important in East Asian Buddhism and in Tibet. In modern Buddhism the idea of interdependence can be followed through various Buddhist thinkers, particularly those concerned with eco-Buddhism. The notion of interdependence is often used in the debate about Buddhism and environmentalism to suggest that the basis for Green Buddhism is the doctrine of interdependence (Gross, 2000a: 412–15; Tucker and Williams, 1997). Eco-Buddhism has its basis in the idea of interdependence (Gross, 2000a: 412–15; Tucker and Williams, 1997). As Simon James suggests, a fundamental feature of modern ecology is that the physical world is not one formed by a set of 'discrete objects', but rather it is made of a dynamic and interconnected web. These concepts resonate with early Buddhist ideas (James, 2013: 602).

I think it is best to understand the idea of interdependence as a hybrid Buddhist doctrine. It can be understood as a synthesis of five Buddhist ideas: dependent-origination (*paṭicca-samuppāda*); not-self (Skt: *anātman*; P: *anattā*); emptiness (Skt: *śūnyatā;* P: *suññatā*); conditionality (Skt: *saṃskāra;* P: *saṅkhāra*); and impermanence (Skt: *anitya*; P: *anicca*).

Dependent-origination (*paṭicca-samuppāda*) is the idea that our current experiences and our future rebirths are shaped by a process of conditions and dependency. Each moment we experience is part of a process, with one condition shaping the next moment. This idea was also used to describe the process of rebirth from one life to the next. A succinct way of describing this process used in the Buddhist texts is the following:

> When this exists, that comes to be; with the arising of this, that arises. When this does not exist, that does not come to be; with the cessation of this, that ceases. (S II 95)

Second, the idea of not-self proposes that there is no enduring self existing in the past, present or the future. The individual is a conditioned phenomenon made up of separate elements that give the appearance of a self (*ātman/ attā*). Sulak Sivaraksa states that the notion of interdependence lies at the heart of Buddhist social activism (Sivaraksa, 1992: 66). Sivaraksa equates interdependence with the doctrine of not-self, and that this leads to 'a concern with social and political matters, and these receive a large share of attention in the teachings of the Buddha' (Sivaraksa, 1992: 66).

Third, the notion of emptiness became prominent in later forms of Buddhism but is found throughout Buddhist history. In many respects, it is another way of describing the dependent nature of all things, and so it could be regarded as a synonym for dependent-origination. This is particularly true for the great Mahāyāna philosopher Nāgārjuna (second–third centuries CE) who stated that whatever is dependently-originated is emptiness, and that this is the middle-way (MMK 24: 18; Garfield, 1995: 304). Phenomena are empty of an enduring essence – we formulate an identity from the constructed parts of entities which are, on final analysis, lacking in essences; emptiness is the abiding characteristic of reality. Once this is realized then one will realize that there is nothing that is worth becoming attached to.

Fourth, the idea that everything is conditioned describes how phenomena are put together, dependent upon something else, for their existence. As 'The discourse about the final awakening of the Buddha' (*Mahāparinibbāna-sutta*, D

II 72–167) records, the last words of the Buddha were 'all conditioned things (saṅkhāra) are subject to decay – strive diligently' (D II 156).

Fifth, this leads to the idea of impermanence. In the Buddhist description of existence, it is stated that one of the key causes of suffering is that all experiences and all phenomena are impermanent (as I discussed in Chapter 2). Nothing endures, things come into existence and then pass away. We might crave continuity but even things that last a long time will eventually fade. Impermanence is a key characteristic of reality.

The doctrine of interdependence is then a hybrid concept, a synthesis of these key Buddhist themes. It combines these ideas and proposes a positive evaluation of the world and our experience of it. This idea resonates with some modern ecological messages, with a sense of wonder in the natural world, and becomes a religious doctrine for the twenty-first century. David McMahan has given a comprehensive and detailed analysis of the history of interdependence as it developed to become a key theme of engaged Buddhism (2009: 149–82). He outlines a number of key influences on its development, including Romanticism, which came to prominence in the nineteenth century and emphasized emotion, imagination and the natural world; Transcendentalism, another nineteenth-century movement in part explaining the goodness of human nature and the natural world; systems theory, a twentieth-century interdisciplinary idea, explaining the interaction of complex systems (and where the source of the term interdependence might be found); deep ecology, originating in the 1970s, proposing a radical reappraisal of how we understand different parts of the ecosystem; and popular accounts of quantum physics, describing the subtle interactions of the physical world (McMahan, 2009: 149).

McMahan also offers three contexts in which the idea of 'interdependence' is used: as 'empirical description', as 'world-affirming wonder', and as an 'ethical imperative' (McMahan, 2009: 150). It is the last of these that is of the most importance to engaged Buddhism, with its obvious ecological and environmental imperatives.

> The many Buddhist and Buddhist–inspired groups engaged in environmental activism routinely cite interdependence or interconnectedness as the conceptual rationale for the link between the dharma and environmentalism. Contemporary discourse on interdependence also carries ethical and political imperatives regarding social and economic justice. (McMahan, 2009: 152)

Interdependence is used by engaged Buddhist activists to argue for the interrelated nature of politics, the environment and the economies of the world. It has become a key theme in engaged Buddhism (Queen, 2002: 234–7; King, 2009: 118; Sivaraksa, 2005: 71; Ingram, 1997). It is the philosophical pivot with which many engaged Buddhist ideas are given meaning. In some ways this understanding of Buddhism goes back to the 1960s when the notion that 'everything is connected' became part of the chorus of New Age philosophy. Ethan Nichtern, founder of the Interdependence Project, uses elements of these ideas, adapting them for mindfulness training and Buddhist activism (Nichtern, 2007).

The founding figure of engaged Buddhism, Thich Nhat Hanh, uses the related term *interbeing* to describe interdependence:

> If you are a poet, you will see clearly that there is a cloud floating in this sheet of paper. Without a cloud, there will be no rain; without rain, the trees cannot grow; and without trees, we cannot make paper. The cloud is essential for the paper to exist. If the cloud is not here, the sheet of paper cannot be here either. So we can say that the cloud and the paper *inter-are*. 'Interbeing' is a word that is not in the dictionary yet, but if we combine the prefix 'inter-' with the verb 'to be,' we have a new verb, inter-be. Without a cloud, we cannot have paper, so we can say that the cloud and the sheet of paper inter-are. (Nhat Hanh, 1988b: 3)

The notion of interdependence described in this famous passage by Thich Nhat Hanh resonates with modern theories of engaged Buddhism. As I have suggested, although the idea of interdependence originated in its developed form in Huayen Buddhism, and it clearly has its roots in the idea of dependent-origination, it cannot be properly understood without combining it with the ideas of not-self, emptiness, conditionality and impermanence. It arguably also has elements originating in wonder and positive evaluation of nature, both the natural world and human nature. It suggests the interconnectedness of the world, of our actions, and the decisions that we make. It also plays on the idea of an empirical and observable analysis. It is to this idea, the scientific nature of engaged Buddhism, to which I will now turn.

A scientific engaged Buddhism

In the modern construction of Buddhism, there has been a well-documented tendency to characterize Buddhism as a scientific religion.[12] Modern Buddhism then is often thought to be compatible with science (McGuire, 2018; Lopez, 2008; Cabezón, 2003). In engaged Buddhism, there is also thought to be a close relationship between Buddhism and science (Cabezón, 2003: 49–51).[13] There is a quote, attributed to Albert Einstein, which has become a mantra promoting the relationship of Buddhism and science:

The religion of the future will be a cosmic religion. It should transcend a personal God and avoid dogmas and theology. Covering both the natural and the spiritual, it should be based on a religious sense arising from the experience of all things, natural and spiritual as a meaningful unity. If there is any religion that would cope with modern scientific needs, it would be Buddhism.

These words are attributed to Albert Einstein, though Donald Lopez suggests they are unlikely to be genuine (Lopez, 2008: 1–2). Even if these ideas are not from Einstein, the message is clear, and one which has resonated with the modern interest in Buddhism – Buddhism is rational and scientific.

Engaged Buddhist thinkers like Buddhadāsa, who, as was explained in the preceding paragraphs, denied the centrality of rebirth in Buddhism, argued that Buddhism and science are compatible:

Buddhadāsa accepts the results of science and tries to bring scientific knowledge within the scope of his reinterpreted version of Buddhism. He does this firstly by claiming that his view of Buddhism is in accord with the findings of science, and secondly by criticizing the animist and Brahmanical aspects of Thai Buddhism as being inconsistent with his scientific and rationalistic interpretation of the scriptures. (Jackson, 2003: 34)

Indeed, Buddhadāsa clearly states that 'Buddhism as such is not a philosophy, it is a science' (Jackson, 2003: 104). This is very much in line with a revised interpretation of Buddhism (Jackson, 2003: 43). In this interpretation, Buddhism is the religion for the modern world, its methods are scientific, it is rational and doctrines like interdependence offer it a contemporary veneer.

Donald Lopez has suggested that there are two main strands to the argument that Buddhism and science are compatible. The first is that Buddhist teachings are not discredited or contradicted by the findings of science, the second is that the teachings of the Buddha in some way anticipated the discoveries of modern science (Lopez, 2008: 2).[14]

Key Buddhist texts have been used to argue for the compatibility of Buddhism and science (Evans, 2007; Fuller, 2004: 35–7). For example, the *Kālāma-sutta* (A I 188–93) is held to be a text in which the Buddha's empirical epistemology shows the rational spirit of Buddhism. It implies that the doctrines of Buddhism can be tested and verified (Jackson, 2003: 43). However, the text is more concerned with justifying ethical behaviour. Its quasi-scientific method is at best secondary.

The idea of the compatibility or complementary nature of engaged Buddhism and science is an interesting theme. Engaged Buddhists will often use it to justify and support their ideas. It also has its dangers. Robert

McGuire has suggested that there is a danger of Buddhism becoming 'demythologised away to nothing' (McGuire, 2018: 385). The idea that Buddhism and science are compatible is likely to originate in the colonial encounter with Buddhism. In the exchange of ideas about the validity of religious traditions, and justifications of religious truths between Buddhists and Christian missionaries, the use of science to defend Buddhism could have been an understandable position taken by Buddhists. This legacy has often continued into engaged Buddhism.

Conclusion

In this chapter I have outlined some of the ways that engaged Buddhism changes some of the key themes of Buddhist metaphysics. We have seen how certain key ideas of Buddhism, notably rebirth and Nirvāna, are adapted. Engaged Buddhism moves away from some of the parameters of traditional forms of Buddhism. The Buddhism of world renunciation in which the individual strives over many lifetimes to achieve awakening is not the concern of the engaged Buddhist. In engaged Buddhism, suffering originates within the mind. This is a Buddhism where suffering is tackled ecologically, politically and within society. Therefore, new interpretations are given of some of the central metaphysical categories of Buddhism. Most importantly, rebirth and awakening are redefined. Engaged Buddhism also introduces hybrid doctrines into Buddhism, most notably the idea of interdependence. As I have suggested, this idea is best understood as a synthesis of five traditional Buddhist ideas: dependent-origination, not-self, emptiness, conditionality and impermanence. It is a key idea of engaged Buddhism. We have innovative evaluations of key ideas in engaged Buddhism. Sometimes this involves dismantling them and reformulating their key themes in a new and engaged conceptual framework. For engaged Buddhists to tackle suffering, this reinterpretation is essential.

Discussion questions

1. Can Buddhism deny rebirth, or is this idea central to Buddhism?

2. What is the difference between Nirvāna in the textual tradition and Nirvāna in engaged Buddhism?

3. How does interdependence describe the world?

Suggestions for further reading

Buddhadāsa, Bhikkhu. 2016. *Nibbāna for Everyone*. Trans. Santikaro Bhikkhu. Bangkok: BIA and Liberation Park with the support of the Buddhadāsa Foundation.

Cabezón, José Ignacio. 2003. 'Buddhism and Science: On the Nature of the Dialogue'. In *Buddhism and Science: Breaking New Ground*, ed. B. Alan Wallace, 35–70. New York: Columbia University Press.

Jackson, Peter A. 2003. *Buddhadāsa: Theravada Buddhism and Modernist Reform in Thailand*. Chiang Mai: Silkworm.

Lopez, Donald S. 2010. *Buddhism and Science: A Guide for the Perplexed*. Chicago: University of Chicago Press.

McMahan, David L. 2008. *The Making of Buddhist Modernism*. New York: Oxford University Press.

Queen, Christopher S. 2002. 'Engaged Buddhism: Agnosticism, Interdependence, Globalization'. In *Westward Dharma: Buddhism Beyond Asia,* ed. Charles S Prebish and Martin Baumann, 324–47. Berkeley: University of California Press.

Quli, Natalie E. 2009. 'Western Self, Asian Other: Modernity, Authenticity, and Nostalgia for "Tradition" in Buddhist Studies'. *Journal of Buddhist Ethics* 16: 1–38.

5

Left, right and the middle way

Engaged Buddhism and politics

The Interdependence Party is a Buddhist political organization formed in Streatham, South London, in 2015. It proposes that because reality is interdependent, it will commit itself to serving the worldwide community – this will enable people of different faiths to live in harmony. It will strive to limit all types of suffering caused by gender, sexuality, race and the destruction of the natural environment. It will treat all individuals with compassion, promoting loving-kindness. It will eradicate greed, hatred and delusion in society by promoting a programme of mindfulness training. It would abolish the slaughter of animals. The party has proposed that a percentage of all earnings will be given to the Saṅgha, to the poor and to those orphaned.[1]

The Interdependence Party does not exist. However, these ideas might help us to focus on how Buddhist ideas are used in politics. This is an important question because up until the twentieth century, it is often held that Buddhism was not political. The term 'politics' is derived from *polis* which has the meaning of 'city-state', and its modern equivalent is 'what concerns the state' (Heywood, 2013: 3).[2] The term has a number of legitimate and wide-ranging meanings. It is the competition over resources, both material and non-material. It is concerned with groups of people making decisions about how these resources are distributed. Politics involves government, public affairs, compromise and consensus, and the exercise of power (Heywood, 2013: 3–12). It often involves protection and the maintenance of order. It is occupied with the making, preserving and amending of general social rules (Heywood, 2013: 2). Though the term has these multiple meanings, it is a social activity and politics is not conducted alone.

Arguments are made that Buddhists were not involved in politics, and that Buddhism is, in essence, apolitical or even antipolitical (Moore, 2016a: 2;

Lele, 2019). Buddhism is understood as other-worldly and a profoundly ascetic religion. The argument is also made that Buddhism is removed from the political sphere in order to protect its sanctity and purity (Larsson, 2015: 44–5). The idea that Buddhism is not political is based on the assumption that the path to awakening and political engagement are incompatible. The argument would then be made that it was with the emergence of engaged Buddhism that Buddhism became political. The suggestion is sometimes made that political engagement came about through the influence of the West (Queen, 1996: 31).

Engaged Buddhists reject what they see as this false version of Buddhism – the notion that it is other-worldly and apolitical. This is seen as an inauthentic caricature of Buddhism.[3] Buddhism has always been an important factor in culture, politics, economics and social welfare. The argument can be made that a disengaged, apolitical Buddhism is a product of modernity and secularism. Its history begins with colonialism when Buddhism was dismissed as unimportant. In turn, an argument is often made that Buddhist social engagement is linked to modernity (Queen, 1996: 18–19; Yarnall, 2000). The engaged Buddhists of the late twentieth and early twenty-first centuries are simply reasserting the political character of Buddhism, which has been side-lined by secularism.

It has been suggested that to separate politics and religion is a modern phenomenon (Shields, 2016: 227). Those who understand political Buddhism as a break with the earlier Buddhist traditions are making the assumption that there is a distinct division between religion and politics. The idea that Buddhism is apolitical is based upon a depoliticization of Buddhism (or removing Buddhism's political connections) made by scholars, observers and adherents of Buddhism (Shields, 2016: 228). Political engaged Buddhists promote the idea that society needs to be Buddhicized in order to imbue it with Buddhist ideas (Main and Lai, 2013: 17). It is possible that this is how Buddhist intuitions have shaped society in the past. Buddhist involvement in politics signifies a Buddhist reform of society. Society should be rebuilt on Buddhist principles and Buddhist ideas. Buddhism plays a central role of society and is a pivotal factor in the political life of a nation. This is in clear distinction to the privately practised Buddhism of much of modern Western culture.

It can be argued that to understand Buddhism as other-worldly and removed from society suits specific agendas, notably non-Buddhist political elites, or notionally Buddhist political movements (those who are culturally Buddhist and pay lip service to its institutions, but relegate its ideas on the political stage). Buddhism is made irrelevant and needs to fight to maintain its integrity and importance (Main and Lai, 2013: 15). Some forms of engaged Buddhism reject any understanding of a secular world that excludes Buddhism. Buddhism is not innately apolitical. Its apparent apolitical nature is possibly the result of modern secular cultures excluding Buddhism (Main and Lai, 2013: 25). Engaged Buddhists understand themselves as having rediscovered Buddhism's political voice. It is possible that Buddhism has always been engaged and is constantly political (Main and Lai, 2013: 15). Before considering this the apolitical caricature of Buddhism must first be considered.

Max Weber and Buddhism

As I have mentioned, an assumption is often made that Buddhism is not involved with politics. This idea is likely to have originated with the nineteenth-century German Sociologist Max Weber (1864–1920). Weber famously characterized Buddhism in the following terms:

> Ancient Buddhism represents in almost all, practically decisive points the characteristic polar opposite of Confucianism as well as of Islam. It is a specifically unpolitical and anti-political status religion, more precisely, a religious 'technology' of wandering and of intellectually-schooled mendicant monks. Like all Indian philosophy and theology it is a 'salvation religion', if one is to use the name 'religion' for an ethical movement without a deity and without a cult. More correctly, it is an ethic with absolute indifference to the question of whether there are 'gods' and how they exist. (Weber, 1958: 206)

Although clearly writing at a time when the Western understanding of Buddhism was in its infancy, Weber's characterization of Buddhism has been very influential (Henry, 2013: 7; Borchert, 2016: 29, note 19; Larsson, 2016: 86, 91; Shields, 2016: 213). In this short passage a number of important and influential points have been made. First, that Buddhism is not political. Second, that it is 'intellectual'. Third, that it is ascetic, or other-worldly. Fourth, that it is concerned primarily with salvation (from the world). Fifth, that it can be understood as an 'ethical movement'. The sixth point follows from this, that it is more of a philosophy rather than a religion. This is a pervasive and enduring portrayal of Buddhism. Finally, the eighth point, that it is not concerned with 'gods' or deities.

We can also find support for Weber's ideas that the Buddhist monk should not be involved in politics, such as its characterization as a pointless activity from early Buddhist texts:

> Bhikkhus, do not engage in the various kinds of pointless talk, that is, talk about kings, thieves, and ministers of state; talk about armies, dangers, and wars;

talk about food, drink, garments, and beds; talk about garlands and scents; talk about relations, vehicles, villages, towns, cities, and countries; talk about women and talk about heroes; street talk and talk by the well; talk about those departed in days gone by; rambling chitchat; speculation about the world and about the sea; talk about becoming this or that. For what reason? Because, bhikkhus, this talk is unbeneficial, irrelevant to the fundamentals of the holy life, and does not lead to revulsion, to dispassion, to cessation, to peace, to direct knowledge, to enlightenment, to Nibbāna. (S V 419–20)

In this passage the message is clear. The life of the Buddhist monk should have nothing to do with social and political engagement. The overcoming of suffering can only be achieved by the individual who is removed from society. This text supports Weber's analysis which characterizes the Buddhist tradition as other-worldly with little concern for politics. This understanding of Buddhism has been influential in the understanding that Buddhism is based upon personal rather than social transformation (King, 2009: 43).

Buddhism and politics

If we consider the history of Buddhist Asia, we soon realize that Buddhists were often incredibly wealthy, engaged in commerce, presided over industries, employed workers, kept slaves, and were intimately involved in Imperial politics in China. Much the same was true in Japan. The adoption of Buddhism by the ruling classes was a strategically political move that we see repeated throughout history. Powerful kings used acts of piety to try to influence the outcomes of their rule. We should then be careful in trying to find normative texts which support the non-involvement of Buddhists in politics. There could be a difference between what Buddhists say they will do, what the Buddha taught and what they did (Schopen, 1997; Elverskog, 2020). Buddhist doctrines like Mappō, which in Japanese Buddhism predicted the decline of the Buddha's teachings, or the idea of the future Buddha, Maitreya, assumed profound political importance in impacting upon the rule of emperors (by predicting their corrupt rule). We should be very careful in accepting the portrayal of Buddhism as apolitical and other-worldly. It is based on a reading of a set of normative texts which might never have reflected the reality of Buddhism as it has historically existed.

Bhikkhu Bodhi is a renowned American scholar monk and founder of Buddhist Global Relief. He has campaigned for modern Buddhists to be actively involved in politics. He has argued that there is a widespread assumption that modern Buddhist should avoid politics. This is based upon the idea that politics is viewed is a distraction from the true Buddhist path (Bodhi, 2018). However, Bodhi rallies against this caricature of Buddhism. He argues that Buddhism must be involved in politics. It is the arena where racism and oppression and militarism and the eco-crises can be fought. For Bodhi, politics is the sphere of action, and, motivated by compassion, the Buddhist should engage with politics. Bhikkhu Bodhi is making an important point to students of Buddhism. He is suggesting that there is a tendency to view Buddhism as non-political. Too often Buddhist practice is aimed at 'inward, subjective experiences geared towards personal transformation' (Bodhi, 2007), which is a modern way of restating Max Weber's description of Buddhism as being ascetic and personal, whereas Buddhists need to tackle suffering caused by 'natural calamities or societal deprivation' (Bodhi, 2007. See also Queen, 2018: 507). Buddhist social engagement originates from an analysis of suffering and how Buddhists should understand the origins and nature of suffering. Looking at the history of Buddhism, we might conclude that Bodhi has a point in highlighting the political involvement of Buddhism down the centuries. From Emperor Aśoka (third century BCE) to Nichiren (1222–82) in Japan, down to the Dalai Lama, there has been both a strong institutional involvement of Buddhism and politics and Buddhists have often had a political voice.

Similar ideas are found in the study of Buddhism and colonialism. In Walpola Rahula's *The Heritage of the Bhikkhu* (which I mentioned in Chapter 1), we find a 'manifesto of socially engaged Buddhism' (Queen, 1996: 14). In it Rahula describes the social role of the Buddhist monk, from the time of the Buddha to the modern world. An important suggestion made by Rahula is that the social role of Buddhist monks was taken over for a number of centuries by colonial powers and, in particular, by missionaries. The social and political positions of the Buddhist monks were in effect 'usurped' by colonial domination. After the fall of the colonial powers, the Buddhist monastics were again able to exercise their social and political roles (see Queen, 1996: 160). This is an interesting idea. Stated simply it is that historians of Buddhism might have been blindsided by the position of Buddhism under colonialism. It follows that the idea that Buddhism has no political interests might be misleading. Of course, during periods of rebellion against colonial powers, there is ample evidence for Buddhist involvement in politics and other social activities (Turner, 2014: 23–44; Larsson, 2015: 54–70).

Buddhism has engaged with various types of political theories and ideologies. These range from Marxism and communism, and political groups opposed to communism. It has embraced fascist and imperialist ideas. It has also been an advocate of democracy (Walton, 2017b: 535). Political groups have made use of Buddhism's flexibility and have adapted its ideas to influence politics.

To the left of the political spectrum, King Norodom Sihanouk in Cambodia in the 1950s and 1960s attempted to formulate a form of Buddhist socialism.

In a similar fashion an alliance of socialist and Buddhist ideas was formulated by the Burmese leader U Nu in the 1960s. U Nu described the goal of socialism as 'returning to this original pure [. . .] state, prior to the appearance of the defilement of craving and the corruption of man, where there are no differences in gender, beauty or possessions' (cited by Houtman, 1999: 268. See also Walton, 2017a: 236).

A theme in these political discourses is that Buddhism is used to aspire to a pure state which eradicates greed, hatred and delusion (as with our fictional Interdependence Party). This in turn leads to a political position which promotes a removal of craving enabling the establishment of a purified society. One interpretation of Buddhist ideas is that they are used to promote equality and eradicate inequality, and privilege based on class and birth. Because Buddhist philosophy has criticized all form of discrimination, we might expect Buddhism to be vocal in its condemnation of racism (Anālayo, 2020).

How Buddhism interacts with politics

There is an abundance of evidence that Buddhism has been profoundly political throughout its history. From Aśoka in India to Nichiren (1222–82) in Japan and from The White Lotus Rebellion in China (1796–1804) to the Buddhist Extinction Rebellion in the twenty-first century, Buddhists have been political.

FIGURE 9 *Buddhist Extinction Rebellion protestors on Waterloo Bridge, London, 18 April 2019. Credit: Photo by Francesca E. Harris.*

This section will consider how Buddhist institutions interact with political institutions.[4] The intention is to give an introductory model of how politics operates in Buddhist cultures. The four points I will outline are the following:

Buddhism has authority over political institutions
↓
Buddhism shares power with political institutions: Mutual respect and protection
↓
Persecution of Buddhism: Opposition and conflict with political authority
↓
Buddhism withdraws from politics

Buddhism has authority over political institutions

In the first scenario, Buddhism has authority over political institutions. In this situation, Buddhist laws override secular laws. The monk is superior to the ruler, which is suggested by this brief passage:

> For those who rely on clan, the *khattiya* (the warrior or ruler) is the best in this world; (but) the person endowed with wisdom and (good) virtue [i.e. the bhikkhu, the Buddhist monk] is the best in the whole universe. (D III 98)

This clearly indicates the superiority of Buddhist monks and, by extension, Buddhist institutions, over non-Buddhist authority. The monk is superior to the politician. Religious authority is superior to secular authority. A similar idea is found in the 'Discourse of the Fruits of the Ascetic Life' (*Samaññaphala-sutta*, D I 47-86) in which a king goes to the Buddha for advice, and the Buddha asserts the superiority of the religious life over the non-religious life. To reflect this authority Buddhism could be made the state religion. This happened briefly in Burma in the early 1960s under U Nu, in which the government became a patron of Buddhism. One of the key features of this was the demand that the state should protect and promote Buddhism (Kawanami, 2016b: 39–40). Thailand in 2007 also became close to implementing Buddhism as the state religion when the idea was almost implemented (Harris, 2016: 3).

Buddhism shares power with political institutions: Mutual respect and protection

In some Buddhist cultures the fate of the nation becomes entwined with the survival of Buddhism. This has been termed 'state-protection Buddhism'

(Harris, 2016: 4). Secular authority and the monastic order work together to the benefit of both. Kings or secular rulers require Buddhist institutions to legitimize their rule, while the Buddhist monastics depend for their material existence on the laity, with the king being the most beneficent among them. Related to this idea has been the historically important 'purifications of the Saṅgha' (Gombrich, 2006: 96–7). As part of this process the monastic order has corrupt monks removed by the decree of the king. The Saṅgha is purified and maintains its sanctity. This interaction of the state and Buddhist governance has been described as a 'soteriological state' (Harris, 2016: 5). A realm on earth is cultivated in which the devout population can practice Buddhism. The example of modern Bhutan and the idea of Gross National Happiness is suggestive of the state and Buddhism having similar ideals:

> The state's responsibility is to provide the best possible conditions to contribute to mental development for the greatest number of people given available resources. It is the job of government to remove obstacles that inhibit an individual's progress toward enlightenment and to reduce unnecessary suffering. (Long, 2019: 114)[5]

Gross National Happiness is neither a simple fulfilment of sensual desires (or simply feeling good), nor is it aligned with a sense of contentment from living the virtuous life. It is a state, mental and/or material, where the Buddha's teachings can be practised – a state of mind in which greed hatred and delusion can be eradicated. Therefore, it is the role of the nation state to provide conditions conducive to the cultivation of happiness, and the pursuit of it is more important that the pursuit of economic or material welfare (Long, 2019: 114). In this example the state and Buddhist institutions work together with mutual respect.

Persecution of Buddhism: Opposition and conflict with political authority

An entirely different scenario is that in which the state persecutes Buddhism and is a threat to Buddhism's existence. In this situation political institutions have authority over Buddhism. Modern examples would be the Chinese Cultural Revolution in the 1960s and 1970s and the Khmer Rouge in Cambodia in the 1970s. In both examples, political institutions and Buddhism were in direct conflict. The reason for the dislike or distrust of Buddhism could be economic, where Buddhist monasticism is seen as a financial strain on society, or xenophobic, where Buddhism's Indian roots are seen as unpatriotic (Harris, 2016: 6). In such cases, there could appear monastic rebellion against political rule. This opposition has been seen in the recent history of Myanmar. The so-called Saffron Revolution saw members of the Burmese Buddhist Saṅgha attempting to overthrow the military rulers of Myanmar. Since these events it could be suggested that Burmese Buddhist culture has returned to a position of mutual respect and protection.

Anti-colonial Buddhist movements are also notable, and these can take the form of a Buddhist millenarianism and messianic movements. This can often take the form of the idea of an imminent return of the Buddha, often in the form of the future Buddha Maitreya. Rebellions coalesce around such figures (Ladwig, 2014: 308–29). Such movements have been important in many countries around Buddhist Asia, particularly in China (Benn, 2014).

Finally, there are also overt and striking episodes in recent Asian history of political activism where monks and lay people undertake extreme forms of political protest. An example of this would be the self-immolation by Tibetans protesting at Chinese occupancy of Tibet (Whalen-Bridge, 2014; Vehaba, 2019). Since 2009, 155 Tibetans have burned themselves alive. This form of protest has a long and controversial history in Buddhism going back to the Vietnam War. In June 1963 the Vietnamese Buddhist monk, Thich Quang Duc, sat at a busy intersection in Saigon and set himself on fire as a protest against the persecution of Buddhism by the Catholic South Vietnam government (Veheba, 2019: 236). A number of Vietnamese monks self-immolated during the following months. Self-immolation has a long history in East Asian Buddhist traditions (Benn, 2007). Finally, a notable political protest, recognized in Buddhist history, is the so-called turning-over of the alms bowl (*pattam nikkujjeyya*). A monk might show displeasure with a lay person by refusing his or her offering (McCarthy, 2008).[6]

In all of these examples, political institutions and Buddhist institutions are in conflict. The aim of the state is to control Buddhism. Buddhism's political stance is to protest and rebel against this coercion.

Buddhism withdraws from politics

The final scenario is for Buddhism to completely withdraw from society. Buddhist monks (and occasionally nuns) have been deliberately disenfranchised in Southeast Asian countries, and this runs counters to the ideal of universal suffrage, that all members of society should be involved in the democratic process. Countering this principle, non-involvement in politics by Buddhist monks preserves their sanctity. In a sense the power of the monk is based upon his disenfranchisement. Monks could become corrupted by politics. The world of politics should not mix with the world of religion (Larsson, 2015: 40–82). When Buddhists withdraw from politics, they are consciously marking the parameters between politics and religion.[7] However, it should be noted that there are prominent modern examples in East Asia of Buddhist reformers actively encouraging the participation of Buddhist monk in politics. Taixu (1890–1947) was a Chinese Buddhist reformer who strongly advocated for monks and nuns to be socially aware, to vote and to be directly involved in politics (Main and Lai, 2013: 20; Ritzinger, 2017). Political action can, in this example, be a religious activity.

These are the four positions, which are in no way exhaustive, but are intended to give rise to further discussion. As we consider these four positions, we can trace a clear movement from overt political involvement, even control of the political process, to complete withdrawal. They are a map of the interaction of Buddhism and politics and could clearly be found in the interaction of religion and politics in other religious traditions. It appears to me that one of the tensions in the study of Buddhism and politics is precisely the idea that religion and politics are separate. This is surely one of the assumptions that engaged Buddhism attempts to discredit. Many of the leading advocates of engaged Buddhism express the idea that to act politically is to be Buddhist. Being Buddhist involves shaping society according to the ideas of Buddhism. I have used the term 'Buddhisize' to express this idea, and I think it expresses the sentiments of Buddhist political thinking. The model offered here is an attempt to describe how this takes place, or, alternatively, how certain Buddhist attitudes might deny this politicization of Buddhism.

'Dictatorial Dhammic Socialism'

In this section I would like to consider an example of how Buddhist ideas are used politically. The discussion is based on the ideas of the influential Thai Buddhist monk Buddhadāsa (1906–93). We have already considered some of his ideas relating to rebirth in Chapter 3.

One of Buddhadāsa's central political discussions is Dictatorial Dhammic Socialism. His starting point was a criticism of liberal democracy. He held that the democratic way of organizing societies was one based upon the freedom to act according to moral defilements (*Natural Cure for Spiritual Disease*, 1986a; Pali: *kilesa*. Bhikkhu Buddhadāsa, 1986b: 81, 84–5; Walton, 2017b: 538; Jackson, 2003: 240). In liberal democracies, according to his critique, individuals will simply follow their desires. Buddhadāsa's political system, when in place, will inhibit natural desires and cravings. He goes on to suggest that in his understanding socialism has a clearer sense of morality than democracy (Buddhadāsa, 1986b: 77–8). The Buddhist ruler must be a morally stable and developed individual. In turn, individuals in society will be morally developed. There is a trickle-down ethical behaviour, or enlightened leadership. The Buddhist monarch imbues his subjects with ethical qualities. As craving and desire are the root cause of an individual's suffering, it follows that they also cause social suffering. They are impediments to personal and social liberation. This is what Buddhadāsa means by Buddhist socialism.

Buddhadāsa famously, and somewhat notoriously, explained this type of socialism as Dictatorial Dhammic Socialism. He used this description because the teachings of the Buddha curtail individuals' destructive desires (Jackson, 2003: 240–1). It is also dictatorial because its methods 'will help to expedite moral solutions to social problems' (Buddhadāsa, 1986b: 83). Specifically, the Buddhist monarch who implements this strict form of Buddhist socialism does so not through tyranny but through moral strength. This monarch, or Buddhist ruler, acts according to the traditional list of 'ten royal virtues' (*dasarājadhamma*: generosity, morality, charity, honesty, gentleness, self-control, non-anger, non-violence, forbearance, non-obstruction), which will be discussed later in this chapter. Buddhadāsa explains what he means by these ideas:

'Dictatorial' means to do something absolutely and decisively (resolutely, unequivocally). This 'absolute' must be correct. If there is Dhamma, it dictates absolutely and correctly. Dictatorship is merely a tool, the means of decisiveness. Thus, dictatorship is neither evil nor good in itself, but depends on the people who use it. If used evilly, it's evil; if used well, it's good. . . . Now we are speaking of the dictatorship which is used in a good way and has Dhamma as the dictator. Would everyone please give justice to the word 'dictator'. (Quoted by Santikaro Bhikkhu, 1996: 174)

The Buddhist monarch, possessing a higher ethical standing than other members of society, has more political authority than other individuals. As he is not elected, he could be termed a karmic leader. The virtue accrued from his good conduct gives him authority. His past ethical conduct makes him the appropriate ruler. Matthew Walton has used the term 'enlightened governance' to describe leadership based upon these principles, in which the morally advanced individual is more fit for leadership and governance (Walton, 2017b: 540). Buddhism has a tendency to promote karmic, enlightened and undemocratic leadership in which politics is imposed by those who govern with wisdom.[8]

If we are troubled by Buddhadāsa's seemingly undemocratic political ideas, it could be suggested that Buddhadāsa was talking metaphorically and that he was referring to an internal dictator, to be used by individuals in society to act selflessly and to be ruthless in their suppression of selfish desires which do not accommodate the needs of the wider society (Walton, 2017b: 538–9).

The 'Two Wheels of the Dhamma'

I would now like to turn to some of the theoretical issues underlying Buddhism and politics. In order to do this, I will be use texts from the Pāli Canon.[9] It should be pointed out that these texts offer a normative system of ideas, which are likely themselves to have served a political function in both their formation and propagation. They were used by elite groups of monastics to impose and preach ideas. These monks were mostly men, educated and often wealthy. We might highlight social and political agendas in their dissemination and preservation.[10]

Although we might examine these texts to gain an understanding of political power in Theravāda Buddhist countries, we should be aware that rulers in premodern Buddhist areas often based their ideology on Indian ideas of statecraft rather than the idealized version of it in Buddhist texts (Bechert, 1973: 89). Buddhist political thinking, at the level of state and the role of monarchs, is a mixture of Buddhist and non-Buddhist elements. The latter elements often originate in Hinduism (Bechert, 1973: 89). There is also a mingling of Buddhist traditions. The popular notion that the king is a Bodhisattva is found in Theravāda traditions and probably originates in Mahāyāna Buddhism (Bechert, 1973: 89). The Pāli material is still of interest in offering a concrete set of ideas in order to describe some Buddhist attitudes to politics.

One of the main features of the description of politics in the Buddhist tradition is its description of 'Two Wheels of Dhamma', which explains the relationship between Buddhism and secular power. The first 'wheel' (cycle or spheres of influence) is 'the wheel of the law' (*dhammacakka*), or the sphere of Buddhist power and discourse, controlled by the Buddhist Saṅgha (Collins, 1998: 473).[11] This is the wheel that the Buddha set in motion in his first teaching, which is preserved in an ancient text with the title 'Setting in Motion the Wheel of the Teachings' (*Dhammacakkapavattana-sutta*, S V 420–4). The second is the 'wheel of command' (*āṇācakka*). The Buddhist king or ruler has a wheel of command, his authority and power.[12] This is the domain of a universal monarch. These are, for want of better terms, the religious and political realms. In slightly more nuanced language, some early Buddhist traditions clearly felt the need to distinguish Buddhism from power and kingship.

The idea of the Two Wheels of the Dhamma are not common in the early Pāli tradition, very rarely occurring in canonical passages. However, historically, they became important. Indeed, these concepts helped Buddhism historically to survive and expand (Keyes, 2013: 18). The two wheels understanding of Buddhist political culture was one what was prevalent around much of South and Southeast Asia from the thirteenth century to the nineteenth century (Keyes, 2013: 20).[13]

In general, this model is an ideal of Theravāda culture, and one, to some extent, adopted by Emperor Aśoka, who is considered to be the first Buddhist ruler, and who gained control of much of India in the third century BCE (Keyes, 2013: 18; Moore, 2015: 41; Jayasuriya, 2008: 55–9; Shaw, 2006: 75; Seneviratna, 1994). It is generally considered that Aśoka had a policy of conquest by righteousness (*dharmavijaya*) rather than conquest by force (*digvijaya*).

This model of Buddhist political and religious culture, and how they maintain and support each other, suggests a realistic encounter of the relationship between Buddhism and politics. They have affinities with the idea of a 'wheel-turning monarch' (Skt. *cakravartin/*P. *cakkavattin*) and the notion of becoming a Buddha. In a biography of the Buddha a prophecy is made that if he stays at home he will become a Wheel-turning monarch, while if he leaves his home, namely, becoming a wandering ascetic, he will become a Buddha (D II 16). There are exclusive destinies available for very advanced spiritual beings, but, in some sense, they require each other to maintain a Buddha's teachings and to promote and sustain the Buddhist religion. The Buddhist tradition seems to have noted both the compatibility and distinction between political and religious realms of human activity.

The *Cakkavatti-Sīhanāda-sutta* (D III 58–79), 'The Lion's Roar of the Turning of the Wheel', contains a description of the wheel-turning monarch; it clearly suggests that Buddhism has authority over political institutions (as in the model laid out in the preceding paragraphs):

Depending on the Dhamma, honouring it, revering it, cherishing it, doing homage to it and venerating it, having the Dhamma as your badge and banner, acknowledging the Dhamma as your master, you should establish guard, ward and protection according to Dhamma for your own household, your troops, your nobles and vassals, for Brahmins (Priests) and householders, ascetics and Brahmins, town and country folk, for beasts and birds. Let no crime prevail in your kingdom, and to those who are in need, give property. And whatever ascetics and Brahmins in your kingdom have renounced the life of sensual infatuation and are devoted to forbearance and gentleness, each one taming himself, each one calming himself and each one striving for the end of craving, if from time to time they should come to you to consult you as to what is wholesome and what is unwholesome, what is blameworthy and what is blameless, what is to be followed and what is not to be followed, and what action will in the long run lead to harm and sorrow, and what to welfare and happiness, you should listen, and tell them to avoid evil (*akusala*) and do what is good (*kusala*). (D III 61)

These are the duties of a wheel-turning monarch. The Buddhist king who rules according to these duties will maintain the wheel treasure, one of seven treasures which the righteous ruler is said to possess.[14] It is perhaps easiest to understand this as an auspicious sign that the king will rule in a righteous fashion. For the Buddhist ruler instils morality in his subjects. The text explains how there will be a number of Buddhist rulers who instil morality in their subjects until one of them is taken over by selfishness. When there is the stability of a Buddhist ruler, people live lives of an exaggerated length (10,000 years). There will then be a period of depravity up to the point where ethical actions are no longer practised. Eventually 'incest, excessive greed and deviant practices' (micchā dhamma) become common. Lack of respect for parents and ascetics increases. Unwholesome action becomes prevalent, and wholesome action disappears.[15] The outcome is that even the term 'wholesome' or 'moral' (kusala) is not known. People do not have the concepts of good and bad. It is quite literally a state beyond good and evil. The lifespan of the population decreases to just ten years and the complete lack of morality results in a nightmare world in which people will behave like animals, full of anger, in which mother kills child, and child kills mother. Eventually, the world is left in the following sorry state:

> And for those of a ten-year life-span there will come to be a 'sword-interval' (sattantarakappa)[16] of seven days, during which they will mistake one another for wild beasts. Sharp swords will appear in their hands and, thinking: 'There is a wild beast!' they will take each other's lives with those swords.

However, some individuals will escape, and over time, begin to practice the five precepts (D III 73–4). The cycle of the descent of the world into depravity is reversed. People adopt good or wholesome actions. They undertake wholesome actions, such as 'refraining from taking what is not given, from sexual misconduct, from lying speech, from slander, from harsh speech, from idle chatter, from covetousness, from ill-will, from wrong-views'. They pay respect to parents and ascetics. People's lifespans and beauty thereby increase – because good actions produce worldly benefits. Their lifespans reach eighty thousand years, and they live in a beautiful land. At this point a new wheel-turning monarch called Sankha will rule, and the next Buddha, Metteyya (Skt. Maitreya), will appear. Eventually Sankha will become a disciple of Mettaya and achieve awakening. As Matthew J. Moore comments:

> There appears to be widespread agreement among scholars that this story represents a novel theory in the history of Indian political thought, often referred to as the Two Wheels of Dhamma – the identification of both religious life and political/social life as being governed by the same underlying moral laws, and the assertion that ultimately the temporal powers were subordinate to the spiritual powers. (Moore, 2015: 41)

Buddhism, in this description, is central to politics and, indeed, makes Buddhist societies supreme over those without Buddhism at their centre. Essentially, members of Buddhist societies follow the Buddhist ethical path and this ensures the stability of their culture. This appears to be the central message of these texts. A Buddhist monarch is a good person who practices the precepts. Because of this, those who he rules over also practice the precepts and other wholesome actions. As soon as the ruler abandons the precepts, so do his subjects, and society descends into chaos. There are clear political messages. If part of politics involves the protection of society, as is generally true, and is certainly one of the commands of a Buddhist ruler, then the way to do this is to be a good individual, who is a morally sound person. And, it seems clear that, to really practice morality, and, therefore to rule over the most stable and virtuous society, nation or state, the ruler should be a Buddhist. Put simply, a Buddhist society is one based upon Buddhist ideas, with a Buddhist ruler, in which the people practice Buddhism.

The supreme Buddhist monarch

One of the central roles of a Buddhist monarch is to protect his society. Indeed, this could be regard as a key feature of political rule. The supremacy of the Buddhist ruler is based upon his conduct, not his birth. As has been shown, Buddhist kingship is based upon a trickle-down affect – the Buddhist ruler's virtue shapes the conduct of his subjects. The conduct of an individual explains the status of the Buddhist ruler, and this conduct shapes that of his subjects.

The details of this are found in the *Aggañña-sutta* (discourse on the knowledge of beginnings) from the *Dīgha-nikāya* (D III 80–98). The ancient non-Buddhist traditions, that we commonly refer to as Hinduism, base their superiority upon a tradition of class distinctions of 'Priests' (*Brāhmins*), 'Warriors' (*Khattiya*), 'Merchants' (*Vessa*) (merchants) and 'Servants' (*Sudda*). As the priests are held to be of a pure birth, they are the highest. The Buddhists, however, point out that one's actions and behaviour are more important to one's purity and place within society (D III 82). The text, as one would expect, supports the superiority of the Buddha's Dhamma. A king should offer service, support and maintain the Buddha and his community of ascetics. The reason for this is made abundantly clear in the text, which boldly states:

Dhamma is the best (*seṭṭho*) thing for people
In this life and the next as well. (D III 84)[17]

Another factor in the esteem of a Buddhist ruler is the respect his society is accorded in neighbouring areas (Long, 2019: 43–6). Though rulers of adjacent areas might be materially superior to those where Buddhism originated, they nonetheless pay reverence and homage to the Buddha (D III 83–4). I think this is the important political message. Followers of the Buddha avoid destructive (pāpa) and unwholesome behaviour, for example, 'taking what was not given, censuring, lying and punishment' (D III 92). They perform constructive and wholesome types of actions. In some ways the text functions as political propaganda, 'because we are a Buddhist nation, society is stable, we have a pleasant life now and are assured good future rebirth'.

The Aggañña-sutta clearly suggests that it is Buddhism that brings goodness to society and that Buddhism produces ethically sound monarchs. The first of these was Mahā-Sammata, given the fanciful etymology 'The People's Choice' (which sounds like an early forerunner of democracy). His appointment, and the subsequent establishment of Buddhism in his kingdom, heralds a culture where people do good deeds and promote what is wholesome, both individually and in society. They meditate and compile books.[18] People will be reborn in heaven according to their conduct, not their status at birth (or their beliefs). It follows that, according to their conduct people will also be born in hell (D III 96). The important ethical and political message is that conduct is the deciding factor of rebirth (as would always be the case in Buddhism) and that society should be led by a Buddhist ruler, who himself practices ethical conduct. Though they use standard doctrinal ideas about karma, the texts politicize ethics and that makes them important. A Buddhist ruler upholds certain ethical standards. These are described as the 'ten royal virtues' (dasarājadhamma) intended to influence a king's actions according to Buddhist principles. These are found in an ancient Buddhist text called the Nandiyamiga Jātaka (J 385):

1. generosity (dāna);

2. morality (sīla);

3. charity (pariccāga);

4. honesty (ajjava);

5. gentleness (maddava);

6. self-control (tapa);

7. non-anger (akkodha);

8. non-violence (ahimsā);

9. forbearance (khanti);

10. non-obstruction (avirodhana).[19]

The early layer of the textual tradition contains one more important clue relating to the politics of early Buddhism. This is found in the notable *Mahāparinibbāna-sutta*. Apart from describing the final days of the Buddha, this *Sutta* also gives the advice of the Buddha on how to maintain good governance. These are the 'seven things ideas that are conducive to welfare' (*aparihāniyā dhammā*) of society. A kingdom that follows these instructions will prosper and not decline.[20]

1. hold regular and frequent assemblies;

2. meet in harmony, break up in harmony, and carry on their business in harmony;

3. do not authorise what has not been authorised already, and do not abolish what has been authorised, but proceed according to what has been authorised by the ancient tradition;

4. honour, respect, revere and salute the elders among them, and consider them worth listening to;

5. do not forcibly abduct others' wives and daughters and compel them to live with them;

6. honour, respect, revere and salute the Vajjian shrines at home and abroad, not withdrawing the proper support made and given before;

7. ensure that proper provision is made for the safety of Arahants, so that such Arahants may come in future to live there, and those already there may dwell in comfort (D II 73–5).

These principles offer an almost unique insight into how the Buddha proposed that a society should be governed. They give a clear indication of what the Buddha proposed for a harmonious society. Taken together with the other ideas we have considered, a relatively clear idea can be gained of the type of ethical leader and the land that he rules, that it found in some Buddhist accounts of good and normative governance. Governance is based upon respect for elders and for the existing traditions, while the leader, in this case a king, is a righteous king, who spreads compassion.

The tension between the 'worldly' and 'supramundane' realms of activity

In some of these descriptions of politics and religion, there is a marked distinction between political and religious worlds. The ancient Buddhist traditions make a distinction between different realms of human activity

(Bechert, 1973: 89). This is central because in engaged Buddhism and other forms of modern Buddhism, this distinction is often removed. As I explained in Chapter 2: 24–7, in doctrinal terms there are two realms of activity: this world, the mundane world of unenlightened activity; and a supramundane world of awakened experience. The mundane world is termed *lokiya*. The term *lokiya* can be translated as 'mundane' or 'belonging to the worlds' (Ñāṇamoli, 1962: 302).[21] The supramundane world is termed *lokuttara*. The term *lokuttara* can be translated as 'supramundane', or 'dissociated from the worlds' (Ñāṇamoli, 1962: 302). The textual tradition accepts these two realms of existence, the mundane world and the supramundane world.

On a basic level one could suggest that when we are living our normal everyday lives, we are likely to be inhabiting the mundane world. However, on listening to a piece of music, on reading a poem, or looking at an inspiring piece of art, we might be elevated to a different realm, one with more clarity, in which the world takes on a different meaning. The Buddhists were perhaps making comparable distinctions in their description of the two worlds.

The tradition elaborates on its description of the mundane (*lokiya*) world. The mundane world is described as having eight 'worldly ideas': 'Gain, non-gain, fame, ill-fame, blame, praise, pleasure, pain' (A IV 157; Nett: 863). Whereas the supramundane world (*lokkutara*) has five supramundane faculties: 'The faith faculty, the energy faculty, the mindfulness faculty, the concentration faculty, the understanding faculty' (S V 193; Nett 865). In many respects, the supramundane world is the realm of the Buddha's teachings, of his Dharma. The religious, Buddhist world is a transcendent realm (Nett. 58). In traditional forms of Buddhism, there is a sharp separation between these realms. The activities of either realm do not mix together. Importantly for our discussion, politics is part of the mundane world while Buddhism is part of the supramundane world. These are distinctions that continue to have relevance in modern forms of state-sponsored Buddhism. Certain activities are set aside from Buddhist monks and are performed by Brahmin priests, such as fertility rites or the consecration of a king (Bechert, 1973: 89).

The distinction between the mundane and supramundane worlds is essential in maintaining the integrity of the path. This need to preserve the sanctity of Buddhism is often reflected in modern Buddhist societies in which the Buddhist monk should not be involved in politics.

In engaged Buddhism, the tension between these two worlds is often lessened or completely removed (Henry, 2013: 10). With this tension removed an outlet for a wider range of Buddhist practice is opened. An individual can practice Buddhism in ways not usually thought to be Buddhist – political Buddhism, eco-engaged Buddhism, ethnocentric engaged Buddhism and the engaged Buddhism of gender and sexuality are given added justification. An important innovation is apparent in the lessening of the tension between these worlds of activity. It means that traditional forms of meditation, such as mindfulness, can be used to tackle political problems – Buddhism has entered into life, and it is to this idea that our attention will now turn.

Mindful politics

Mindfulness and meditation is an area that has received a lot of attention by scholars looking for links between Buddhism and politics. Both Houtman (1999) and Moore (2016b) have made important contributions in the study of mindfulness and politics.[22] Houtman argues that meditation has been part of political culture used by opposition members in Myanmar to retain resoluteness and calmness in their protest against military rule. Meditation is also used to counter the extreme political views that pervade political discourse. Meditation, or 'mental culture', can be a tool to enable a political discourse based upon Buddhist values. Buddhism is used, quite straightforwardly, to shape the character of political debate. This has some similarities to the ideas encountered in Chapter 3, and how the problem of holding strictly to rigid views can be a danger for engaged Buddhist practice.

Matthew Moore suggests that the modern mindfulness movement has parallels and allies with the politics of the left (Moore, 2016b).[23] Moore explains that the politics of the left has many similarities with the rudimentary ideas of Buddhism. These include non-violence, pacifism, a democratic community (the Saṅgha), moral equality, vegetarianism and an ecological message. All of these ideas, suggests Moore, make Buddhism 'a good ally for the West' (Moore, 2016b: 276). Of course, as always, we might point out, as Moore does, that ideas of the liberal left might not so readily find amenable concepts in Buddhism. The Buddhist ideas mentioned, when we look at them in more detail, have nuances and, indeed, are different – for instance, the historically valid idea that Buddhists have generally supported an absolute (if idealized) monarch – from many of the cherished ideas and ideals of the left-leaning thinking of the West. Questions remain as to whether Buddhism will maintain its Buddhist roots in political discourse, or if it will become disconnected from traditional forms of practice (Moore, 2016b: 278). While a political allegiance between Buddhist mindfulness movements and politics is possible, it is clear that some of the ideals held by both may often be superficial. However, as Houtman's study has suggested, the use of meditative techniques by native traditions of mental culture, and by this, I mean Asian Buddhist groups, may be suggestive of underlying Buddhist ideas shaping political discourse. There might be Buddhist mindfulness movements engaging in political discourse, but there is arguably an emphasis in these movements where Buddhism is employed as a form of therapy to cure minds, rather than an overt form of protest using Buddhist ideas.

Conclusion

If the Buddha were to run for office, he might face some criticism. Isn't his religious tradition one that is not sullied by the reality of power and corruption? In the influential characterization of Buddhism, originating with Max Weber, Buddhism is apolitical; it is removed from society and preaches a message of world renunciation. This is a place from which Buddhism cannot be moved as it will destroy the focus of the Buddhist path. Historically, some of these assumptions are sound enough, and there is a reading of Buddhist history which supports this ideal. In this reading, the political face of Buddhism was influenced by the West, primarily by Christianity, particularly during the colonial period. However, as our model of possible interactions of Buddhism and politics has suggested, there are a number of different ways that the Buddhist encounter with society could have occurred, and the idealized version of Buddhist removal from politics is one option among several. As scholars like Gregory Schopen have argued, Buddhist were involved in power, authority, the gaining of political favour, the affairs of the court and the state (Schopen, 1997). Indeed, considering its popularity, it has been extremely successful in these activities. Buddhism proclaimed an alternative discourse, both historically and in its modern formations. Historically, among other things, it taught the political message that that rule was achieved through conduct, not birth. A harmonious society is based upon the leadership of the righteous king. This monarch, through his pious actions, will protect and defend the Buddhist state. In engaged Buddhism an equally progressive sentiment (although in some ways one opposed to the rigidity of traditional Buddhist culture) adds to its popularity. Buddhism sheds much of its conservative baggage and becomes the religion of choice of the political left. Buddhism in Asia is often conservative and preserves traditional values. However, politically engaged Buddhism has a message of radicalism in which traditional cultural and political values are questioned. It is a politics based upon mindfulness and the relentless overturning of entrenched views and opinions. Buddhism, in this light, offers a politically diverse set of values, based upon egalitarianism and equality, with very important anti-racist messages. An image of the Buddha taking the knee could easily be imagined. Buddhism does not necessarily carry a set of agendas of what is politically right or wrong, though I suggested at the beginning of this chapter, with the imaginary Interdependence Party, that this is possible. Buddhism's politics is based upon changing and adapting entrenched positions and set agendas. It promotes an awareness of multiple forms of prejudice. This, I would suggest, is the setting of Buddhist political involvement.

Political engaged Buddhism can mean many things. It could be used to support authoritarian ideas to the right of the political spectrum and be aligned to the political left. It would be a mistake to not appreciate the diverse political landscape of Buddhism.

Discussion questions

1. Is Buddhism apolitical?

2. Is Buddhism aligned to a particular political position?

3. Which forms of governance does Buddhism most easily support?

Suggestions for further reading

Borchert, Thomas. 2007. 'Buddhism, Politics and Nationalism in the Twentieth and Twenty-First Centuries'. *Religion Compass* 1 (5): 529–46.

Friedlander, Peter. 2009. 'Buddhism and Politics'. In *Routledge Handbook of Religion and Politics,* ed. Jeffrey Haynes, 11–25. New York: Routledge.

Harris, Ian Charles. 2016. 'Introduction to Buddhism and the Political Process: Patterns of Interaction'. In *Buddhism and the Political Process,* ed. Hiroko Kawanami, 1–10. New York: Palgrave Macmillan.

Larsson, Tomas. 2016. 'Buddha or the Ballot: The Buddhist Exception to Universal Suffrage in Contemporary Asia'. In *Buddhism and the Political Process,* ed. Hiroko Kawanami, 78–96. Basingstoke: Palgrave Macmillan.

Moore, Matthew J. 2016a. *Buddhism and Political Theory.* New York: Oxford University Press.

Walton, Matthew J. 2017b. 'Buddhism, Nationalism, and Governance'. In *The Oxford Handbook of Contemporary Buddhism,* ed. Michael Jerryson, 532–45. New York: Oxford University Press.

6

Eco-engaged Buddhism

There is an ancient Buddhist Sutra, a discourse containing the teachings of the Buddha which has an ecological message. This text predicts how in a future time there will be an environmental disaster, much like what is being experienced in the twenty-first century. This period is known in Indian religious traditions as the 'dark time' or *kali yuga*. At this point in human history, an ancient Buddha known as the Great Sun Buddha (some scholars think he is the Buddha Vairocana) will appear in his true form, as Smokey the Bear. After describing the ecological disaster that will appear on earth, and explaining that those threatened by pollution should chant the great mantra, the *mahāmantra* of Smokey the Bear – 'drown their butts, crush their butts' (perhaps part of the early discourse on Buddhism and violence), the Sutra then states that

> Now those who recite this Sutra and then try to put it into practice
> will accumulate merit as countless as the sands of Arizona and
> Nevada,
> Will help save the planet Earth from total oil slick,
> Will enter the age of harmony of humans and nature,
> Will win the tender love and caress of men, women, and beasts,
> Will always have ripe blackberries to eat and a sunny spot under a pine tree
>   to sit at,
> AND IN THE END WILL WIN HIGHEST PERFECT ENLIGHTENMENT
> Thus have we heard. (Hunt-Badiner, 1990: 476)

Sadly, like the Interdependence Party, this Sutra is not genuine. This parody of a Buddhist text closely echoes Mahāyāna sutras, particularly *Prajñāpāramitā* texts, is useful in highlighting one of the ways in which engaged Buddhist thinkers and activists use Buddhist ideas to tackle the environmental crisis. It is not part of any Buddhist canon, unless we wish to count it as part of a green or an eco-engaged Buddhist canon. Its title is Smokey the Bear Sutra and was written in 1969 by Gary Snyder. Snyder, who was part of a 1960s literary movement known as the Beats, was the hero of Jack Kerouac's novel *The Dharma Bums*. He is one of the early proponents of the Buddhist ecological movement (Harris, 1995a: 200–3). This group of writers and artists were, in many ways, early pioneers in the migration of Buddhism to the West. Some of the themes they emphasized continue to be of great relevance.

The history of eco-engaged Buddhism

In this chapter I will consider how engaged Buddhists tackle the suffering caused by the modern ecological crisis. This has been described as global *dukkha* (Habito, 2007: 138–9). We might use several terms to describe this movement: Green Buddhism or Green Buddhists, ecological Dharma or eco-Dharma,[1] or eco-Buddhism (Holder, 2007: 113; Harris, 1995b; Ives, 2009a: 170; Kaza, 2019). Earth Saṅgha is a term used to suggest the wider phenomenon of Buddhism and ecology, together with eco-friendly Buddhism (Johnston, 2006: 70). The term 'Terrayāna' or 'earth vehicle' was coined by Kenneth Kraft and suggests the idea that the alliance of Buddhism and ecology is a new vehicle, a *yāna*, the ecology or green vehicle, signifying a this-worldly liberation to overcome global *dukkha* (Kraft, 2000: 501). I will use the term 'eco-engaged Buddhism' (or occasionally eco-Buddhism) to refer to these movements – Buddhism with an ecological message. The term is intended to highlight the ecological and environmental Buddhist movements that actively tackle the modern ecological crises.

There is a large body of both academic and practical writing on eco-Buddhism. Three important anthologies appeared over the course of a decade from 1990. The first was *Dharma Gaia* (Hunt-Badiner, 1990). This was followed by *Buddhism and Ecology* (Tucker and Williams, 1997) and *Dharma Rain* (Kaza and Kraft, 2000).[2] For those wishing to familiarize themselves with the field of study, Johnston (2006) gives a very comprehensive survey of the literature available on Buddhism and environmentalism together with a detailed history of the Buddhist environmental movement. Ian Harris (1995a) casts a critical eye over the field of study and laid much of the methodological groundwork for the study of eco-Buddhism in his many articles on the subject. Seth Devere Clippard (2011) provides another excellent overview of eco-Buddhism. Other important studies will be considered as we encounter them in this chapter.

Two overlapping terms are being used in this chapter, ecology and environmentalism. In very general terms, ecology is the scientific study of the world's ecosystems, whereas environmentalism is the reaction to these

FIGURE 10 *An image used by Buddhist Global relief to stress eco-engaged Buddhism. Credit: Thanks to Robin Wethe Altman for permission to use her artwork.*

findings, often by activists, to ecological problems. This is important for the study of Buddhist ecology and environmentalism. When we are talking about ecology, the arguments are understood on an abstract level; when we talk about environmentalism we are referring to the actions that Buddhists take (Darlington, 2016: 489). In this chapter I will be talking about both.

An obvious point needs to be made at the outset, which is something of a dilemma for eco-engaged Buddhism. The point is that eco-engaged Buddhism is tackling problems, such as climate change, deforestation, pollution and the extinction of species, that did not exist in the time of the Buddha (Holder, 2007: 115). These are problems that did not become apparent for another two thousand years, so, how could the Buddhism of the ancient texts have a response to them? This difficulty should be acknowledged and raising it might help to alleviate some of the tensions in the study of eco-engaged Buddhism. It is a dilemma in many aspects of modern Buddhism, in studies of gender, sexuality and politics. It can also inhibit the discussion of the Buddhist response to modern ethical problems. In considering eco-engaged Buddhism, it needs to be evaluated in terms of strategies to alleviate suffering caused by the destruction of the natural environment. Consideration must be given to whether its doctrines and teachings can counter ecological problems. Clearly, we will not find historical records of the Buddha making pronouncements about deforestation, but we will find compassionate attitudes within the Buddhist texts which can be applied to the alleviation of suffering caused by the ecological crises. These will imply ways of reacting to the natural environment that lends itself to a greening of Buddhism. Eco-engaged Buddhist movements such as the Global Buddhist Climate Change Collective (gbccc.org) and One Earth (oneearthsangha.org) are motivated by the Buddha's teachings to tackle global suffering caused by the ecological crisis. These are the issues addressed by eco-engaged Buddhism.

Themes in the study of eco-engaged Buddhism

The study of eco-engaged Buddhism is split into a number of themes. We might single out a particular text as displaying environmental concerns. For example, there are attempts to locate Buddhist environmentalism in the wider Buddhist textual tradition, mostly Chinese and Tibetan, where affinities with nature are generally thought to be more pronounced than in the Pāli canon (Kaza and Kenneth, 2000: 9–78).

An alternative is to choose a particular doctrine which, it is claimed, exhibits ecological awareness. The notion of interdependence is usually held to be the main candidate to accomplish this for eco-engaged Buddhism. Many Buddhist environmentalists are influenced by the notion that the key idea of ecology is that all things in the environment are intimately interconnected, and this ecological conception of the world is in line with the early Buddhist understanding of it (James, 2013: 601). I have outlined the idea of engaged Buddhism's relationship with what I have termed the hybrid idea of interdependence in Chapter 3 and I will expand on this idea below.

Finally, it might be held that because some Buddhists lived close to nature they had an environmental awareness (Darlington, 2016: 488). Proponents of eco-Buddhism will often suggest a strong affinity between ancient Buddhist monastic communities and their proximity and appreciation of the natural environment. It has been suggested that an affinity between Buddhism and nature is found, in particular, in East Asian Buddhism. This is likely to have been due to the influence of the indigenous traditions of China, particularly Daoism, with its this-worldly aesthetic in poetry and art (James, 2013: 604). As Buddhism migrated into China and Japan, the influence of the natural environment on Buddhist teachings becomes prominent (James, 2013: 604). The idea is put forward that nature is accorded religious value in China and

Japan. There is a metaphysical shift in East Asian Buddhism which influences a Buddhist appreciation of nature. This results in an evaluation of nature not found in Indian Buddhism (Harris, 1995a: 201).

However, the argument can also be made that the natural environment was the basis for human liberation; therefore, its importance was soteriological. Its value was based on it fulfilling this function – its wildness promotes spiritual practice, therefore it is protected. There is an anthropocentric reason to care for the natural environment. It is based on the idea that humans are central to religious narratives – it is not eco-centric, based on the idea that ecology and the natural environment are central. This criticism would hold that Buddhism does not display a close affinity to nature but uses the world as a location of religious contemplation. The natural environment, particularly isolated forests and jungles, was simply used for solitary meditation (James, 2013: 603; Harris, 2000: 122). It is a realm of impermanence and suffering. As with engaged Buddhist encounters with society, Buddhism's relationship with the natural environment could be criticized on the grounds that Buddhism's focus is on eradicating suffering in the mind – the natural environment is used either to achieve liberation, or to escape from it. In Indian Buddhism arguments were not made for the preservation of the natural environment; there was no concept of sustainability. The value given to the natural environment was based on its location for religious exercise. It was often considered a place of danger and isolation where virtuoso Buddhist monks could accomplish rigorous meditative exercises. Tiyavanich Kamala has written a vivid account of the twentieth-century forest ascetics in Thailand that gives an idea of the historical use of the natural environment by Buddhist practitioners (Kamala, 1997).

Eco-engaged Buddhist ideas

Eco-engaged Buddhism claims that there are Buddhist teachings and ideas that can be used to counter the destruction of the natural environment. I have already suggested how Buddhist communities valued the natural environment as a location to practice the Buddhist path (though I have pointed out how the use of nature might not be the same as valuing nature). I would like to focus on the wider Buddhist understanding of nature. Thich Nhat Hanh has suggested that 'harming nature is harming ourselves, and vice versa' (Nhat Hanh, 1988: 41; Ives, 2013: 552). Eco-engaged Buddhists will often use this idea on both an aesthetic and metaphysical level to suggest that Buddhism has a profound connection with nature (Eckel, 1997). This is true in the aesthetic appreciation of nature across Buddhist Asia.

In considering this topic, several ideas soon become apparent: (1) Buddhist teachings might inspire art and poetry where an allegiance with nature is expressed; (2) There might be claims to a more philosophical relationship between Buddhism and nature – for example, the doctrine of not-self might be used to break down barriers between the individual and nature. The doctrine of Buddha-nature, which I will consider in the paragraphs that follow, could also be used in a similar way; (3) There are claims that Buddhist teachings can be used to alleviate the suffering caused by the destruction of forests or the pollution of cities; (4) The widespread Buddhist idea of not harming plants because animals and insects live among them could be used in a practical sense to fight the destruction of the environment (Schmithausen, 1997: 28; Darlington, 2016: 488, 490; Lucas, 2006: 75); (5) All of these ideas culminate in the assumption that Buddhism is inherently eco-friendly. This distinguishes it from the notion that there is a pathology inherent in Western appropriations of nature, which can only be overcome by creating a Buddhist ecological and green identity, and this can most readily be structured by Buddhist ideas (Harris, 1995a: 202). This ecological Buddhist identity has been termed an 'eco-self', or a 'greening of the self' (Macy, 1990).[3] The world needs to be populated by *ecosattvas* to counter the environmental crisis (Loy, 2019: 12). This position is also maintained by One Earth Sangha's EcoSattva training (oneearthsangha.org). One Earth Sangha uses the idea of interdependence to explore the suffering caused by the eco-crises. It offers guidance and Buddhist healing remedies to overcome what it describes as eco-suffering.

We might conclude that although early Buddhist communities had affinities with the natural world it is difficult to find ecological theories or environmental concerns in the various textual canons of early Buddhism. However, there has been historical affinities between Buddhism and the natural world. There are also Buddhist ideas that could suggest how Buddhist doctrines could be used to counter the eco-crises.

Eco-engaged Buddhism and interdependence

In eco-engaged Buddhism, meditation and mindfulness are used as a way to break through to environmental awareness (Anālayo, 2019: 75–7). Using language similar to those in which fixed views are transcended, Christopher Ives suggests that meditation leads to 'nonconceptual awareness' that is 'profoundly ecological' (Ives, 2013: 551, citing Pitt, 1990: 104). It is through meditation that one achieves what Joanna Macy has called 'the greening of the self' (Ives, 2013: 551, citing Macy, 1990: 53). This greening of the self goes beyond a culturally conditioned sense of self, which is not in touch with ecological concerns. Macy describes the Buddhist version of this greening of the self as based upon dependent-origination, which she appears to equate with interdependence and the image of Indra's net, from Huayan Buddhism, the so-called Flower Garden school of Chinese Buddhism (Macy, 1990: 60–1; see Williams, 2009: 129–48).[4] I discussed this idea in Chapter 3. In this section I will discuss the centrality of interdependence to eco-engaged Buddhism.[5]

Eco-engaged Buddhism suggests that Buddhism has several key doctrines that can be deployed by environmental activists: Compassion, loving-kindness, generosity, renunciation, sympathetic joy and interdependence. Interdependence is the preferred translation of the term *paṭicca-samuppāda* in eco-engaged Buddhism rather than the more usual 'dependent-origination' (see, for example Macy, 1991). Sallie B. King equates the ideas of dependent-origination and interdependence (King, 2009: 13–14).[6] It is not difficult to see why interdependence is the preferred translation of *paṭicca-samuppāda* in eco-Buddhism. It is because of the basic idea in ecology that entities in the natural world are interrelated (Clippard, 2011: 218).[7] The term interdependence is then used to suggest this meaning. It has a resonance for the environmental movement (Clippard, 2011: 218).

Some scholars, most notably Gross (2003) and Macy (1991), have argued strongly that the Buddha himself taught a doctrine on interdependence and that this is central to Buddhist ecology movements. Gross holds that the idea of interdependence is one of the most fundamental teachings of the Buddha, which he realized on the night of his awakening (Gross, 2003: 337).[8] Buddhism has a central doctrine asserting the interrelatedness, the interconnectedness of all things, peoples and environments. Therefore, Buddhism has a strong ecological message that can be used by environmental activists. It has its roots in an ancient Chinese analogy from Huayan Buddhism in which all phenomena in the universe are interconnected and woven together in an intricate net of interdependence (see the discussion in Chapter 3. See also Ingram, 1997). The term interdependence serves the purposes of eco-engaged Buddhism; it connects many of its key values. Sallie B. King, one of the most prominent writers on engaged Buddhism over the last twenty years, explains that the concept of interdependence is the most important idea expressing the compatibility between Buddhism and the ecology movement. It expresses the idea that things do not exist in isolation and that there is a mutual dependence between them (King, 2009: 118). King, like other commentators on engaged Buddhism, argues that the notion of interdependence is central to engaged Buddhist ecological thought – without questioning the validity of the idea and the innovation needed to make it fit the agendas of eco-Buddhism. This idea, that the doctrine of interdependence is a key Buddhist idea throughout Buddhist history, is a central motif of engaged Buddhism and ecology. It offers a rational and holistic interpretation of Buddhist philosophy; a green Buddhism with, as it were, an earth Saṅgha[9] at its centre (Johnston, 2006: 72).

Sulak Sivaraksa has stated that the 'concept of interdependent co-arising is the crux of Buddhist understanding. Nothing is formed in isolation and, like the jeweled net of Indra. Each individual reflects every other infinitely' (Sivaraksa, 2005: 71). Sivaraksa explains his interpretation of interdependence using other Buddhist ideas such as the evaluation of the precarious nature of the self being a conditioned phenomenon in Buddhism (utilizing Thich Nhat Hanh's idea of interbeing in his discussion. Sivaraksa, 2005: 71). In Sivaraksa's analysis interdependence and the idea of not-self (Pali: *anattā*; Sanskrit: *anātman*) express ideas of fluidity and mutual dependence that are at the heart of eco-Buddhism. In many ways similar ideas are adapted in eco-Buddhism to those utilized in other areas of engaged Buddhism (such as gender and sexuality).

Eco-engaged Buddhist writers give an optimistic interpretation of the web of conditionality. It is not to be transcended but acts as a trigger or impetus for environmental concern. The conditioned nature of existence is not a signifier of suffering, but a phenomenon that fosters environmental concern, one of wonder and meaning. The same is true of the idea of not-self, which in our model of interdependence as a hybrid Buddhist doctrine was central (see Chapter 3). Not-self is interpreted as an idea that can foster non-selfish environmental concern. These might not be traditional evaluations but there is nothing particularly wrong with Buddhist ideas being used to tackle modern problems, particularly those affecting the environment.

The way that dependent-origination is equated with interdependence is not without its detractors. For example, Lambert Schmithausen considered how dependent-origination[10] was understood in early Buddhism (Schmithausen, 1997). He argues convincingly that the doctrine was originally intended to suggest a path of liberation for individual human beings (Schmithausen, 1997: 12). He goes on to suggest that without a radical reinterpretation it could not provide a basis for ecological problems (Schmithausen, 1997: 12–13). He suggests that the idea that all things are interconnected in the present moment is not an idea found in the early texts of Buddhism, and occurs much later in China (Schmithausen, 1997: 13).[11]

Despite these objections, many eco-engaged Buddhists, and engaged Buddhists in general, use the idea of interdependence as the prevailing and key doctrine of Buddhism. It expresses a solidarity with the modern ecological crises and chimes well with many of its themes. One could argue that the doctrine of interdependence gives Buddhism a positive evaluation of the natural environment. Through it, ecosystems are invested with value.

Themes in the study of Buddhist environmentalism

The doctrine of Buddha-nature

There are several Buddhist doctrines popular in East Asia that lend themselves to an eco-Buddhist message. The idea of Buddha-nature is based upon the premise that sentient beings, humans and animals intrinsically possess Buddhahood, though in a hidden form (Schmithausen, 1991: 22). This could lead to the idea that plants, animals and rivers also possess Buddha-nature. This clearly could have influenced the spread of vegetarianism in China and such an attitude also has environmental ramifications (Schmithausen, 1991: 24). Some Chinese Buddhist teachers even suggest that plants are already Buddhas, though this would be a problematic idea in early Buddhism (Schmithausen, 1991: 22).

It could also be argued that Mahāyāna Buddhist ideas like the philosophical notion of 'non-duality', which downplays the idea that we are separate and distinct, or Nagārjuna's argument that Nirvāna and Saṃsāra are on the final analysis identical, could also promote a fruitful dialogue between Buddhism and environmentalism. The emphasis on the Bodhisattva as individuals striving to alleviate all human suffering also lends itself to ecological concerns (Habito, 2007: 134–5). All of these teachings suggest that as Buddhism spread around Asia, ideas became important that could be sympathetic to the natural world.

The importance of such doctrines to 'eco-religiosity' (Harris, 1995b: 174) or 'eco-spirituality' and the ways it could shape Buddhist environmental thinking is compelling. This idea suggests a connection between humans and the natural environment which is religiously significant. In Indian forms of Buddhism, the analysis of the natural environment was in many cases negative and, more often than not, as I have explained earlier, anthropocentric in nature (Harris, 1991, 1994a, 1995b, 1997; Schmithausen 1991, 1997). However, East Asian Buddhist ideas such as Buddha-nature suggest an intrinsic value given to nature. It promotes eco-religiosity. Nature is ontologically loaded with Buddhahood. This can broadly be described as an identification with nature (Ives, 2009a: 169–72). Having its roots in Buddha-nature and using interdependence and the idea of not-self, eco-engaged Buddhists evoke ideas of a non-dual experience of the environment in which self-interest is diminished.[12]

The argument could also be made that nature, in its spontaneity, which so inspired East Asian Buddhist poetry, also evokes impermanence. Therefore, it is being used as an object of contemplation to suggest wider Buddhist doctrinal themes and is not being given real value on its own terms.

Thai tree ordination

The fundamental premise of eco-engaged Buddhist movements is the idea that compassion and loving-kindness can instinctively be widened to include the natural world. Susan Darlington considers how Buddhist monks in modern Thailand tackle environmental problems in order to alleviate suffering. The suffering they wish to alleviate is caused, for example, by deforestation which leads to a cycle of poverty and debt, and farmers being forced to grow cash crops in ways that are destructive to the environment by government banks (Darlington, 2016: 499). In these situations, Buddhist monks understand their responsibility is to alleviate the communities' suffering. Some Buddhist monks, faced with suffering caused by the destruction of the environment and its related problems, tackle the suffering of Buddhist communities. The point has been made that compassion for sentient beings entails caring for the ecosystems in which they live (Holder, 2007: 125). This is the context of Thai tree ordinations.

Tree ordination ceremonies

One of the most widely studied areas of the Buddhist approach to environmental issues has been the Thai tree ordination movement, in which Buddhist monks symbolically ordain trees (Darlington, 1998: 7). Amid growing deforestation in Thailand from the mid-1980s onwards, a small group of Buddhist monks began to focus on environmental problems. On a basic level this movement is based upon the symbolic ordination of trees to protect them from deforestation. Individual trees are ritually ordained to give them a status similar to that of Buddhist monks. As Buddhist monks are held with such high esteem in Thai culture, these rituals stop the destruction of trees. As one would not harm a Buddhist monk, so an ordained tree is similarly protected and revered. Clearly those performing these rituals are not literally ordaining the trees – this would not be countenanced by Buddhist teachings. The trees are being given a symbolic status to suggest their sanctity. The intention is to promote environmental awareness, not to make the trees into monks.[13] This caused villagers to view nature in entirely different ways. This is an extremely notable example of eco-engaged Buddhism, and I would like to give more details of this movement.

In Buddhist Asia the natural environment has long been thought to be inhabited by various spirits which individuals interact with. In Thai Buddhist cosmology, which borrows much from general Buddhist ideas, there are three fundamental levels of experience: heavenly realms inhabited by celestial

FIGURE 11 *Thai tree ordination. The plaque reads 'To destroy the forest is to destroy the nation.' Credit: Susan Darlington.*

beings known as *thewada*, the earth inhabited by humans and hell realms inhabited by lower beings known as *phi*. Humans interact with these spirits, which are mostly benign and friendly. However, if provoked they can become malevolent. Thai Buddhists therefore perform a number of rituals to keep these spirits passive. The spirits are usually located in the natural environment, such as trees and rivers. There is then a compelling concern with the natural environment.

The first tree ordination occurred in Mae Chai in Northern Thailand in 1988. An environmental monk, who I would describe as an eco-engaged Buddhist, Phrakhru Manas, performed the ritual. He placed tree saplings at the base of an image of the Buddha in order to sanctify them. After this, they were planted, and, due to their sacred nature, were protected. The saplings were given the title of ordained tress (in Thai: *ton mai thi buat lao*. Darlington, 2012: 61). The central point of these rituals was that the destruction of the tree, or any part of the forest, would result in Buddhist demerit (Thai: *baap*). It would basically cause harm to the individual in this life or the next. Quite often, robes are wrapped around sacred Bodhi trees, the tree under which the Buddha is held to have achieved awakening. The innovation in these ceremonies is that the status of the tree is changed. Prior to its ritual ordination, it was not a sacred object (Darlington, 1998: 8–9). In one case a plaque was nailed to a tree after its ordination which translated as 'To destroy the forest is to destroy life, one's rebirth, or the nation' (Darlington, 1998: 10; 2012: 75). Issues of activism and religious and national identity are clearly evoked by aspects of Thai tree ordinations. These ceremonies culminated in a project to ordain fifty million trees to mark the Thai king's fiftieth year of reign in 1996–7 (Darlington, 2012: 69).

It is clear that the status of the tree has not specifically been changed, from a tree to an ordained tree or even a monk, but that it has been sanctified. However, villagers often consider the trees as ordained (Darlington, 2012: 61–2, 64). The tree ordinations adapted rituals to incorporate very common protective chants known in Pāli as *paritta*. These rituals involve the chanting of specific Buddhist texts to foster individual and communal well-being and are very common in South and Southeast Asia. When performed during tree ordinations, they bless the trees and transform them into sacred objects. Similar rituals are performed for rivers with long-life ceremonies.

In Buddhist countries some monks have then become aware of various ecological issues such as deforestation and problems caused by intensive chemical use in the growing of crops and the effects these practices have on wildlife populations (Darlington, 2012: 167). All of these are environmental problems that cause suffering to Buddhist and non-Buddhist communities. It is on this premise that the Buddhist environmental movement is given validity. Buddhist monks involved in the environmental movement are concerned with the suffering caused by the destruction of the natural environment. Their practices are based on the most basic Buddhist instinct, that of compassion. Buddhist rituals and symbols are employed to alleviate environmental suffering (Darlington, 2012: 167).

The formation of eco-engaged Buddhist monks is important. The concepts of 'environmental monks' (Thai: *phra nak anuraksa thamachat)* grew from, and have similarities with, 'development monks' (Thai: *phra nak phatthana*, Darlington, 2012: 6–7). The concept of development monks originated in the 1970s while the concept of environmental monks developed in the 1980s (Darlington, 2012: 50). Development monks, which is not an official category

FIGURE 12 *Buddhist monks ordaining a tree in Northern Thailand. Credit: Susan Darlington.*

within the Thai Buddhist Saṅgha, tackled, in general, the economic causes of suffering in the form of government development programmes, which were seen by them as overly materialistic. On the other hand, the later environmental monks – again, not an official Thai Buddhist Saṅgha category – tackled the environmental causes of suffering (Darlington, 2012: 108). Though this is a rather simplistic picture of these two movements, these categories are of some interest to engaged Buddhism. They indicate how engaged Buddhism can be led by monastics and that the Saṅgha can, at least unofficially, cultivate engaged Buddhist movements that operate outside of their usual activities in Buddhist societies, which is often highly traditional and conservative. Both groups have been at the forefront of promoting grass roots engaged Buddhism in Thailand for a number of decades.[14]

A number of points can be made about the phenomenon of Thai tree ordination. First, it originated with a small group of Buddhist monks who were reacting to the suffering of their community. These monks primarily acted to alleviate suffering rather than generate or offer merit. They adapted traditional Buddhist rituals and used the villagers' belief in spirits to symbolically change the way the local communities understood their natural environment. Many Buddhist rituals are based on the idea that the Buddha, his teachings, and the Saṅgha can protect one from danger and ensure a better future rebirth. By adapting these rituals to ensure the protection of the forest, the forest is in turn sanctified and suffering alleviated. Finally, and perhaps most importantly, the Buddhist monks became involved in suffering in this life and not in ensuring a better future rebirth. One of the key themes of engaged Buddhism is precisely this reorientation of the causes of suffering. Buddhist practice is oriented to this life, to the overcoming of suffering in the here and now.

Eco-engaged Buddhism

In this chapter I have described Buddhist reactions to the environmental crises. I have explained some of the strategies used by Buddhism to tackle ecological problems. Questions have been raised about the validity of these practices by seeking environmental ideas in the historical textual traditions (Elverskog, 2020). Alternatively, should eco-engaged Buddhism be understood as a new form of Buddhism?[15] It might be argued that eco-engaged Buddhism is neither a departure from the early tradition, nor a new form of Buddhism, but the natural extension of Buddhism's focus on alleviating suffering. It has been shown how eco-engaged Buddhism makes use of the hybrid Buddhist doctrine of interdependence. In adapting the meaning of dependent-origination, the Buddhist environmental movement is using a number of Buddhist ideas to counter the destruction of the natural environment. If interdependence is a hybrid Buddhist doctrine, then it can be understood as expressing a number of key Buddhist ideas and not simply as an aberration found in later Chinese Buddhism.

Early Buddhism is not likely to display an environmental awareness. In the past the natural environment was not the primary place where suffering originated. Of course, there is a stronger and more fundamental argument that, even if the natural environment had been a cause of suffering at the time of the Buddha, then his concern would still be to focus upon the internal causes of this suffering – on the mind, as is the case with much of Buddhist teachings. Leaving this wider issue to one side for a moment, in eco-engaged Buddhism strategies are used to alleviate the suffering caused by the destruction of the natural environment. The idea of interdependence, compassion, loving-kindness, not-self, Buddha-nature and ideal of the Bodhisattva could certainly be fruitful in this dialogue. As I have suggested, symbolic rituals can be used to sanctify trees, to suggest their spiritual nature, their importance in alleviating suffering. It is on these points that eco-engaged Buddhism finds its message and has value in the modern ecological debate.

Discussion questions

1. Is Buddhism environmentally friendly?

2. Which Buddhist ideas promote an eco-friendly message?

3. Are there areas in which Buddhism has negative attitudes concerning the natural environment?

Suggestions for further reading

Darlington, Susan M. 2016. 'Contemporary Buddhism and Ecology'. In *The Oxford Handbook of Contemporary Buddhism,* ed. Michael Jerryson, 487–503. New York: Oxford University Press.

Elverskog, Johan. 2020. *The Buddha's Footprint: An Environmental History of Asia.* Philadelphia: University of Pennsylvania Press.

Harris, Ian Charles. 1995b. 'Getting to Grips with Buddhist Environmentalism: A Provisional Typology'. *Journal of Buddhist Ethics* 2: 173–90.

Ives, Christopher. 2013. 'Resources for Buddhist Environmental Ethics'. *Journal of Buddhist Ethics* 20: 541–71.

Johnston, Lucas. 2006. 'The "Nature" of Buddhism: A Survey of Relevant Literature and Themes'. *Worldviews: Environment, Culture, Religion* 10 (1): 69–99.

Schmithausen, Lambert. 1997. 'The Early Buddhist Tradition and Ecological Ethics'. *Journal of Buddhist Ethics* 4: 1–74.

7

Suffering, sexuality and gender

This chapter will discuss engaged Buddhism, sexuality and gender.[1] Any discussion of sexuality and gender issues in Buddhist history is complex. On the one hand, we might expect the Buddhist perspective to be one of liberality and equality. Buddhism does not hold prejudices against sexualities and gendered identities. On the other hand, traditional Buddhist debates on gender have nuances and assumptions that are not part of the modern debate on issues of sexuality and gender. For example, deviance from heteronormativity (the belief that heterosexual behaviour is normal), based upon the gender binary of relationships between men and women, is often problematic in a number of ways in Buddhist culture and society – primarily in the context of karma and sexual misconduct. I will explore issues to do with gender, LGBTIAQ+ engaged Buddhism and trans* Buddhism and ideas related to gender and sexuality/sexualities. I will suggest how engaged Buddhism needs to adapt and change fundamental Buddhist ideas. A basic problem for engaged Buddhism is the traditional interpretation of karma. Therefore, the idea of engaged Buddhist karma will be suggested to alleviate some of the prevalent discriminations against genders and sexualities found in Buddhism.

There are a number of good places to begin a study of gender and sexuality in Buddhism – some specifically on gender, others discussing sexuality and gender. The study of gender and Buddhism was pioneered by I. B. Horner in *Women Under Primitive Buddhism* (1930). Other notable studies include Diana Paul, *Women in Buddhism* (1989); José Cabezón, *Sexuality and Gender* (1992); Rita Gross, *Buddhism After Patriarchy* (1993) and Bernard Faure, *The Power of Denial* (2003). José Cabezón's more recent *Sexuality in Classical South Asian Buddhism* (2017) is also important.[2] Other scholarship on sexuality and gender has appeared in recent years, and these will be considered in the relevant discussions below.

At the outset of this chapter, it should be stated that Buddhism, historically, often displays patriarchal and misogynistic narratives. The tradition is often

FIGURE 13 *Rainbodhi symbol, an LGBTQIA+ Buddhist Community, based in Sydney, Australia. Credit: Rainbodhi Logo designed by Ben Crompton.*

dominated by male voices (Gross, 2014: 472). It is sometimes androcentric – male themes and biases dominate its culture – rather than gynocentric, in which the female voice is prominent (Langenberg, 2019). Engaged Buddhists have questioned and challenged Buddhism's conservatism on issues of sexuality and gender discrimination (Romberg, 2002: 166–7). They also campaign to promote a liberal and egalitarian discourse on gender, proposing that all sexualities and genders have equal value. Engaged Buddhism stresses that there should be no discrimination on the basis of sexuality or gender. This chapter will explain some of the issues related to the female gender but will spend more time exploring the suffering caused by discrimination against other gender and sexual identities. It will show how engaged Buddhist gender movements campaign against discrimination as part of the wider LGBTIAQ+ debate.[3]

Buddhism and sexual desire

Buddhism understands sexual activity as problematic on a fundamental level because it is considered to be an expression of craving. Craving is the fundamental cause of suffering and therefore sex causes suffering. We could argue that sex, in the sense of having sex, is not a form of craving but an expression of love between two people. However, on a basic level, Buddhism does not approach sexual activity in this way. Its focus is often on the lustful and craving elements of sex.

A notable early text is the *Ādittapariyāya-sutta* (S IV, 19–20), often referred to as the 'Fire Sutta', or the 'discourse on burning' (Langenberg, 2018: 568). In it we find the following criticism of craving, including sexual desire:

> Bhikkhus, all is burning. And what, bhikkhus, is the all that is burning? The eye is burning, forms are burning, eye-consciousness is burning, eye-contact is burning, and whatever feeling arises with eye-contact as condition – whether pleasant or painful or neither-painful-nor-pleasant-that too is burning. Burning with what? Burning with the fire of lust (*raga*), with the fire of hatred, with the fire of delusion; burning with birth, aging, and death; with sorrow, lamentation, pain, displeasure, and despair, I say. (S IV 19)

Fire can easily get out of hand and become uncontrollable, like sexual desire; this is part of its danger. It is not craving per se which is the problem, but its uncontrollable nature. Another notable textual example of the dangers of sexual desire is found in the *Sutta-nipāta* (Sn. 766–71):

> Whoever avoids sensual pleasures, as if avoiding the head of a snake with his foot, he, being mindful, passes beyond attachment to this world. (Sn. 768)[4]

Another good way to describe Buddhist attitudes to sex and desire is with reference to the five precepts *(pañcasīla)*. These are guidelines that Buddhists follow in their daily lives. There are clear and very important distinctions between the conduct of a monastic (monk or nun) and that of the lay people (the un-ordained Buddhist community). For example, a monastic should abstain from all sexual activity, and there are strict and precise descriptions of how this rule can be broken (see Gyatso, 2005). In the following, I would briefly like to provide an overview of the general understanding of how a Buddhist layperson should act in relation to sex. The five precepts are:

1. To refrain from harming living creatures.

2. To refrain from taking what is not given.

3. To refrain from sexual misconduct.

4. To refrain from false speech.

5. To refrain from intoxicants that cause heedlessness.

The third precept is stating that the Buddhist should 'refrain from sexual misconduct' (*kāmesu-micchācāra*).[5] In general, sex is unethical, a form of behaviour to be avoided, if it involves inappropriate partners, organs, times or places. It is prohibited in the following ways:

1. If the women is 'under protection of others' (adultery, or a member of one's own family);[6]

2. Voyeurism ('where many people have gathered');

3. By using an improper orifice ('by way of the mouth or the anus');

4. In an improper place (a monastery, a shrine, etc.);

5. Too often ('more than five successive times').[7]

As I have already suggested, one could argue that Buddhism does not have a problem with sex, in and of itself. However, sex causes a number of problems. First and foremost is that it leads to craving and attachment, for more sex and for the objects of sexual attraction. And craving and attachment are, based upon the very first principles of Buddhism, the causes of suffering. All sexual relationships are, on a fundamental level, equally harmful as they are an expression of craving and attachment. Also, sex and desire perpetuates *saṃsāra*. There is a generative criticism of it – it leads to reproduction. This aspect of sex and desire is often in the foreground of Buddhist criticisms of it.

A related point is that sex leads to children, husbands, wives, a home and domestic duties. Therefore, the ideal of celibacy (*brahmacariya*) was often proposed in Buddhism. The *Brahmajāla-sutta* mentions that the Buddha abandons non-celibacy or 'unchastity' (*abrahmacariya*):

> Abandoning unchastity, the ascetic Gotama lives far from it, aloof from the village-practice of sex (*methunā*). (D I 4)

It is celibacy which distinguishes a lay person from the monastic who follows the strict monastic code. In essence, celibacy is the ideal (Jackson, 1998: 61).

Sex and reproduction detract the individual from the alleviation of suffering (Gross, 2014: 479). The aim of the Buddhist life is to cultivate certain states of mind that allow one to see the processes of conditionality, craving and attachment. In Buddhist thought this is described as 'seeing things as they really are'. The household life, founded on procreation, responsibility, and worldly status is not conducive to promoting such insight. Therefore, on a fundamental level, sex is curtailed in different but complementary ways for both the monastic and the lay person.[8]

Female gender: Equality and discrimination

A theme in Buddhist history is that women are socially and spiritually inferior to men.[9] To be born as a female is considered to be an inferior rebirth. A similar evaluation is extended to the spiritual realm, and it is argued that women are soteriologically inferior to men and that to achieve the pinnacle of the religious life a male rebirth is necessary (Appleton, 2011: 47). Female inferiority is sometimes explained in terms of the result of negative or unwholesome karma from a previous birth.

There are a number of texts which propose female inferiority in early Buddhism, and indeed throughout Buddhist history. A key passage is one in which the Buddha is asked by his aunt, Mahāpajāpatī, if an order of nuns, a female Saṅgha, can be established.[10] The Buddha refuses three times. There then occurs a conversation between the Buddha and his close attendant Ānanda. During the conversation the Buddha concedes that a woman can achieve awakening (Nirvāna). He is persuaded to allow for the ordination of women if they accept eight special training rules (gurudhammas). All of these rules mean that nuns must accept monks as their superiors. For example:

> A nun who has been ordained (even) for a century must greet respectfully, rise up from her seat, salute with joined palms, do proper homage to a monk ordained but that day. And this rule is to be honoured, respected, revered, venerated, never to be transgressed during her life. (A IV 276)

The Buddha also explains that his teachings, which would have survived for a thousand years, will now only last for five hundred years. The reason for this is straightforward – the ordination of women. In effect the establishment of the order of nuns will hasten the decline of the Buddha's teachings. This is compared to when a disease attacks a whole field of rice and the rice does not last long (A IV 278–9). This is perhaps the most notorious misogynistic passage. As Janet Gyatso points out, it is preserved in all surviving monastic traditions (Gyatso, 2003: 91, note 2).[11]

Another gendered narrative is the idea that to be a Buddha one needs to be a man. This concept is based upon the notion that a Buddha has thirty-two physical marks on his body, one of these is that he has a penis in a sheath.[12] By definition, a Buddha is a man.

> He understands: 'It is impossible, it cannot happen that a woman could be an Accomplished One, a Fully Enlightened One – there is no such possibility.' And he understands: 'It is possible that a man might be an Accomplished One, a Fully Enlightened One – there is such a possibility.' (M III 65)[13]

A woman can achieve awakening, this has already been established in the conversation between the Buddha and Ānanda in relation to the establishment of the order of nuns. There is an important distinction between an Arahant (who has achieved awakening) and a Buddha (and a Bodhisattva as the tradition develops). This is that a Buddha, unlike an Arahant, is a great teacher and can lead others to awakening. There might be significant issues of authority in the contrast of male versus female, and these are being superimposed onto the doctrinal contrast of a Buddha/Bodhisattva versus an Arahant.

There is also a biological impediment to a woman becoming a Buddha. A Buddha simply cannot have a female body (Collett, 2018: 562). He is a great man, an ideal man, an image of male beauty (Powers, 2009: 173). In Theravāda traditions the question is whether women can become Buddhas, and in Mahāyāna traditions, whether they can become Bodhisattvas.[14] Nancy Schuster has explained that 'the 32 marks were, in Buddhist tradition, the key to visual identification of a Buddha, and were indispensable to the depiction of the Buddha in art and to the visualization of the Buddha in meditation' (Schuster, 2005: 332; quoted by Powers, 2009: 173).

There is also a story suggesting the impurity of women as a notable Mahāyāna text explains:

> Completely perfected Buddhas are not women. And why? Precisely because a bodhisattva, from the time he has passed beyond the first incalculable age (of his career) has completely abandoned the state of womanhood. Ascending (thereafter) to the most excellent throne of enlightenment, he is never again reborn as a woman. All women are by nature full of defilement and of weak intelligence. And not by one who is full of defilement and of weak intelligence is completely perfected Buddhahood attained. (*The Bodhisattvabhūmi of Asaṅga*. Translation by Willis, 1985: 69, slightly adapted by Collett, 2018: 560)

The *Kamboja-sutta* further questions the character of women by stating that 'women are prone to anger; women are envious; women are miserly; women are unwise'.[15] They ensnare the minds of men 'with their glances and smiles' (A III 69), and they are a danger to men, because they are so tempting,[16] and their real quality is to be a good wife (A IV 265). A notorious series of passages occurs in two *Sappa-suttas* at A III 260–1. In these, women (*mātugāma*) are compared to a black snake (*kaṇhasappa*); women are described as

> Impure, foul-smelling, frightening, dangerous, and they betray friends, they are wrathful, hostile, of virulent venom, double-tongued, and they betray friends. (A III 260–1)

The analogy with the black snake appears to be particularly problematic. One could argue that these passages are interpolations – they were put into the Buddhist canon at a later point by a group of Buddhist monks who were themselves misogynistic.

There are also many examples where women are portrayed in a positive way,[17] and this is particularly true of their religious qualities (Collett, 2018: 560–1). So, across all Buddhist traditions there are both positive and negative evaluations of the religious potential of women. However, in all Buddhist traditions, suggestions of the inferiority of women are also clear.

Gender and culture

Some scholars, while accepting that there is gender discrimination in the history of Buddhism, argue that this is a phenomenon that has grown from the native culture in which Buddhism flourished. In this argument there is no gender discrimination in the foundational doctrines of Buddhism. Perhaps the best proponent of this idea is Alice Collett, who has summarized this thesis in the following way:

> [A]lthough the idea of the inferiority of women is one that is very much alive today in some Buddhist traditions, just as it has been historically, it is a doctrinally and ethically unsubstantiated view. I aim to demonstrate that the reasons posited for female inferiority are unfounded and that there is no doctrinal or ethical basis for it within tradition. In fact, the opposite is instead the case; the arguments made in favour of female inferiority in no way accord with core Buddhist doctrine and the central ethical tenets of the tradition. This is so much the case that an obvious conclusion to be drawn is that the ideas about female inferiority came into Buddhism through ingestion of norms and mores of traditional societies rather than as an integral part of Buddhist ontological or ideological principles. (Collett, 2018: 552)

Collett is arguing that the discrimination against women in Buddhist traditions is due to cultural influence.[18] In a way, culture has muddied the clear waters of the Buddhist tradition. She states quite clearly that the idea of the inferiority of women, found in many Buddhist cultures (and, one must suggest Buddhist textual traditions), are 'undoctrinal' and 'unethical' according to the underlying doctrines and ethics of the Pāli Canon (Collett, 2018: 553). Social norms which degenerate women are subsumed into the Pāli Canon (Collett, 2018: 554):

Given that the idea of women being inferior comes from the notion that female nature is the problem, and this is both undoctrinal and does not chime with Buddhist ethics nor the principles that underlie moral decision-making, this suggests that the negativity towards women and sporadic misogyny we come across in Pāli literature has likely found its way in via ingestion of the traditional (non-Buddhist) view of women found in ancient South Asian societies, rather than for a doctrinally motivated or ethically significant reason grounded in Buddhist principles or teaching. (Collett, 2018: 559)

If I understand Collett correctly she is arguing that Buddhism is doctrinally and philosophically genderless, or at least that it would not support any form of gender discrimination. Buddhism's misogyny is a cultural accretion:

To say a woman is inferior to a man because of her (static and unchangeable) 'female nature' is therefore to deny the quintessence of Buddhism. (Collett, 2018: 559)

There is no static, gendered 'nature' according to the doctrine of dependent-origination. Such an idea is alien to Buddhism. There are very real methodological issues with Collett's ideas of how to even separate 'pure doctrine' from 'cultural accretion' and the presuppositions in doing so, as well as issues of how selective and arbitrary this process can be. Nonetheless, she is one of the few scholars to challenge misogyny in the Buddhist texts.

There is still the question of how misogynistic passages found their way into Buddhism. Philosophically, there is a strong case to suggest that Buddhism held the genders to be equal. But, historically, culturally and in some texts the genders are not equal. As Roger Corless has stated, Buddhism preaches but does not often practice non-duality (Corless, 2000: 278; Vella, 2019: 63).

Buddhism gives two different answers to the question of gender equality. It might be appropriate to think in terms of us receiving different answers because we are posing the question to separate parts of the Buddhist tradition. One is philosophical, attempting to explain and understand the truths of the Buddha's teachings. The other is narrative, with social, political and cultural interests.

To address the misogynistic passages directly, a nuanced understanding might be to acknowledge the societal, political and cultural context that these passages were addressing. They could simply be reflections of the interests of male monastics who aimed to embellish their positions as leaders of Buddhist culture. Therefore, they denigrated the status of women and in so doing lessened the threat of competition for status from the female monastics. The passages are not reflections of philosophical interests.

The difficulty for engaged Buddhists is that, culturally or otherwise, misogynistic and androcentric ideas are prevalent in both the textual and historical traditions of Buddhism. However, it should be pointed out that engaged Buddhists, like many modern Buddhist movements, are centred on the philosophical tradition, as it is often considered that this is the place where a true type of Buddhism, free from the trappings of culture and status, is found.

Sakyadhita: Campaigning for gender equality

Sakyadhita is an engaged Buddhist group that campaigns for gender equality. The term Sakyadhita means 'daughters of the Buddha'.[19] Their key focus is the establishment (or reestablishment) of the order of nuns in Buddhist Asia. The order of nuns was established during the lifetime of the Buddha and survives in China, Korea and in some forms of Vietnamese Buddhism. It originally lasted for around 1,500 years in Sri Lanka but died out around the eleventh century. It was never properly established in Tibet or in most of Southeast Asia (Gross, 2014: 476). A Buddhist nun in these countries is a woman who adopts eight or ten precepts, basically the ordination of a novice. These are referred to with different designations in each country, *dasa sil mata* in Sri Lanka, *mae chi* in Thailand and *thilashin* in Myanmar.

Although complex, a summary of the situation is the following. For a female to be ordained, there needs to be a group of nuns who have been ordained for a number of years. This is clearly not possible in a region where there are no ordained nuns (Harvey, 1990: 23). The debate about female ordination often centres around legalistic issues to do with having a true transmission of the teaching, and members of the Saṅgha needing to authenticate the ordination. It is possible to 'import' the lineage from other countries, but there is often opposition to this. Therefore, a major concern of Sakyadhita is to promote the full ordination of women. They also take on a number of other issues such as sexual violence against women and the establishment of female Buddhist communities around the world.

Homosexuality in Buddhist history: Karmic sexuality

When we turn to more general issues to do with sexuality in Buddhism, a number of assumptions are apparent.[20] For example, we might assume that

Buddhism has a tolerant attitude to different types of sexual orientation, that gender will not be a fixed category, and that there is an openness to types of queerness.[21] Tolerance is central to Buddhism, and it could justifiably be assumed that Buddhists would practise tolerance towards different sexualities (Hu, 2016: 662). Buddhism emphasizes tolerance and compassion and has key doctrines which counter discrimination.

If sexual identity causes suffering, then this clearly fits within the remit of engaged Buddhism.[22] In general, many societies have adopted 'heteronormativity'. This is the idea, as I have mentioned, that heterosexual activity, relationships between people of the opposite sex, are normal, standard and accepted by society as a whole. José Cabezón has suggested that Buddhism in general has been neutral in its view of homosexuality:

> Despite the ambivalence concerning homosexuality in Buddhist history, the evidence seems to suggest that as a whole Buddhism has been for the most part neutral on the question of homosexuality. The principal question for Buddhism has not been one of heterosexuality vs. homosexuality but one of sexuality vs. celibacy. In this sense, homosexuality when condemned is condemned more for being an instance of sexuality than for being homos (involving partners of the same sex). The fact that Buddhism has been essentially neutral in this regard does not imply that the cultures in which Buddhism arose and flourished have always been neutral. Some, at certain times, have been tolerant of same-sex-relations; others have not. However because of the essential neutrality of the Buddhist tradition in this regard, it has adapted to particular sociocultural norms, so that throughout its history we find a wide gamut of opinions concerning homosexual activity, ranging from condemnation (never to the point of active persecution) to praise. (Cabezón, 1998: 30. See also: 43)[23]

Cabezón offers what we might take to be a liberal view of homosexuality in Buddhism. In this account Buddhism takes a neutral view of homosexuality, neither condemning nor promoting it.

Other scholars such as Peter Harvey have taken issue with this conclusion by suggesting that, in different Buddhist cultural contexts, homosexuality is condemned (Harvey, 2000: 423–33).[24] A representative quote from Harvey's analysis is from the popular Chinese monk Ven. Master Hsüan Hua (1918–95), who stated that 'homosexuality . . . plants the seeds which lead to rebirth in the lower realms of existence' (Harvey, 2000: 426). In Buddhist Asia homosexuality is viewed as the result of bad actions in a previous life, and as something which can be 'cured'.

One key issue is whether homosexuality is considered to be a form of sexual misconduct in Buddhism. Some modern Buddhists, such as the Dalai

Lama, clearly indicate that they consider homosexuality to be a form of sexual misconduct (Conkin, 1998: 352; Yip and Smith, 2010: 130). The Dalai Lama has equated homosexuality with sexual misconduct (Harvey, 2000: 432–4; see also Conkin, 1998: 351–6).[25] This is based upon sexual misconduct being defined as sex using 'an improper orifice' (by way of the mouth or the anus). In this context homosexuality, or at least forms of homosexual sex, breaks the lay Buddhist precepts.

Buddhist views of homosexuality range from condemnation to more liberal and accepting attitudes. First, there are traditional Buddhist teachers, often from Asia, who inherit negative views of homosexuality from traditional Buddhist cultures. This prejudice has a number of factors but has a clear foundation in the idea that homosexuality is karmic in nature. The attraction of men towards men and women towards women is the outcome of unwholesome actions performed in a past life. We might coin the term 'karmic sexuality' to describe this phenomenon.

In mainstream Theravāda Buddhist traditions, we sometimes find homosexuality being condemned. For example, Buddhadāsa, the fifth-century Indian commentator on the Pāli canon defined 'wrong-practices' (micchā-dhammo) as 'desire and attachment in men for men, in women for women' (Harvey, 2000: 421; Zwilling, 1998: 53).[26] As Harvey suggests, the condemnation of homosexuality between men is present, but not conclusive. On lesbianism, the Indian Buddhist texts are almost silent (Harvey, 2000: 422).

Peter Jackson (1998: 79–81) offers an account of popular Thai Buddhist attitudes to the origins of homosexuality, which summarizes many of the important arguments about homosexuality in Buddhist history. He suggests that there are two attitudes to homosexuality. The first emphasizes that homosexuality is the result of past unwholesome actions in a previous life. The second that homosexuality is a conscious violation of the ethical principles of Buddhism (Jackson, 1998: 79). Basing his analysis on contemporary Thai accounts, Jackson outlines some of the general assumptions about the karmic origins of homosexuality. The unwholesome actions that cause homosexuality are 'adultery, being a prostitute, sexually interfering with one's children or being sexually irresponsible, such as a man not caring for a woman who becomes pregnant by him' (Jackson, 1998: 79). This represents some Buddhist attitudes to the causes of homosexuality. Clearly, there is a sense of condemnation against individuals being homosexual. The idea is that an individual has committed unwholesome actions and is now experiencing the consequences of those actions in a past life. Homosexuality is then a karmic debt that needs to be paid (Jackson, 1998: 80). In many ways, and again these are general attitudes, homosexuality is a consequence of sexual misconduct according to some standard Buddhist accounts (Jackson, 1998: 83). As we will see, transgenderism is also often thought to have karmic origins in Buddhism.

Buddhism and (homo)sexuality: Liberal views

Following from this, one could argue that in Buddhist reformist movements there is often a need to de-emphasize karma (Jackson, 1998: 84). Karma can become a weapon of discrimination and a way to justify inequality (Hu, 2011: 95). In traditional Buddhis culture, karma is used to explain why individuals are who they are and this includes their gender and sexuality. It can also become a problematic idea in the context of violence against women in traditional and modern Buddhist cultures (Khuankaew, 2009). In engaged Buddhism, there are arguments against karmic descriptions of individuals. By karmic descriptions I mean those traditional narratives that explain people based upon a rigid evaluation of how their actions in the past cause the present person. Engaged Buddhism requires a revaluation of karma. Various alliances are envisaged in the search of a rainbow Buddha or a pink Buddha (Harrold, 2019).

The Australian Buddhist monk Venerable Sujato argues forcefully for the acceptance of a wide range of sexualities. In his essay promoting marriage equality, he quotes the Fo Guang Shan[27] founder, Master Hsin Yun, who gives a more liberal view of homosexuality from a Buddhist perspective:

> People often ask me what I think about homosexuality. They wonder, is it right, is it wrong? The answer is, it is neither right nor wrong. It is just something that people do. If people are not harming each other, their private lives are their own business; we should be tolerant of them and not reject them. (Quoted by Sujato, 2012: n.p.)

Sujato goes on to make the point that discrimination against homosexuals has no place in Buddhism:

> Sadly enough, modern generations of Buddhists and Hindus are now doing this work for them [those Christian missionaries who condemned homosexuality in Asia], oblivious to their own more accepting and compassionate past. When a Thai monk like Thattajiwo, one of the leaders of Dhammakaya, rails against the 'sexual perverts', who have called down the kammic justice of AIDS . . . upon them, oblivious of the pit of sin they have fallen into, and the even greater sufferings that await them in future disease-ridden hells of torment, he is merely parroting the frothing excesses of Christian and Islamic fundamentalists. . . . Such apocalyptic and condemnatory 'ethics' have no basis in the Buddha's teaching. (Sujato, 2012: n.p.)

Sujato is making the simple but important point that Buddhism is based upon the idea of compassion and that discrimination has no place in it as a living religion. In this more liberal setting, homophobic cultural assumptions are downplayed. Indeed, it is often assumed that Buddhism is not homonegative, even though historical and cultural evidence suggests otherwise. As with female gender discrimination, Buddhism is not philosophically homophobic, but culturally homonegative ideas are sometimes prominent (Yip and Smith, 2010: 111). These cultural assumptions are not confined to Asian cultures; there are also many Western cultural assumptions displaying intolerance to LGBTIAQ+ sexualities.

Acceptance of homosexuality, sexual freedom and non-binary gender choice is very much part of the ethos of modern Buddhist practitioners, particularly in the West. It is often taken for granted by modern liberal Buddhists that Buddhism has no discriminatory doctrinal baggage and that Buddhist teachings can be used in a form of activism against gender discrimination. Leonard Zwilling argues that the assumed liberal attitudes to homosexuality in Buddhism are based primarily on the liberal attitudes of Western Dharma teachers, not on Asian Buddhist views of same-sex relations (Zwilling, 1998: 45). However, as we shall see, philosophically and doctrinally there are much more open attitudes.

This is related to a point made by Amy Langenberg (Langenberg, 2018), who argues that Buddhism is antinatalist. Antinatalism offers a negative evaluation of birth and procreation. It proposes that reproduction has no soteriological or moral value (Langenberg, 2018: 572–3) and that this leads to a more open attitude, even open to different types of sex and sexuality:

> As Buddhist thinking and practice develops in ancient India (and interacts with the cultures of Tibet and beyond), the Buddha emerges as a sex symbol of sorts, bodhisattvas are advised to use sex as a teaching tool when appropriate, and sexuality is eventually harnessed to the soteriological aims of Buddhism. (Langenberg, 2018: 578)

The allusion here is to types of tantric practice which were practised in India and became prominent in Tibet. In some tantric practices, sex is used as a vehicle to liberation. Langenberg uses the example to make a wider point about Buddhism. This is that sexuality, and indeed sexiness (of people, particularly the Buddha), might have been more central in Buddhist history than is usually supposed. She uses the work of John Powers (Powers, 2009) to suggest how physical beauty is stressed, and he is described as 'handsome, comely, and graceful' (M II 165; Langenberg, 2018: 579; Powers, 2009: 3).

Tantra, and tantric sex, is highly symbolic in nature. While it might evoke some general question about the place of sexuality in Buddhist traditions, it has not been a primary vehicle for engaged Buddhist practice and activists movements.[28]

LGBTIAQ+ Buddhism: Philosophical themes of gender and sexuality

A major theme addressed in Buddhism and sexuality, and one in which engaged Buddhists have a strong and important voice, focuses on LGBTIAQ+ Buddhism. In this conversation, engaged Buddhist writers challenge traditional forms of Buddhism in which there are rigid binaries between male and female. Engaged Buddhism attempts to challenge heteronormativity (Gleig, 2012: 198).

Amy Paris Langenberg has pointed out how contemporary LGBTIAQ+ (I will continue to use the longer acronym even though the scholars I am citing often use LGBTQI) Buddhists are occasionally in disagreement with cultural and historical Buddhist traditions:

> Another vital conversation in contemporary Buddhism is fuelled by individuals expressing non-normative gender and sexual identities in Buddhist communities. American and European LGBTQ Buddhists have been reading traditional sources against their own visions of gender non-binary, non-gender conforming communities, and diverse sexual orientations and expressions. For instance, some queer Buddhists simply reject Buddhist rules against homosexuality as 'cultural Buddhism' and draw instead on the doctrines of no-self and emptiness to validate their queerness. (Langenberg, 2018: 587–8)

There are two themes to follow in the encounter between LGBTIAQ+ sexualities and Buddhism. First, there is the philosophical point that Buddhism teaches a non-dual, non-essentialist philosophy. This could be termed the theoretical queering of Buddhism (Gleig, 2012: 199). Second is the idea central to Buddhism that discrimination is anathema – any discrimination goes against the fundamental tenets of Buddhism. Can these two ideas be used to show that Buddhism is supportive of LGBTIAQ+ sexualities and identities?

A basic premise of Buddhist philosophy, particularly in the Mahāyāna school known as Yogācāra, is that the mind distorts the true nature of reality. It makes binary assumptions, when, in reality, the mind needs to become freed from adopting positions. Roger Corless compares this to a view of life freed from the gendered categories of male and female (2004: 239). These arguments lead Corless to suggest that the Dharma is queer (2004: 240). Buddhism, quite fundamentally, is a middle-way between extremes and positions – a queer perspective is at the heart of Buddhism. Buddhism's arguments about the non-viability of 'positions' have been discussed in Chapter 2. To have a position is to have an attachment. Thinkers like Corless bring these traditional ideas into the service of formulating a queer Dharma and in so doing give some sustained philosophical theory to LGBTIAQ+ Buddhist thinking.

A central theme of LGBTIAQ+ Buddhist identity is the idea that in Buddhist philosophy there is clear support for non-binary thinking.[29] This is often termed the non-essentialist philosophy of Buddhism. Buddhism, at the fundamental level, has the idea that the universe is a conditioned phenomenon in which there are no basic distinctions between its individual parts. Doctrines suggestive of this include 'not-self', dependent-origination, emptiness, non-duality, and Buddha-nature (which is held to be genderless). In fact, similar ideas are used to support eco-engaged Buddhism. Based upon these ideas it is suggested that Buddhism is gender-neutral, and indeed these central ideas of Buddhist philosophy can be used as queer doctrines. For example, queer identity, with its 'deconstruction of a normative sense of self' (Gleig, 2012: 207), resonates with the Buddhist teaching of not-self.

John Powers discusses genderless ideas found in the 'Discourse Spoken by Vimalakīrti' (*Vimalakīrtinirdeśa Sūtra*), suggesting that in this Buddhist text, dating from around the second century CE, there is an anticipation of the 'analyses deconstructing gender categories by centuries' (Powers, 2009: 136). As the Buddha states in the *Vimalakīrti*: 'Phenomena are neither male nor female' (Powers, 2008: 136). Commenting upon these texts Reiko Ohnuma observes that

> Thus, in these episodes, the man's mistake is not in adhering to the dictum that a woman could not become a Buddha, but in adhering to any ultimate distinction between 'man' and 'woman', 'Buddha' and 'non-Buddha', at all. (Ohnuma, 2000: 127)

Neither men nor women are 'better' – the binary distinctions are 'empty'. There is an 'emptiness-critique' (Ohnuma, 2000: 129) of binary genders, and in particular of the superiority of male over female genders.[30] It should also be mentioned that the apparent negation or deconstruction of gender altogether can also be a way of deftly sidestepping the possibility of equality between genders, minimizing inequality as an issue and enabling its neglect.

I have outlined the idea that Buddhism has a philosophical basis in non-duality, which lessens the idea that the universe and human experience are based upon firm and immutable essences. I would now like to suggest that an analysis of three ideas could be used by LGBTIAQ+ Buddhists to enforce their ideas that Buddhism could be used to support a queer philosophy.

First, the key doctrine of 'not-self' (*anātman/anattā*) incorporating the idea of the fluidity of identity and gender. Second, the Mahāyāna notion of 'Buddha-nature' *(tathāgatagarbha)*, the idea that there is an underlying essence of Buddhahood in each individual.[31] Third, the idea of two-levels of truth, conventional truth (samvrti-satya/sammuti-sacca) and ultimate truth (paramārtha-satya/paramattha-sacca).

The idea of not-self questions the reality of gender identities. The self is a fluid and conditioned phenomenon. It is constantly in a state of change and flux. It is made of individual factors and the idea of a permanent and enduring 'self' collapses when things are seen as they really are. The language we use does not apply to a substantial reality. It is clearly explained how a Buddha uses terms like 'I' and 'me' in a conventional way, without supposing an underlying substance, a 'self'.[32]

The idea of Buddha-nature similarly questions the distinctive importance and ontological value of self-identity. On its basic level it suggests that individuals are not what they appear to be and that hidden beneath self-identity is a true nature, an awakened essence, covered in the excesses of conditioning and continual rebirths. David Loy uses similar strategies when he states that 'all of us have the same Buddha-nature', and that this 'implies not only the liberation and empowerment of women but opposition to all gender-based discrimination, including gay, lesbian, and transsexual rights' (Loy, 2003: 38).

Finally, and perhaps most importantly, on the conventional level there is a self, and its accompanying gender, but on the ultimate level there is no 'self' or accompanying gender. Reality can be encountered on different levels. When based upon greed, hatred and delusion, it is gendered, cultural and selfish. When based upon generosity, compassion and wisdom, it is non-gendered, universal and without an individual conditioned self.

All three categories can inform much of the debate about identity in the Buddhist setting and are of great use in LGBTQIA+ engaged Buddhism. We are encountering a point in Buddhist thought at which many of the tensions between modern and culturally influenced Buddhist discourse are being interrogated. In culturally influenced Buddhist discourse, issues of gender, ethnicity, race, sexuality and nationality often override more fundamental concerns of Buddhist philosophy. In modern discourse a universal vision of reality is primary.

Ann Gleig reports that the LGBTIAQ+ Buddhists that she has interviewed expressed that their queer identities facilitated an expression of the Buddhist Dharma. They described a compatibility between 'foundational Buddhist teachings' and their queer identities (Gleig, 2012: 207). This identity is based upon a resonance between Buddhist philosophy and non-binary identities – that is, a modern Buddhist identity as opposed to traditional or institutional forms of Buddhism. This reorientation of Buddhism to certain key doctrines, what is termed 'non-essentialist' philosophy, is used at a number of points in engaged Buddhism. Discrimination against non-binary gender identities is not supported by key Buddhist ideas. This is similar to the idea that misogyny is not supported, which I outlined earlier. This is the case on a number of levels.

Fundamental Buddhist doctrines do not support reified static positions, be they gender, sexuality, race or ethnicity. Second, and as will be evident in the paragraphs that follow, in terms of compassion and loving-kindness, any form of attitude which is prejudiced against forms of identity seems to run counter to Buddhist religious attitudes.

One way of understanding the difference between LGBTIAQ+ Buddhist identity, which is open to different sexualities, and traditional Buddhist identity, which tends towards homophobia, is to consider the focus of each group. As I have suggested, LGBTQI Buddhist focus upon fundamental philosophical ideas. Many Buddhist practitioners in Buddhist societies focus upon karma and rebirth. Their uses and experiences of Buddhist teachings are fundamentally different. Engaged Buddhist LGBTIAQ+ groups want to alleviate the suffering caused by social discrimination, while the latter want to alleviate the suffering caused by repeated rebirths. Both are valid practices, but give different understandings of human sexuality. There is what Ann Gleig has termed a 'disjuncture' between the two groups (2012: 207). Buddhist ideas, it is proposed, lessen or even eliminate gender binaries; they 'undo dualistic ways of thinking' (Gleig, 2012: 198). The Dharma is, in essence, queer, because of its non-essentialist philosophy:

> The anti-essentialist stance of Buddhism means that LGBTQI people can de-emphasise sexuality and gender identity issues; in fact identity *per se*. (Yip and Smith, 2010: 137)

In discussing LGBTIAQ+ Buddhism, we are talking about a form of engaged Buddhist discourse which is often in tension with traditional forms of Buddhism in which gender binaries are prominent. One could simply evaluate them as two distinct forms of Buddhism, historically and culturally isolated from each other. However, these new and emerging LGBTIAQ+ Buddhist identities become a key factor in engaged Buddhism. The suffering caused by the practising of alternative sexualities is a legitimate expression of Buddhist activism, in which Buddhism can offer a number of philosophical and doctrinal arguments for its alleviation.

Suffering caused by heteronormativity in engaged Buddhism

Those with LGBTIAQ+ identities offer a number of key experiences that resonate with core Buddhist teachings to do with suffering. Engaged Buddhists have actively campaigned against the suffering caused by discrimination against LGBTIAQ+ Buddhists. A notable example of this is the Burmese-born Taiwanese Buddhist nun Bhikshuni Chao-Hwei. She has campaigned in recent years for LGBTIAQ+ rights, including gay marriage, in Taiwan (Hu, 2016: 663–6). She campaigns for LGBTIAQ+ rights on the grounds that suffering is caused by discrimination based upon heteronormative culture and society (Hu, 2016: 664).[33] In many ways this is a natural Buddhist response to suffering that we can expect to find in engaged Buddhism. As we have seen, there is suffering caused by the ecological crisis, there is suffering caused by political discrimination, and there is suffering caused by heteronormativity. Discrimination and Buddhist teachings against it make LGBTIAQ+ rights a legitimate focus for Buddhist activism (Hu, 2016: 665–6). Chao-Hwei argues:

> As Buddhists, we should follow the Buddha in protecting beings and should and should be compassionate and use our power to help LGBT individuals alleviate suffering and attain happiness. (Quoted in Hu, 2016: 669)

Chao-Hwei gained an international reputation in 2012, when she performed a same-sex marriage ceremony for a lesbian couple (International Network of Engaged Buddhists, 2012: 31).

Venerable Sujato, who is involved in many engaged Buddhist activities, has a message similar to that of Bhikshuni Chao-Hwei. He argues that for Buddhism homosexuality should not be a divisive issue. Buddhism's concern is with compassion and to reaching out to those who are suffering, those who are marginalized in society, and this often includes those who identify as LGBTIAQ+. He suggests that Buddhists have a moral imperative to help those who suffer (Sujato, 2012: n.p.).

Trans*-Buddhism

Transgender is an umbrella term for those whose experience or understanding of their gender is different to that which was assigned at birth. As an example, a transgender man is an individual who was assigned the female gender at birth but lives and experiences the world as a man. Used as an umbrella term, it denotes this transition between assigned gender and the lived experience of gender (Krempasky, Renson, and Schubert, 2016).

In recent years there has been a growing trans-Buddhist movement (Manders and Marston, 2019). Sometimes trans* (i.e. 'trans-asterisk') is used, to denote 'trans' but leaves open whether it is 'transgender', 'transsexual', etc. As we have seen, identity can be a defining factor in causing and alleviating suffering in a Buddhist context; therefore addressing suffering caused by gender and identity can be described as part of engaged Buddhism.

Some would suggest that on a popular level Buddhism has a ready-made trans-icon in the form of the gender-bending Buddhist icon Bodhisattva of compassion, Avalokiteśvara, with his adaptation into the female Guanyin in China (Bailey, 2009; Enke, 2019).[34] In India and Tibet Avalokiteśvara was the male Bodhisattva symbolizing compassion (in Tibet he was known as Chenrezig). When Buddhism migrated to China, over a long historical period, Avalokiteśvara transformed into Guanyin, who is female.[35] The usefulness of Avalokiteśvara/ Guanyin being a symbol of Buddhist LGBTIAQ+ activism is obvious, as the transformation raises questions regarding the substantive reality of gender (Hu, 2016: 673). It could, for example, express the idea used in some Buddhist traditions of a Bodhisattva taking various forms of rebirth out of compassion to help sentient beings (Vella, 2019: 61).[36] Here we have a Bodhisattva whose gender changes from male to female. As we shall see, there is an abundance of gender changes in Buddhist narrative history.[37] The theme of using Bodhisattvas as activists is a common one in engaged Buddhism (Jones, 2003: 18–20; Jenkins, 2003). We could describe eco-sattvas in ecology movements, and gender-sattvas, queer-sattvas or trans*-sattvas might also be suggested in engaged Buddhist gender and sexuality movements.

Bee Scherer has suggested the term metagenderism in relation to gender change. By this Scherer means there is a discussion of gender beyond the polarities of male and female in Buddhism (Scherer, 2006). Engaged Buddhists attempt to break down binary gender identities and find in Buddhism conceptual support for non-binary gender identities:

> The Buddha's paradigm as set in the early monastic discipline and the Buddhist multi-voiced debate on gender equality provides a springboard for a modern Buddhist inclusive anthropology and the spiritual state beyond gender polarities, which I propose to call 'metagenderism'. (Scherer, 2006: 65)

Scherer suggests that in Tibetan models of what they term 'soteriological androgyny' Tibetan tantric rituals embrace a 'transcendence of gender' in the quest for liberation (Scherer, 2006: 74). The idea that an individual is fixed in their gender from birth might be offered an entirely different conceptual vocabulary by some Buddhist discourses.

Types of gendered persons

To understand engaged Buddhist views of gender and sexuality we need to consider the types of genders described in Buddhism. The origins of male and female genders is described in the *Aggañña-sutta* (D III 80–98). At the beginning of the world cycle, people are sexless, they have no set genders. However, over time, binary genders emerge:

> Neither moon nor sun appeared, no constellations or stars appeared, night and day were not distinguished, nor months and fortnights, no years or seasons, and no male and female, beings being reckoned just as beings. (D III 86)

Then, due to greed and desire, the different genders arose (D III 88).[38] The ancient Buddhist traditions also recognized different non-binary gender categories. First, there is the category of a 'hermaphrodite' (*ubhato-byañjanaka*), literally, 'having the characteristics of both sexes' (Harvey, 2000: 412–13; Jackson, 1998: 63–9). These can be described as an 'intersex person' (Anderson, 2017). A hermaphrodite cannot be ordained as a Buddhist monk. Traditionally the reason for this is the possibility of them tempting monks or nuns into having sex (Harvey, 2000: 413). Sometimes this gender category has been understood as 'bisexual' (Harvey, 2000: 413; Jackson, 1998: 67).

Another gender category is a 'eunuch' (*paṇḍaka*) and implies 'one without testicles' (Harvey, 2000: 413–19; Zwilling, 1998: 48–50). The term is translated by José Cabezón as 'queer' (Cabezón, 2017: 13) and by John Powers as 'sexual deviant' (Powers, 2019: 736). Eunuchs are described by the compilers of the Buddhist texts as engaging in sexual practices considered depraved or perverted, such as men performing oral sex on other men (Powers, 2019: 736). They are sometimes described as lacking the sexual characteristics, presumably the sexual organs, of either a male or a female. A *paṇḍaka* (male or female) cannot be ordained as a monk or nun (Harvey, 2000: 414–15). The reason for this appears to be that their ordination would damage the reputation of the Saṅgha, due to their supposed promiscuity. They are often characterized as effeminate and sexually dangerous (Zwilling, 1992: 204). They are described by Cabezón as 'a class of people who are deemed deviant by virtue of their nonnormative bodies or desires' (2017: 13). The Buddhist canon goes into greater detail about genders:

> Three kinds of females: human women, non-human females, female animals. Three kinds of hermaphrodites: human hermaphrodites, non-human hermaphrodites, animal hermaphrodites. Three kinds of eunuchs: human eunuchs, non-human eunuchs, animal eunuchs. Three kinds of males: human males, nonhuman males, animal males. There is an offence involving defeat if he commits sexual intercourse with human women in three ways. Also with non-human women and with female animals. Also with human, non-human and animal hermaphrodites. (Vin III 28)

The text is describing all possible gender types (Harvey, 2000: 414; Scherer, 2006: 68). The idea of these different gender types leaves open the theoretical possibility that trans* Buddhism, as part of the wider spectrum of engaged Buddhism, has key resources to fight gender discrimination, even though the categories themselves may not have been formulated with this intention.

Gender transformation in Buddhist history

With its description of these various types of genders, it is perhaps not surprising that Buddhist texts sometimes describe how genders can change over lifetimes, or even during the current life. In the Pāli material, gender change is possible in the present life, from male to female, and from female to male. Gender is in principle a fluid idea in Buddhism. Due to the idea of an endless cycle of rebirths, there is a natural reflection on this fluidity of gender. In a famous passage it is stated that 'there are no men who have not, at some time or the other, been women; and no women who have not, at some time or other, been men' (Burlingame, 1921: 24). However, there is also an ingrained negativity apparent in these discussions. Gender in the present life is determined by the person's past actions, by karma, and acts performed in the present life can also change the individual's gender. There are notable instances of a female having the aspiration to be reborn as a man in order to be reborn in a heavenly realm. These themes are found in the *Sakkapañha-sutta* (D II 263–89):

> There was, Lord, right here in Kapilavatthu a Sakyan girl called Gopikā who had faith in the Buddha, the Dhamma and the Saṅgha, and who observed the precepts scrupulously. She rejected the status of a woman and developed the thought of becoming a man. Then, after her death, at the breaking-up of the body, she went to a happy destination, being reborn in a heaven-state among the Thirty-Three Gods, as one of our sons, becoming known as Gopaka the son of the devas. (D II 271)

This passage is notable for the way in which, to gain a heavenly rebirth, the female needs to become a male. In later Mahāyāna texts the theme is emphasized that to become a Buddha then the person needs to be male, so there is the necessity for a gender change, from female to male, before Buddhahood can be achieved (Hae-ju, 1999). This change can happen quite suddenly. Indeed, many of the gender changes in the Buddhist canon are quickly achieved, often instantaneous (Faure, 2003: 100). In the later commentarial literature, the story is found of a householder called Soreyya, who in fact changes gender twice, from male to female, then back again. Eventually he becomes an Arahant, a Buddhist saint.[39] An important doctrinal factor in gender change, particularly when it occurs from female to male, relates to the thirty-two marks of a great man. These are the physical characteristics shared by all Buddhas and wheel-turning monarchs. In this understanding, as was mentioned earlier, a Buddha has a penis. This idea is likely to have influenced some of the episodes of gender change (Collett, 2018: 562).

Much of the Vinaya descriptions of gender change are legalistic in nature. These texts need to regulate laws about the penalties committed by different genders. Therefore, the specifics of an individual's gender need to be known when a particular offence is committed (Gyatso, 2003: 110):

> Now at that time the sexual features of a woman appeared on a certain monk. They told the Blessed One about this matter. [He said,] 'Monks, I allow the same teacher, the same ordination, the same rainy seasons together with the nuns. I allow reinstatement among the nuns for those offenses that nuns share in common with monks. According to those offenses of monks that are not shared in common with nuns, there is no offense.'
>
> Now at that time, the sexual features of a man appeared on a certain nun. They told the Blessed One about this matter. [He said,] 'Monks, I allow the same teacher, the same ordination, the same rainy seasons in relation to the monks. I allow reinstatement among the monks for those offenses that monks share in common with the nuns. According to those offences of nuns that not shared in common with monks, there is no offense.' (Vin III.35. Translated Anderson, 2017)[40]

Clearly at stake here is the definition of individuals as male and female and how Vinaya rules are followed according to gender.

As the gender of a person can change from one life to the next, there are also reported cases of gender-changing within their current life. As a general rule, the reason for the change in gender is karmic. By this is meant that the change is caused by an individual's behaviour. Gender change is also used to suggest that there is no such thing as 'male' and 'female'. This is a prominent theme in key Mahāyāna texts (Anderson, 2017). Naomi Appleton explains how 'magical sex-change' occurring in these texts is used to suggest the illusory nature of gender (Appleton, 2011: 32). One of the key passages is the following from the famous and influential Lotus Sūtra:

> Then, at that moment, before the elder Śariputra and the entire world, King Sagara's daughter's female organs vanished, and the male organs became visible. She appeared as a bodhisattva. (Quoted by Faure, 2003: 100)

Even though these texts might be describing the illusory nature of gender, and therefore be important to engaged Buddhist debates, there is a problem considered by Anālayo about the karmic method used in gender transformations (Anālayo, 2014). He discusses the value judgement, made in the commentaries but not in the canonical texts (in the later rather than the earlier traditions), about the good karmic fortune in a female becoming a man, and the bad karmic fortune of a man becoming a woman. Anālayo suggests that the value judgement is made in the later tradition in which the loss of male gender is the result of a strong unwholesome action, and the gaining of maleness the result of strong wholesome actions (Anālayo, 2014: 113).[41] John Powers reports on other episodes in the wider Indian and Chinese Buddhist contexts where a female body is rejected and a male body acquired (Powers, 2009: 138–9):

> Texts in which gender change is discussed evince an underlying concern with the fragility of the male state and the threat of losing what one has gained from past good deeds. An inadvertent thought can reverse one's positive karma and result in immediate gender shift. In addition, inattention in the present life or failure to recognize the tenuousness of one's current endowment can lead one to squander a male birth on sensual pleasures or to engage in acts of arrogance or violence that will result in future retribution, perhaps as a female or a lower form of life. For every story of a woman who successfully escapes the female condition and is predicted to be blessed with male physiques in subsequent existences, there are many cautionary tales of men who are changed into women or cursed to spend future lives in female forms. (Powers, 2009: 139–40)

The negative nature of female rebirth is clear from Power's overview. While the fluidity of gender and the non-dualistic nature of Buddhist philosophy offers arguments in favour of trans* Buddhism, the question of karma and sexuality are a major obstacle for engaged Buddhism. While the fluidity of gender might, on a certain level, be useful to LGBTIAQ+ Buddhists, in suggesting the illusory nature of gender, their actual understanding in Buddhist texts might be problematic. Doctrinally they often point to the superiority of the male gender. However, they are still of importance in showing how gender change is possible in Buddhism.

LGBTIAQ+ mindful activism: Traditional karma and secular karma

There is then a problem for trans* Buddhism, and related engaged Buddhist LGBTIAQ+ movements, with the central idea of karma. One way of understanding engaged Buddhist LGBTIAQ+ activism is in the need to de-activate karma. By this I mean that karma is often a problematic idea and one which gay and transgender Buddhists find problematic to Buddhist practice. Buddhist culture often suggests that there is a karmic reason for homosexuality and queerness. There is a widespread assumption that an individual's gender and sexuality have karmic causes. Therefore, part of Buddhist LGBTIAQ+ activism might be prompted by a need to eradicate or adapt key Buddhist ideas (Vella, 2019: 61). In this context, it is traditional forms of Buddhism which are part of the problem to LGBTIAQ+ Buddhist practice.[42] As we have seen the non-dual philosophy of Buddhism is an attraction to LGBTIAQ+ Buddhists, but ideas related to karma are often a hindrance. In response, LGBTIAQ+ Buddhists will often explain the idea of karma as operating in this life, not over many lifetimes. The notion of karma might be used to suggest that individuals should take personal responsibility for their actions.[43]

Two engaged Buddhist academics who adapt the idea of karma are Karen Alexander and Jonathan Yescavage, who explain how they understand karma as a positive attitude which promotes 'personal responsibility'. This could be described as engaged Buddhist karma to distinguish it from traditional ideas of karma which often justify discrimination. This understanding of karma focuses it on something active in the present moment. This form of engaged Buddhist LGBTIAQ+ activism is one that fights what might be termed metaphysical prejudice. By this I mean religious doctrines that promote intolerance against minority groups such as those from LGBTIAQ+ communities. Alexander and Yescavage explain this different attitude as follows: 'a [. . .] karmic approach requires that we take responsibility for our actions and recognize their effects on others and ourselves' (Alexander and Yescavage, 2010: 155).

Those identifying as LGBTIAQ+ might face criticism from traditional religious traditions (including Buddhism). Responding to intolerant attitudes to LGBTIAQ+ individuals by fundamentalist and conservative religious groups they explain that

On many occasions, we have felt deep anger, even rage, at such comments. We know what it is like to grow up with such religious fundamentalism, and we understand – personally – how such views can lead young queer people to contemplate leaving home, severing ties with family and friends and even suicide. For us, such antiqueer religious attitudes are not only bigoted, but also contribute unbelievably to the suffering of people who are trying to understand how to love others. (Alexander and Yescavage, 2010: 155–6)

The target of their engaged Buddhist activism would be prejudice and intolerance. The means towards this, suggested by Alexander and Yescavage, is for LGBTIAQ+ Buddhists to model themselves on Bodhisattvas (a theme I mentioned earlier) whom they equate with activists, to fight gender-based discrimination (Alexander and Yescavage, 2010: 158).

Alexander and Yescavage, as LGBTIAQ+ Buddhist activists, formulate three strategies, similar in some respects to aspects of Thich Nath Hanh's fourteen principles of engaged Buddhism.

> First, be mindful. Be mindful of anger, harmful or prideful attachment to particular goals, and of lingering resentments. Even too much 'pride' in one's identity – as an activist, as a member of the group for which you are an activist – can lead to increasing attachment to particular concrete goals as opposed to cultivating compassion.
>
> Second, work on transforming 'us against them' thinking. It's too tempting at times to demonize those who are working against us. This bipolarity only isolates from others and prevents us from exploring potentially useful common ground. Consider, instead, how we are all interdependent.
>
> Third, to extend the point we just made, be grateful to your enemies. After all, they can teach us much, most particularly, how to evolve spiritually. Those who may at first seem to be working against us actually can offer us unique opportunities to practice compassion and to recognize our common humanity. (Alexander and Yescavage, 2010: 164)

There appears to be the idea that, by eradicating rigidness in morality and ethics, through an openness to new and caring relationships, there are parallels with fundamental Buddhist principles.[44] Some LGBTIAQ+ Buddhists have suggested problems with the Buddhist Saṅgha being gender binary in nature, and the prejudice this causes people who do not identify within this duality (Vanh, 2019: 233). Buddhism offers pathways to compassion and healing for LGBTIAQ+ Buddhists, and this should be used as the means to counter the suffering caused by gender and sexuality prejudice.

How can LGBTIAQ+ Buddhists practice freely and openly in Buddhist communities? This question is taken up by Ray Buckner who has written lucidly about his experiences of being a transgender Buddhist (Buckner, 2017). His main point is about a trans* Buddhist being visible, which I take to mean adopting their own identity, being who they are, not who society, or an imposed gender, suggests they should be. Through this visibility, Buckner argues, a trans-Buddhist can connect with other marginalized individuals, and so help in alleviating suffering. As a trans engaged Buddhist practice, this could be interpreted as a legitimate Buddhist practice.

LGBTIAQ+ Buddhists and loving-kindness

A key text of Buddhism is the 'Discourse on Loving-Kindness', known in Pāli as the *Mettā-sutta*. This text has been used by engaged Buddhists to express the centrality of tolerance and compassion during Buddhist political protests. It has also been used by LGBTQIA+ Buddhists, and particularly trans-Buddhists, to suggest how society should respect their identities:

Mettā-sutta

This is what should be done
By one who is skilled in goodness,
And who seeks the path of peace:
Let them be able and upright,
Straightforward and gentle in speech,
Humble and not conceited,
Contented and easily satisfied,
Unburdened with duties and frugal in their ways.
Peaceful and calm and wise and skilful,
Not proud or demanding in nature.
Let them not do the slightest thing
That the wise would later reprove.
Wishing: In gladness and in safety,
May all beings be at ease.
Whatever living beings there may be;
Whether they are weak or strong, omitting none,
The great or the mighty, medium, short or small,
The seen and the unseen,
Those living near and far away,
Those born and to-be-born –
May all beings be at ease!

Let none deceive another,
Or despise any being in any state.
Let none through anger or ill-will
Wish harm upon another.
Even as a mother protects with her life
Her child, her only child,
So with a boundless heart
Should one cherish all living beings;
Radiating kindness over the entire world:
Spreading upwards to the skies,
And downwards to the depths;

Outwards and unbounded,
Freed from hatred and ill-will.
Whether standing or walking, seated or lying down
Free from drowsiness,
One should sustain this recollection.
This is said to be the sublime abiding.
By not holding to fixed views,
The pure-hearted one, having clarity of vision,
Being freed from all sense desires,
Is not born again into this world.[45]

In the Transbuddhist.org's *Developing Trans Competence Guide* (Krempasky, Renson, and Schubert, 2016), emphasis is given to the section of the text suggesting that loving-kindness should be shown to all living beings, without exception, weak, strong, mighty, medium, short or small. It is perhaps easy to see why such an essential part of the Buddhist canon should be used by trans-Buddhists. No matter how different individual beings are, the text clearly argues, they should be shown loving-kindness (for a Mahāyāna perspective see Vella, 2019: 63).

The *Developing Trans Competence Guide* describes its vision of a 'trans inclusive sangha':

> I feel connected to my sangha because I can trust them to treat me appropriately and with respect. When I introduce myself to someone, I trust that they will not assume the wrong pronouns for me regardless of how my body looks to them. When I speak up in a question and answer session, I trust that no one will misgender me based on how my voice sounds to them. I know that if someone says something disrespectful to me, that other sangha members and leaders in the sangha will understand and how to address it. My sangha is a place where I don't worry about encountering the transphobia and cissexism that I often encounter in the world. I can focus on practice and connection, and feel relaxed in my body, not on guard for disrespect.

This short passage illustrates many of the key themes we find throughout Buddhism and is also suggestive of the ways in which we might use Buddhist doctrines to counter trans and more general LGBTIAQ+ discrimination.

Buddhism and the #MeToo movement

One final area of sexuality and gender in recent years that has been tackled by engaged Buddhists is the #MeToo movement.[46] The #MeToo hashtag came to prominence in 2017 and is a movement which targets sexual harassment and sexual assault. Victims are able to describe their experiences and often to name the person who committed the assault.[47]

Like in other areas of public life, Buddhism has not escaped scrutiny and controversy. There have been many notable cases of leading Buddhist teachers being investigated for various forms of abuse of power, including sexual misbehaviour. With the basic premise that Buddhism addresses suffering, the suffering caused by Buddhist teachers is a factor in engaged Buddhism.[48] As we have seen, engaged Buddhists have a voice in all aspects of sexuality and gender, and therefore they should scrutinize the abuse of power within Buddhist communities.

In July 2018 *The New York Times* carried the headline 'The "King" of Shambala Buddhism is Undone by Abuse Report'.[49] It described abuse allegations against female devotees by Sakyong Mipham Rinpoche, who is the leader of Shambhala International. Shambhala International has over 200 meditation centres around the world. According to reports the worldwide #MeToo movement prompted members to come forward with reports of allegations.[50]

The allegations were based upon reports compiled by a Buddhist group known as Buddhist Project Sunshine, which deals with sexual misconduct within the Tibetan Buddhist group, Shambhala, of which Shambhala International is a part.[51] Buddhist Project Sunshine describes itself as a 'grass roots initiative to bring healing light to sexualized violence in the global Buddhist community'. Its Twitter feed describes ongoing sexual abuse claims against Shambhala. The Shambhala lineage of modern Tibetan Buddhism traces its roots to the controversial teacher Chögyam Trungpa who was Sakyong Mipham Rinpoche's father. It is a lay form of Buddhist practice, with charismatic leaders and unconventional ways of teaching. Sakyong Mipham Rinpoche founded the organization in 2000.

Other abuse allegations against prominent Buddhist teachers, in America, the UK and China have also occurred recently. Notable is the famous Tibetan teacher Sogyal Rinpoche, author of the bestselling *Tibetan Book of Living and Dying* and the leading teacher of the Rigpa Tibetan Buddhist community.[52] In the UK Dennis Lingwood, better known as Sangharakshita, founder of the Friends of the Western Buddhist Order (more recently known as 'Triratna'), has also faced serious allegations.

As Sarah H. Jacoby has commented, 'It is no exaggeration to say that Buddhism is having its #MeToo moment.'[53] As she goes on to say, it seems like Buddhist practitioners had known about the abuse committed by Buddhist teachers, perhaps for decades.

A number of factors seem obvious when we consider how these controversies became possible. First, the fundamental guru–student relationship that is central to these movements is open to abuse. Second, the practice of sexual techniques and rituals in some Buddhist movements, such as tantric practices. Third, the use of different teachings and practices to promote the lessening of fixed views and opinions and to lessen attachment to the 'self'.[54] These final techniques play into some of the themes in our study of engaged Buddhism. At a certain level Buddhism is suspicious of holding to views and opinions. I have described this in Chapter 2. In abuse settings this idea could be manipulated against innocent students of Buddhism being coerced into situations in which their practice is based upon giving up sexual inhibitions.

Following on from this I would like to consider whether there is a distinctively Buddhist #MeToo movement. It seems obvious that a Buddhist #MeToo movement should be part of engaged Buddhism. In previous chapters we have encountered philosophical and ecological Buddhist responses to suffering. In the current chapter I have suggested how engaged Buddhism encounters issues of sexuality and gender. With the growing #MeToo movement, can we discover legitimate Buddhist ideas that counter sexual harassment?

Elizabeth Monson, an American Buddhist teacher, has addressed some aspects of the Buddhist #MeToo movement's ideas about how to tackle sexual harassment.[55] Monson shapes her ideas in the context of building a Buddhism for the West. She stresses the Buddhist idea of how each individual must be responsible for their thoughts and actions. A basic premise of a Buddhist #MeToo movement would be the emphasis on karma and how actions have consequences. We have seen the ways in which LGBTIAQ+ Buddhists utilize karma. A basic idea of Buddhism is that there are certain unwholesome courses of action, of body, speech and mind. This is fundamental to Buddhist teachings and could be validly used as a basis to tackle sexual misconduct within Buddhist communities. Monson introduces the basic Buddhist idea of 'awareness' to counter what is at a basic level the charisma used by many Buddhist teachers. Buddhist teachers and, to an extent, Buddhist monks, in the West and in many traditional Buddhist cultures, are seen as embodiments of the Buddha. The possibility of the abuse of this power must have been historically prevalent, and the Buddhist #MeToo movement is simply a reflection on this. For Monson there should be a reflection on the destructiveness of unwholesome actions, and a questioning of the conduct of Buddhist teachers. A distinctively Buddhist #MeToo movement is still in its infancy. There have been movements in recent years, including #ShambhalaMeToo and the #MeTooGuru campaign exploring sexual exploitation in Buddhist groups.

There are clearly historical and emerging sexual controversies in modern Western Buddhism. Given the close relationship between Buddhist monks and laypeople around Buddhist Asia, it can be predicted that Buddhist reactions to sexual harassment in Asian Buddhist communities will sadly become more prominent. Ann Gleig and Amy Langenberg are currently conducting research into sexual abuse in American Buddhism and their findings will greatly add to this debate.

Conclusion

In this chapter we have considered certain ideas to do with gender and sexuality in Buddhism. As a starting point gender and sexuality are part of the wider engaged Buddhist movement. LGBTIAQ+ Buddhism, trans*-Buddhism, and Buddhism concerned with gender discrimination against females tackle related forms of suffering. This suffering, in part, is based upon discrimination. At a basic level, one's biological gender or one's LGBTIAQ+ gender identity becomes a target of discrimination which causes suffering. On the one hand, Buddhist traditions offer some relief from this discrimination. There are key teachings on non-duality, suggesting the fluidity of genders and LGBTIAQ+ identities. There are further ideas to do with gender change which are striking in the Buddhist textual traditions. Over the course of lifetimes, gender does change; we have all experienced different genders in the Buddhist analysis – we have been born male and female, and Buddhism also offers various alternative forms of gender. However, the Buddha was a man – he had a male body. As the Buddha is obviously central to Buddhist traditions, male rebirth is often valued more than that of females. Added to this is the idea that gender is related to karma. In a very crude way, we might suggest that a male rebirth is related to good ethical actions performed in a previous life. The doctrine of karma proposes that sexuality which is not heteronormative is in some senses the result of unwholesome activity in a previous life.

In LGBTIAQ+ engaged Buddhism, and those fighting gender prejudice, there must be a resolution of the dilemma posed by this traditional idea of karma, which accuses and metaphysically victimizes LGBTIAQ+ Buddhists and women. Engaged Buddhism will often use a different model of karma, engaged Buddhist karma, which focusses on the present moment, and finds in Buddhism a comfort and refuge. What I am calling engaged Buddhist karma de-activates karma of its judgemental bias and focuses upon its use in structuring behaviour in the present life. In engaged Buddhism ancient biases that inflict discrimination against women and alternative sexualities are replaced with a different model of karma. We have already discussed how ideas of rebirth often need a reorientation in engaged Buddhism. The themes of adaptation are also central to trans*, LGBTIAQ+ and related gender issues in engaged Buddhism. In engaged Buddhism, karma needs to be used, not to describe wider contexts of rebirth, but as a form of reflection on prejudice and suffering. Engaged Buddhist karma needs to shape one's current behaviour, and not be a predictor of one's future rebirth.

Discussion questions

1. Is the idea of karma an insurmountable problem for LGBTIAQ+ Buddhism?

2. Does the Buddhist idea of gender change help in the removal of trans*-Buddhist suffering?

3. Should the removal of discrimination be central to Buddhism or does its roots in Buddhist culture give it a measure of validity?

Suggestions for further reading

Anālayo, Bhikkhu. 2014. 'Karma and Female Birth.' *Journal of Buddhist Ethics*: 109–53.

Anderson, Carol. 2017. 'Changing Sex or Changing Gender in Pāli Buddhist Literature.' *The Scholar and Feminist Online*. 14 (2): 231–51.

Cabezón, José. 2017. *Sexuality in Classical South Asian Buddhism*. Somerville, MA: Wisdom Publications.

Collett, Alice. 2018. 'Buddhism and Women.' In *The Oxford Handbook of Buddhist Ethics*, ed. Daniel Cozort and James Mark Shields, 552–66. New York: Oxford University Press.

Corless, Roger. 2004. 'Towards a Queer Dharmology of Sex.' *Culture and Religion* 5 (2): 229–43.

Gleig, Ann. 2012. 'Queering Buddhism or Buddhist De-Queering?.' *Theology & Sexuality*, 18 (3): 198–214.

Gross, Rita. 1993. *Buddhism After Patriarchy: A Feminist History, Analysis, and Reconstruction of Buddhism*. Albany: State University of New York Press.

Gyatso, Janet. 2005. 'Sex.' In *Critical Terms for the Study of Buddhism*, ed. Donald S. Lopez, 271–90. Chicago: The University of Chicago Press.

Langenberg, Amy P. 2018. 'Buddhism and Sexuality.' In *The Oxford Handbook of Buddhist Ethics*, eds. Daniel Cozort and James Mark Shield, 567–91. New York: Oxford University Press.

8

Ethnocentric engaged Buddhism

The teachings of the Buddha contain a universal philosophy of peace and compassion which can be applied across diverse cultures during different historical periods. Therefore, the idea that Buddhism can be used to support the ideology of one ethnic or political group contradicts many of our assumptions about Buddhism. In this chapter I will describe a set of Buddhist narratives emerging in Southeast Asian Buddhism which leads to a radical form of Buddhism which is often at odds with accepted ideas about Buddhism.[1] They are also fundamental in the emergence of Buddhist identity in Southeast Asia. They challenge notions of what it means to be Buddhist. These new identities do not have their foundations in a rational and universal version of the Buddha's teachings. They are also not part of the more usual types of engaged Buddhism. Their origins are much more local and specific. They form part of the encounter between Buddhism, ethnicity and nationalism.[2]

Ethnocentric engaged Buddhism is the term I use to describe a localized form of engaged Buddhism which is often at odds with more universalistic understandings of engaged Buddhism. The term describes new and emerging Buddhist identities which are often protectionist in their outlook. They also embrace forms of action which are sometimes in considerable tension with more passive forms of Buddhist behaviour. My use of these ideas also problematizes the tendency to understand engaged Buddhism as predominantly positive, non-violent. As Jessica Main and Rongdao Lai have argued:

Movements with a variety of modern ideological standpoints and political positions can possess a socially engaged soteriology in which social action is itself liberating. Each socio-political situation is complex, however, giving rise to nationalistic social engagement in some cases and pacifist engagement in others. (Main and Lai, 2013: 4)

The categories of good or bad, passive or violent, should not be a defining consideration in evaluating specific groups as types of engaged Buddhism. Engaged Buddhists do not need to be pacifists (Main and Lai, 2013: 26). They often are, but they need not be. The national and ethnic concerns of the groups I consider in this chapter evoke a rhetoric of intolerance and discrimination which is often violent in its expression. The description of these forms of engaged Buddhism has the aim of understanding Buddhist ideas and practices that contribute to the emergence of chauvinistic and nationalistic engaged Buddhist practices. By studying these forms of engaged Buddhism, I intend to widen the vocabulary of precisely what constitutes engaged Buddhism. Engaged Buddhism is not simply a phenomenon in which Buddhist ideas are used to promote social harmony and justice and to convey Buddhist ideas about the modern ecological crisis. Engaged Buddhists can propose Buddhist ideas on more controversial ideas to do with race, ethnicity and political ideas about the nature of Buddhist communities.

There are ethnocentric forms of engaged Buddhism, nationalistic forms of engaged Buddhism and protectionist forms of engaged Buddhism. Engaged Buddhism is usually considered to consist of Buddhist movements that are far removed from the interests of the nation state. Engaged Buddhism is personal and meditative. In this chapter I am questioning the model of engaged Buddhism that frames it as personal, meditative and removed from the interests of the nation state (Main and Lai, 2013: 10).

Indeed, the two defining features of engaged Buddhism that Main and Lai suggest, non-violence and independence from the nation state, needs to be re-evaluated if we are to understand the wider ramifications of engaged Buddhism (Main and Lai, 2013: 10). Buddhism is an active and pervasive factor in Buddhist culture, and, as I suggested in Chapter 4, Buddhism is decisive in culture, economics and social welfare. In modern Buddhist cultures there is an attempt to 'Buddhasize' society (Main and Lai, 2013: 17).[3] In opposition to the secularization of modern Buddhist societies, ethnocentric engaged Buddhists are involved in reaffirming Buddhism's position at the centre of Buddhist culture.

There could be legitimate objections to my use of these Buddhist movements in the study of engaged Buddhism. It might be suggested that the description of ethnocentric Buddhism and its related movements do not have a place in a book describing engaged Buddhism. Engaged Buddhism is compassionate in nature, and the subjects discussed in this and the subsequent chapter describe an enraged or angry form of Buddhism. I would disagree. Returning to some of the themes in Chapter 1, engaged Buddhism describes Buddhism entering into society. It can do so passively, using Buddhist ideas to overcome suffering in the world, or, its footsteps can be harsh – the bare feet of the Buddhist monk, being replaced by the boots of the aggressor (who might

FIGURE 14 *Buddhists for Black Lives Matter, Los Angeles City Hall, Downtown Los Angeles, June 2020. Credit: Nina Mueller and Buddhistdoor Global.*

also be a monk). Engaged Buddhism can be universal or chauvinistic, offer the hand of peace, such as Buddhists taking part in the Black Lives Matter Movement, or be heavy handed, motivated by the defence and protection of Buddhism. Both are expressions of Buddhism that leave the monastery; both are engaged Buddhism.

Buddhist identity

The forms of Buddhist rhetoric I am concerned with in this chapter shape Buddhist identity and are often used politically and put into the service of particular groups. These groups have both religious and political agendas which often overlap. They emerge from key ideas related to cultural, national and ethnic agendas. Pivotal is the idea that the teachings of the Buddha are under threat and need to be protected (Foxeus, 2019: 668). Therefore I would suggest they can be termed protectionist engaged Buddhism, though the usual term I use is ethnocentric engaged Buddhism.

Let me explain how Buddhist identity is typically described in most Asian Buddhist contexts. In an important sense, Buddhist identity is a set of sacred allegiances. These are usually expressed in terms of going for refuge to the Buddha, Dhamma and Saṅgha:

> I go to the Buddha for refuge. I go to the Dhamma for refuge. I go to the Saṅgha for refuge. A second time I go to the Buddha for refuge. A second time I go to the Dhamma for refuge. A second time I go to the Saṅgha for refuge. A third time I go to the Buddha for refuge. A third time I go to the Dhamma for refuge. A third time I go to the Saṅgha for refuge.[4]

Going for refuge could be considered as a signifier of Buddhist identity. It is a mark of dedication and identification, a way of committing oneself to the Buddhist path. It is an acceptance of the reality of suffering (*dukkha*) and to the idea that the Buddha's teachings are the way to alleviate it. It is, in effect, an adherence to the principles of the Buddhist religion.

Buddhist identity in modern Myanmar

In modern Myanmar Buddhist groups are reacting in radical ways to questions of identity and a new religious discourse is emerging. The most prominent reaction has been from a movement under the broad heading of the Organization to Protect Race and Religion (*myo barthar tharthanar*), often known by the Burmese acronym MaBaTha (Walton and Hayward, 2014: 14). This group is fronted by the prominent Buddhist monk Ashin Wirathu. Ashin Wirathu is a Mandalay-based monk based at Ma Soe Yein monastery. Mandalay is a large city in the north of Myanmar. He was imprisoned for a number of years between 2003–12 for preaching sermons that were considered to incite violence. In recent years he has become prominent as the unofficial spokesman for MaBaTha (Walton and Hayward 2014: 13). The Organisation for the Protection of Race and Religion grew out of various groups such as the Patriotic Burmese Monks Union and from an earlier nationwide organization within Myanmar known as the 969 movement. The latter group campaigned around Myanmar in recent years, encouraging Burmese citizens to only frequent Buddhist-owned businesses and to purchase goods displaying the symbol of the 969 movement, signifying that the premises were owned by Buddhists. This symbol is the Buddhist or *sāsana* flag, with the Burmese digits '969' superimposed on it. It has been a very common sight around modern Myanmar.[5] The flag originated in late nineteenth-century Sri Lanka and it was adopted by the World Fellowship of Buddhists in 1952 as the international Buddhist flag. Its colours are meant to represent a halo around the Buddha when he achieved awakening (Gombrich, 2006: 184).

FIGURE 15 *The nationalistic Burmese Buddhist monk, Ashin Wirathu, Mandalay, 1 June 2015. Credit: Taken by the author.*

Highlighting the main objectives of the MaBaTha and 969 movements, Ashin Wirathu stated in a sermon in February 2014:

> If you buy a good from a Muslim shop, your money just doesn't stop there [that] money will eventually be used against you to destroy your race and religion. That money will be used to get a Buddhist-Burmese woman, and she will very soon be coerced or even forced to convert to Islam. [Once Muslims] become overly populous, they will overwhelm us and take over our country and make it an evil Islamic nation.[6]

Groups like the MaBaTha and the 969 movement are part of a phenomenon in which Theravāda Buddhism is used as an ideological vehicle. As Thomas Borchert has observed, Theravāda Buddhism is often used 'to deepen ethnic distinctions in society and to give advantages to a particular ethnic or national group' (Borchert, 2014: 600). This in turn has led to occurrences of conflicts based upon the conflation of ethnic and religious identities (Borchert, 2014: 601). The recent phenomenon of Theravāda ideology being politicized could be viewed as a deviation from the more familiar form of Buddhist practice. However, recent events in Buddhist Asia might also suggest that Theravāda Buddhism can foster a strong sense of Buddhist identity and that this has been important in Theravāda Buddhist history.[7] The suggestion could also be made that it has been a theme in the wider Buddhist history of Asia.

Ashin Wirathu, MaBaTha and the 969 movement offer a distinctive form of Buddhism emerging in Southeast Asia. This is one in which racial and national identity (or a mixture of these) is central.[8] All these related movements offer a rhetoric of intolerance, discrimination and, as suggested in the quote above from Ashin Wirathu, an overt form of Islamophobia.[9] The departure of these movements from a more international Theravāda outlook is due to a focus upon ethnic, racial and related forms of local and specific identities. Indeed, as Borchert has suggested, global forms of Buddhism are a relatively new phenomenon and that 'this transnational face of Buddhism masks very local forms of Buddhism' (Borchert, 2007: 531). Buddhism has often supported local ethnic identities which can be a source of violence and conflict.

An alternative but complementary approach is taken by Matthew Walton, who notes that, in discussions of Buddhist nationalism, the rhetoric used in defending Buddhist identity is not usually based on Buddhist doctrine but 'more closely connected to particular cultural traditions or identities' (Walton, 2017b: 542).

It appears that an analysis of Buddhism in modern Myanmar might reveal otherwise hidden agendas in the history of Buddhism. This is not the Buddhism of the popular imagination. It is a Buddhism in which alternative themes are prominent. It is a Buddhism in which the preservation and defence of the sāsana (the Buddha's teachings, the Buddhist 'religion') is more important than the ascetic ideal of escaping from the cycle of rebirths. These radical forms of Buddhism do not conform to the Buddhism of the Western imagination. As David Steinberg has suggested:

> The Western schoolbook approach which views textual Buddhism as pacifistic, meditative and non-violent misses the dynamic of Buddhism in Myanmar as a socio-political force. It is as naïve as interpreting the history of Western Europe on the basis of the Sermon on the Mount. (Steinberg, 2014)[10]

If we put aside our romantic idea of Buddhism, how surprised should we be by these Buddhist ideas? For example, Buddhism has often, if not always, been allied to rulers, kings and emperors. There is little historical evidence of the world-renouncing ascetic tradition having ever existed except in an elite and small (though notionally important) group (Fogelin, 2015). There is even less evidence for an egalitarian, liberal, multicultural and 'secular' Buddhist society. In Buddhist countries, the Saṅgha has very real power, and modern Myanmar might offer us an insight into how Buddhist culture functioned in the past. I am not suggesting the extremism of MaBaTha type movements might have ever been the norm, but narratives of ethnic and religious identity surely have existed. The question I turn to now is how we are to understand the rhetoric of these groups.

Ethnocentric engaged Buddhism

The term ethnocentric engaged Buddhism can be used to describe the particular phenomenon I have been considering in the history of Buddhism. There are other terms that could be used to describe this form of Buddhism. Hiroko Kawanami has proposed the idea of Buddhist communalism and has described the historical origination of the idea in modern Myanmar (Kawanami, 2016b: 31–55). The term chauvinistic Buddhism also embraces many of its ideas and practices (ee King, 2009: 3). The reason I am using the term ethnocentric engaged Buddhism is to suggest that these types of Buddhism are part of the engaged Buddhist movement. They should be understood in this way because they tackle suffering in society. We might disagree with their methods and their teachings, but this should not preclude them from being legitimate forms of engaged Buddhism.

Thomas Borchert suggests that there is a tendency in studies of Buddhism to bracket out notions of ethnicity, and more broadly culture, as 'epiphenomenal' (Borchert, 2014: 594). This implies that they are not central to the doctrinal and textual core of Buddhist traditions. At the heart of this tendency is the idea that Buddhism does not categorize people into different groups. However, as Borchert notes, the discussion of race, ethnicity and Buddhism is similar to the discussion of Buddhism and violence. In both discussions, when Buddhism is violent, or supports racial or ethnic divisions, then this is considered to be a deviation from 'authentic Buddhism' (Borchert, 2014: 594–5).

I am using the term ethnocentric engaged Buddhism to describe a particular type of engaged Buddhism in which ethnicity is central to the formulation of Buddhist identity. In turn, this ethnocentric Buddhist identity prompts a particular type of engaged Buddhism. In using this term, I need to briefly consider what is meant by ethnicity. Richard Jenkins has summarized Max Weber's influential description of ethnic groups in the following way: 'An ethnic group is based (. . .) on the *belief* shared by its members that, however distantly, they are of common descent' (Jenkins, 1997: 9–10). As Jenkins goes on to note, Weber's arguments suggest that political activity brings people together as an ethnic group. People belong to particular ethnic groups because they act together, therefore, 'the pursuit of collective interests (. . .) encourage ethnic identification' (Jenkins, 1997: 10; Hutchinson and Smith, 1996: 35). A more detailed working definition of ethnicity is given by Baranove and Yelvington:

> Ethnicity may be best conceived of as a set of ideas concerning a group's real or imagined cultural links with an ancestral past. It suggests identification with a certain group based on cultural and historical traditions, including language and religion, and provides basic insights into the nature and origins of a group of people as well as explanations for their modern beliefs, behaviours and accomplishments. Inherent in the concepts the notion that members of a distinct ethnic group share some set of common characteristics that sets them apart from the broader society. (Baranove and Yelvington, 2003: 225)

Ethnicity is a set of cultural, political and historical identities. The term ethnocentric engaged Buddhism points to the ideological and political narratives in which Buddhist identity is intrinsically linked to national and ethnic identity. In this respect Richard Rorty is worth quoting:

> To be ethnocentric is to divide the human race into people to whom one must justify one's beliefs and others. The first group – one's *ethnos* – comprises those who share enough of one's beliefs to make fruitful conversation possible. In this sense, everyone is ethnocentric when engaged in actual debate, no matter how much realist rhetoric about objectivity he produces in his study. (Rorty, 1989: 44)[11]

In this use, there are shared cultural and ethnic characteristics which distinguish Buddhists from non-Buddhists. These ideas can be used to create what has been described as an 'ethnic state' (Robinne, 2019: 287–92), or, in my terminology, an ethnocentric engaged Buddhist state.

The term ethnocentric engaged Buddhism signals the combination of features of Buddhist and national identities producing distinct ethno-Buddhist identities. For example, in Thailand there is the idea of 'nation, religion, monarch' (*chat-sāsana-phramahakasat*; Liow, 2016: 108) and in Myanmar 'nation, language and religion' (*amyo-barthar-tharthanar*).[12] In both of these examples the idea of adherence and allegiance to Buddhism (the *sāsana*. Burmese: *tharthanar*) is linked to other factors in the formation of identity. These new and emerging Theravāda Buddhist narratives in Myanmar promote forms of Buddhist nationalism which, as I have suggested, are a challenge to the prevailing notions of Buddhism in the West.[13]

The defence of one's religion is linked to these other themes of national and ethnic identity – to defend one is to defend the other. This phenomenon is clearly seen in some of the rhetoric I outlined earlier in relation to Ashin Wirathu and the MaBaTha movement. Fundamental questions in relation to these discourses are ideas of belonging and identity (Schober, 2017: 160; Robinne, 2019: 287–92). The formation of modern Burmese Buddhist identity is complex. Juliane Schober quotes a 1914 speech by U May Ong, who was then the Rector of Rangoon University and professed that the Burman possess 'race, language, Buddhism and erudition' and that 'We Burmese are Buddhists' (Schober, 2017: 163. See also Gravers, 2013: 48). According to Schober this early expression of Burmese identity has shaped discourses in the formation of Buddhist nationalism. It is a key factor in the idea that race, ethnicity and Buddhist identity are primary factors in what it means to be Burmese (Schober, 2017: 163–4).[14]

The point is that while ethical behaviour is central to Buddhist identity other factors relating to ethnicity and culture are also important. These other factors can promote a type of Buddhism which can be termed ethnocentric engaged Buddhism.

The ideas of ethnocentric engaged Buddhism

There are a number of possible factors and ideas that could shape the formation of ethnocentric engaged Buddhism. Not all of these are available in each cultural context. Some are available across Buddhist Asia, some confined to a particular area. I will outline seven themes. (1) The idea of the 'True Dhamma/Dharma' (saddharma/saddhamma); (2) The idea of the disappearance of the Dharma/Dhamma; (3) The idea that the teachings can be corrupted and are subject to decline; (4) The idea of a collective Buddhist identity; (5) The idea that Buddhism is under threat and needs to be protected; (6) The idea of the threat of conversion; (7) The idea that Buddhism is linked to ethnicity.

These are prominent themes that might contribute to a form of Buddhism that commits violence and discriminates against other ethnic and religious groups. I am not claiming that all, or, indeed, any of these factors are present in a given situation. My suggestion is that these ideas are available in Buddhist culture and that they might influence violent forms of engaged Buddhism. They are themes that might contribute to an understanding of militant forms of engaged Buddhism in Asia. Just as there are a number of factors that contribute to more peaceful and tolerant Buddhist movements, such as teachings on compassion and loving-kindness, the doctrine of not-self which lessens selfish activity, etc., so these ideas might lead to a sectarian and chauvinistic type of Buddhism.

(1) The idea of the 'True Dhamma/Dharma' (*saddharma/saddhamma*) has been a theme throughout Buddhist history. In its developed form, it suggests that there is a complete and perfect version of the teachings of the Buddha preserved in one particular place. In East Asian Buddhism a particular text is considered to contain the essential teachings of the Buddha (or a Buddha). The *Saddharmapundarika Sūtra* (the so-called *Lotus Sutra*) is the best known example of this phenomenon in East Asia (Nattier, 1991: 66; Williams, 2009: 149–71). This text is considered the perfect and final teaching of the Buddha – the culmination of his message. It is thought to have great power in expediating liberation. In Theravāda Buddhism the Pāli Canon could also be considered to preserve the essential word of the Buddha. Buddhist nationalism could be built upon this idea. The point is that Buddhist identity can be based on texts, Buddhist symbols or places of pilgrimage to create a lineage back to the Buddha (see Strong, 2004).

(2) The second key theme of ethnocentric engaged Buddhism is that the teachings of the Buddha will not last indefinitely and has a limited and predictable history. In its developed form this is the idea of the disappearance or decline of the teachings of the Buddha (*sāsana–antaradhāna*, Nattier, 1991: 122). The teachings of the Buddha will last a finite period of time. In the early traditions, it is explained that the Buddha's teachings will survive for five hundred years, while in some East Asian traditions it is stated that his teachings will last as long as ten thousand years (Nattier, 1991: 28–9).

Famously, in the Pāli canon, the reason that the Buddha's teachings will only last five hundred years is the formation of the order of Buddhist nuns or, more correctly, the admittance of women into the Buddhist Saṅgha. This notorious passage states the following:

> If [. . .] women had not obtained the going forth from the household life into homelessness in the Dhamma and discipline proclaimed by the Tathāgata [the Buddha; if the order of nuns had not been established], the spiritual life would have been of long duration; the good Dhamma would have stood firm even for a thousand years. However [. . .] because women have gone forth from the household life into homelessness in the Dhamma and discipline proclaimed by the Tathāgata, now the spiritual life will not be of long duration; the good Dhamma will last only five hundred years. (A IV 278)

Leaving aside the difficult questions that this passage raises (is there evidence of misogyny is early Buddhism? Were these sentiments placed in the text at a later date by monks who had problems with the female gender, as I discussed briefly in Chapter 7?), a possible implication of such ideas is the urgency for a given people to preserve and defend the teachings of the Buddha with its imminent demise long ago predicted by the Buddha himself. Ethnocentric engaged Buddhists need to act to preserve the Buddha's teachings, to protect his monastic order – Buddhism is in danger; there is a call to arms, a rhetoric of impending disaster, Buddhists must act in order that Buddhism survives.

(3) The third related theme of ethnocentric engaged Buddhism is the idea that the teachings themselves can be corrupted and are subject to decline. This idea is written into the Buddhist narrative DNA. Jan Nattier suggests seven categories which summarize the reason for this decline:

> 1. the admission of women into the monastic community; 2. lack of respect toward various elements of the Buddhist tradition; 3. Lack of diligence in meditation practice; 4. carelessness in the transmission of the teachings; 5. the emergence of divisions in the Sangha; 6. the emergence of a false or 'counterfeit' Dharma; and 7. excessive association with secular society. (Nattier, 1991: 120)

The teachings of the Buddha do not disappear due to a lack of belief, or the prevalence of mistaken beliefs, but because of bad and misguided behaviour (Jerryson, 2016a: 270). The causes of this corruption are often internal, caused by members of the Buddhist community – for example, undisciplined monks. The decline might also be due to monks becoming too involved in secular society (more details given in Fuller, 2018: 28–32).

(4) The fourth idea of ethnocentric engaged Buddhism is the idea of a collective Buddhist identity. Alicia Turner suggests that a key factor in the formulation of Buddhist identity is the idea of communal belonging (2014: 7–9). This idea originated in descriptions of the ethical actions of the Buddha found in a variety of Buddhist texts such as the Jātakas (descriptions of the previous lives of the Buddha) and the historical lineage Vaṃsa texts of Sri Lanka which, Turner suggests,

> [E]ncouraged listeners to appreciate how the benefits and possibilities of the Buddha's sāsana [the Buddha's teachings, the Buddhist religion] they enjoyed were the result of the sacrifices and devotion of previous generations. The text worked to inculcate a sense of gratitude to those who came before that constructed Buddhists as collective heirs of the past to promote the sāsana and created an obligation to continue the effort for future generations. (Turner, 2014: 8)

Benedict Anderson's *Imagined Communities* (Anderson, 2006) has been one of the most influential books on the idea of the nation for well over a decade, and he has shaped many scholar's ideas, including Turner's. In Anderson's pioneering work he describes the nation as an imagined political community.

An important aspect of this imagined community is an 'image of communion' in the minds of each member, even though most of them will not know or meet the other members of the nation (Turner, 2014: 8). As Anderson argues about imagined communities:

> It is imagined as a community, because, regardless of the actual inequality and exploitation that may prevail in each, the nation is always conceived as a deep, horizontal comradeship. Ultimately it is this fraternity that makes it possible [. . .] for so many millions of people, not so much to kill, as willingly to die for such limited imaginings. (Anderson, 2006: 7)

We can make sense of modern ethnocentric engaged Buddhism through the perspective offered by Benedict Anderson. In the formulation of Buddhist identity, there is an imagined identity, a construction, an amalgamation of traditional narratives and modern ones. Buddhist identity becomes a focus for ethnocentric engaged Buddhism which forms alliances around it.

(5) The fifth idea of ethnocentric engaged Buddhism is the notion that Buddhism is under threat and needs to be protected. The term protectionist engaged Buddhism could be used to describe this phenomenon. Iselin Frydenlund has used the term 'Buddhist protectionist ideology' (Frydenlund, 2018: 3).[15] The threat in much of modern Buddhist Asia is perceived to be from Islam. In turn, Buddhist monks like Ashin Wirathu are held to be defenders of Buddhism. These self-proclaimed protectors of Buddhism can use arguments to justify their actions and rhetoric to defend Buddhist institutions. Matthew Walton and Michael Jerryson describe Ashin Wirathu's popular preaching in the following terms:

> He draws on narratives that make reference to Buddhism, but not directly to its doctrine; he appeals to a more nebulous notion of Buddhist cultural and political identity, and an even more specific *Burmese* Buddhist identity. This identity is rooted in a particular historical self-understanding, yet is affected by a set of global narratives about Islam, Buddhism, and Burmese Buddhists' places in the world. (Walton and Jerryson, 2016: 796)

Using these ideas, Buddhist monks can justify their political engagement when it is used in defence of Buddhism, and precisely this is protectionist engaged Buddhism.

The protection of Buddhism often finds expression in relation to the defence and protection of Buddhist women. In a recent article Gerard McCarthy and Jacqueline Menager have described how, over a number of decades, Buddhist Myanmar has had a 'discourse focused on the need to protect and promote the reproduction – literally and metaphorically – of Myanmar as a Buddhist nation'

(McCarthy and Menager, 2017: 396). This highlights the gendered narrative in which Muslim men are seen as a threat to Buddhist women. Mikael Gravers suggests that in modern Myanmar there is a mixing of narratives. First, the traditional ones focused upon the decline of the Buddha's teaching. Second, the globalized idea that Islam is a threat to the survival of Buddhism (Gravers, 2015: 1–2).[16]

(6) The sixth idea of ethnocentric engaged Buddhism is the threat of conversion. An example of this is the four laws which were enacted in Myanmar in 2015. The four laws are: 'the Population Control Law, the Conversion Law, the Buddhist Women's Special Marriage Law and the Monogamy Law'. It is the second of these, the conversion law that is of interest in the description of ethnocentric engaged Buddhism (McCarthy and Menager, 2017: 397).[17] As Susan Hayward and Matthew Walton explain:

> The Religious Conversion Law requires those wishing to convert to complete a government application and be subjected to an interview with at least five members of an oversight committee to demonstrate that they were not coerced into conversion. The law also criminalizes coercive conversion of other people. (Hayward and Walton, 2016: 71)

Iselin Frydenlund suggests that the conversion laws are a reaction to the Islamic practice of requiring conversion to Islam by Buddhists in Islamic cultures (Frydenlund, 2017: 7).[18] These laws gained public support, partly through propaganda spread by members of MaBaTha. The formulation of these laws has been part of MaBaTha's campaign for many years (Frydenlund, 2017: 6).

The importance of this aspect of ethnocentric engaged Buddhism is that they express a fear within some Buddhist movements of other religious groups. Non-Buddhist religions need to be controlled, tamed and moderated. The idea of a multicultural religiously plural society is treated with suspicion by many of these Buddhist groups. This idea is part of the protectionist tendency apparent in ethnocentric engaged Buddhism. These ideas play upon fears that Buddhism is under threat – that it is facing a period of decline during which the Buddha's teachings will be lost and that it needs protecting, primarily from Buddhists converting to Islam, culminating finally in the idea that a particular ethnic group can protect and defend Buddhism.

(7) In ethnocentric engaged Buddhism, Buddhist identity is associated with ethnicity. A particular ethnic group is under threat and needs to preserve the teachings of the Buddha. Other ethnic groups, unless they come under the control of the dominant Buddhist group, are a danger. In certain contexts, to be Buddhist is to be part of a distinct ethnic group. This in turn gives rise to a natural sense of Buddhist nationalism. What is essential to the tradition

is emphasized, for example, preserving Buddhist culture, and Buddhist fundamentalism comes to the fore in which the 'other' is polarized as a threat to the future of Buddhism.

Buddhist culture can produce a form of Buddhism which stresses local and ethnic concerns. These local expressions of Buddhism are occasionally violent, personal and chauvinistic which have little to do with the core ethical values of a more universal Buddhist message. These are forms of engaged Buddhism. Because they are local, have ethnic identities, and promote cultural interests, the ways in which they engage with the world in order to alleviate suffering is distinctly at odds with the more universal messages of Buddhism.

Ethnocentric engaged Buddhism: A summary

The factors contributing to ethnocentric engaged Buddhism contribute to the emergence of attitudes which appear to contradict the more compassionate teachings of Buddhism. There is a temptation to assume that these modern movements are not genuinely Buddhist in nature. However, I have suggested that there are ideas and concepts within traditional forms of Buddhism that can be used to justify extreme reactions to other religions to shape a radical form of Buddhist identity.

By using the term ethnocentric engaged Buddhism, I hope to suggest historical and doctrinal themes and narratives within Buddhism that might help to explain this phenomenon. Buddhism would, we might expect, react calmly, and with kindness and compassion to the presence of other religions and ethnic groups. This seems to lie at the heart of the teachings of the Buddha. However, I have suggested that there are mechanisms in place in Buddhist texts, doctrinal history and culture that would, at the very least, allow for other ways of forming Buddhist identity.

I have suggested that there is a form of engaged Buddhism which is often, though not always, at odds with other forms of Buddhism. These forms of engaged Buddhism clearly fit into a description of Buddhist engagement. They attempt to alleviate forms of suffering. The suffering they address is the suffering caused by radical evaluations of Buddhist identity. To be a Buddhist is to support, honour and preserve the three jewels of Buddhism: the Buddha, his teachings and the community of monastics. Without the survival of these three jewels, there will be no chance to eradicate suffering. Buddhism needs to be protected, and I have used the alternative term protectionist engaged Buddhism to describe this phenomenon. Without preserving Buddhism, suffering cannot be alleviated, greed, hatred and delusion will prevail and the Buddhist path to awakening will be extinguished.

Discussion questions

1. Can the protection of Buddhism be used to justify violence?

2. Are ethnocentric engaged Buddhist movements examples of engaged Buddhism?

3. How is Buddhist identity united with ethnic identity?

Suggestions for further reading

Borchert, Thomas. 2014. 'The Buddha's Precepts on Respecting Other Races and Religions? Thinking about the Relationship of Ethnicity and Theravāda Buddhism'. *Journal of Social Issues in Southeast Asia* 29 (3): 591–626.
Cheah, Joseph. 2016. 'Buddhism, Race, and Ethnicity'. In *The Oxford Handbook of Contemporary Buddhism*, ed. Michael Jerryson, 650–61. New York: Oxford University Press.
Foxeus, Niklas. 2019. 'The Buddha was a Devoted Nationalist: Buddhist Nationalism, *Ressentiment*, and Defending Buddhism in Myanmar'. *Religion* 49 (4): 661–90.
Fuller, Paul. 2018. 'The Narratives of Ethnocentric Buddhist Identity'. *The Journal of the British Association of Religious Studies* 20: 19–44.
Jerryson, Michael. 2015. 'Buddhists and Violence: Historical Continuity/Academic Incongruities'. *Religion Compass* 9: 141–50.
Schonthal, Benjamin and Matthew J. Walton. 2016. 'The (New) Buddhist Nationalisms? Symmetries and Specificities in Sri Lanka and Myanmar'. *Contemporary Buddhism* 17 (1): 81–115.

9

Buddhism on the edge, Buddhists offended

Engaged Buddhism and blasphemy

In this chapter I would like to consider another controversial feature of engaged Buddhism. It involves the misappropriation of Buddhist sacred objects and has many similarities to the idea of blasphemy in other religious traditions (Robinne, 2019: 307). It has become commonplace for images of the Buddha to be used as decorations in various contexts in modern societies. Statues of the Buddha are found around people's homes. Images of the Buddha are often used as tattoos (Jerryson, 2016b: 121). Finally, they can be used in the fashion industry (Shields, 2010). There are some Buddhist groups, such as the Knowing Buddha Organization (knowingbuddha.org), founded in Thailand in 2010, which campaign against the commercialization of Buddhism (Jerryson, 2016b: 121). This suggests that Asian Buddhist communities take offence to the misuse of Buddhist material culture.

The idea of blasphemy is not usually associated with Buddhism.[1] However, this chapter will suggest that it is a more prevalent idea in the Pāli canon and in modern Southeast Asia than is usually assumed.[2] It seems clear that the Pāli canon at the very least anticipates some of the recent Buddhist rhetoric about blasphemy in modern Southeast Asian engaged Buddhism. Recent events can be understood within the broader context of the earlier Pāli canonical texts and are foreshadowed by textual passages, even if these are not directly known by key figures in recent Buddhist movements.[3]

The Pāli canon forms the textual basis of Theravāda Buddhism, the school of Buddhism practised in South and Southeast Asia. It also forms the textual

FIGURE 16 *Publicity poster used by the Knowing Buddha Organization in Thailand. The Knowing Buddha Organization campaign against the improper use of Buddhist images. Credit: Used with permission of Montira Yotee from the Knowing Buddha Organization.*

basis of modern Burmese Buddhism.[4] As in the previous chapter the focus will be on Burmese Buddhism. However, I hope these ideas can be applied to other Buddhist communities around Asia.

There are many terms in the Pāli canon that refer to 'disrespect' committed against venerated objects or people, and some of these cover ideas that come close to the notion of blasphemy that we find in the Abrahamic religions. It therefore seems reasonable to compare ideas in the Pāli canon and to consider how these might also manifest in general attitudes and patterns of behaviour in modern Burma and in what I have termed ethnocentric engaged Buddhist movements.

I am not suggesting that a direct causal connection exists between passages in the Pāli canon and that these are acted upon in a specific way in modern Buddhist attitudes to blasphemy and disrespect. I am, however, suggesting that the tradition mediated through the Pāli canon forms an important part of what Steven Collins has termed the 'Pāli imaginaire' (Collins, 1998). This denotes an ideology contained in the Pāli textual tradition which, over the centuries, 'moved downwards, and at some point before or during the modern period became a "popular" or peasant religion' (Collins, 1998: 565–6). Collins is indicating a subtle process by which an elite textual tradition, with a focus on the Pāli canon, can permeate and influence forms of behaviour in modern religious culture. It is such a process that I am arguing for in this chapter, though I am not suggesting that a particular text influenced a particular type of behaviour.[5]

My contention is that we can note ideas and concepts that have to do with blasphemy in the Pāli canon and that similar ideas and attitudes are expressed by monks of the Theravāda tradition in modern Burma. These ideas and practices form part of the Pāli conceptual world, or the 'Pāli imaginaire'. The Pāli canon can be used to explain in technical terms why Burmese Buddhists might become offended by a lack of respect shown towards images of the Buddha, for example, though the monks themselves might not be aware of the passages in the Pāli canon. I am using the examples from the Pāli canon to suggest how the actions of the monks might be justified by the textual tradition, not to suggest that the monks are using the Pāli canon to justify their actions.

In the previous chapter I suggested that there are specific conceptual ideas found in the earlier Buddhist traditions which could be used to understand some of the actions of modern ethnocentric or protectionist engaged Buddhists. I was not suggesting that those involved in modern engaged Buddhism were directly acting upon these ideas, but that they could anticipate or influence modern Buddhist movements.

It is my argument throughout this chapter that there is a prevalent attitude throughout Theravāda Buddhist history, which is found in the Pāli canon and in mainstream religious practice. This attitude is one in which the teachings of the Buddha and sacred Buddhist objects should be protected (part of the conceptual vocabulary of protectionist engaged Buddhism). When it is thought that disrespect is shown towards the Buddha and his teachings, then a reaction to this can be shown towards the perpetrators of the act of disrespect. This reaction, in modern Myanmar, can be violent. My idea is that passages describing these ideas in the Pāli canon have not generally been given much attention. I do not suggest that these passages are quoted by modern Burmese Buddhists in terms of a justification for blasphemous attitudes; however, they do anticipate modern religious attitudes. If we reflect upon these passages in the Pāli canon we will gain an insight into Southeast Asian Buddhist culture, part of the conceptual world of Theravāda Buddhism. There is not a direct link whereby notions found in the Pāli canon are enacted upon by modern Burmese proponents of Buddhism. Rather the actions of modern Buddhism could be legitimized by passages in the Pāli canon.

In summary, these activities are undertaken by engaged Buddhism, and this is not a term denoting a specific ideological position and, even less, a recommended or commendable moral position. Rather, it encompasses a wide range of activities, and blasphemy is one of these.

Blasphemy and Buddhism?

The widespread assumption that Buddhism has no concept of blasphemy is based upon the idea that the central focus in Buddhism is on achieving a detached state of mind. The idea of non-attachment is a basic teaching that is prevalent in the textual traditions of Buddhism. It would then follow that for a Buddhist to become offended, for example, by a perceived misuse of an image of the Buddha would, in a quite fundamental way, go against the central attitude of non-attachment which Buddhism aims to promote.[6] In simple terms the idea that blasphemy can be committed against Buddhism seems to run counter to assumptions about what Buddhism is, namely, a religious discipline which aims at the overcoming of all forms of mental rigidity. However, this understanding ignores an equally legitimate conceptual framework in which offence is shown to types of disrespect aimed at Buddhism. The latter framework, like that of non-attachment, also finds a place in the Pāli canon and in modern Burmese engaged Buddhist discourse. Both the rhetoric of non-attachment and meditative calm and that of condemning the manipulation and misuse of Buddhist sacred objects has a footing in the Pāli canon and modern Burmese engaged Buddhist thinking. It is this narrative of offence, disrespect and blasphemy which is my primary focus in this chapter.

Blasphemy, culture and identity

Scholars make an important point about the history of blasphemy and, in particular, blasphemy laws. This is that, in committing blasphemy, the accused is not simply offending the religion but also offending the state, nation or country in which religion takes a central place (Ross, 2012: 4). When religion and state form close ritual, legal and ceremonial alliances, as it does across many modern Buddhist cultures, then the notion of blasphemy becomes an issue of some importance.

Buddhism, as it exists in many Asian countries, has not undergone a rigorous process of secularization. By this I mean that aspects of culture that are separated and exist as independent entities in modern cultures do not resemble their Asian counterparts. As this has not taken place, notions of religion, nation and identity are closely linked. In this situation, the rights of the group or of the culture are not separated from the sensibilities of the religion. In fact, religious and cultural identities are often indistinguishable for Asian Buddhists. This is in stark contrast to the modern perception of Buddhism in which Buddhism is perceived as having little to do with culture and society.[7]

In many parts of Asia, Buddhism is very much part of an individual's identity, as I explained in the previous chapter. This can take the form of it being part of both cultural and national identity. As Rebecca Ross asks, 'is religion a choice, or is it a cultural identity?' (Ross, 2012: 8). The former, in which one's religion is a choice, fits into a secularized modern form of Buddhism, which aligns itself to the modern Western encounter with Buddhism. The latter, in which religion (the *sāsana*), culture and identity have close and overlapping meanings, is more easily identifiable in modern and pre-modern Asian Buddhist societies. One might suggest the following to make these categories clearer. Traditional forms of Buddhism are based upon a complex group of ideas and practices. Prominent are ideas and practices that emphasize the generation of merit in order to have a better rebirth – the ideas that the Buddha, his teachings and his monastic community have the power to avert danger, hardship and misfortune. Modern forms of Buddhism often emphasize contemplative exercises in the form of meditation. Their focus is often on attaining a state of peace and well-being in the present life, even in the present moment. I outlined some of these ideas at the outset of Chapter 3 and the discussion of modern Buddhism. Modern Buddhism will often stress the supposed scientific and rational nature of the Buddha and his teachings, while traditional forms of Buddhism will often be more concerned with the miraculous and supernatural elements associated with Buddhism.

It is often difficult to find justifications for notions similar to blasphemy in the Buddhist textual tradition. However, I would like to challenge this assumption and show that there are several episodes where disrespect is shown towards, for example, the Buddha, Dharma and Saṅgha in which ideas similar to blasphemy are clearly apparent. Therefore, there is a precedent for the practices of ethnocentric engaged Buddhism. A more subtle way of stating this is to suggest that, on the evidence of the passages used in this chapter, in accusing others of committing blasphemy, to use Steven Collins terms 'there is nothing in this which is inimical to the Buddhism of the Pāli imaginaire' (Collins, 1998: 567). There are also modern incidents in which the idea of blasphemy being a workable idea in Buddhism becomes clear. I think that it is essential in our understanding of engaged Buddhism that we begin to appreciate that ideas similar to blasphemy were, in a subtle way, present throughout Buddhist history, or at least formed possible conceptual components of Buddhist culture. This is important as it challenges some of our most cherished ideas about precisely what Buddhism is and how it has been practised throughout its history.

As I will show, there are passages in the Pāli canon in which ideas similar to blasphemy are apparent. This would suggest that, in Buddhist history, Buddhist communities might, and on the evidence probably did, interact with other religious communities and cultures in ways that we might not have expected. This is certainly true in modern Burma/Myanmar. Burmese Buddhists are acting in ways that they should not act *if* there is no notion similar to blasphemy in the Buddhist tradition, in the Pāli canon, and in Buddhist culture. However, it is precisely the argument of this chapter that there is a notion similar to blasphemy found throughout Buddhist history, even though the actors in these episodes are not directly aware of the textual tradition which would give legitimacy to their actions. My point is not that they, the Buddhist monks, are using the Pāli canon to justify their actions, but that the Pāli canon has passages that could be used to give this legitimacy. A Buddhist might abstain from drinking alcohol and advise others that they should also abstain, but might not be aware of the reasons for this, or the textual passages which validate such precepts. The Pāli canon will offer various injunctions that one should indeed abstain from taking alcohol. In turn, there will be passages describing how ingesting intoxicants causes heedlessness and confusion and this lack of clarity will hinder the individual from reflecting upon the nature of suffering. Similarly, a modern Buddhist might argue that respect should be shown towards the Buddha, the Dhamma and the Saṅgha but not be able to point to a canonical text that explains precisely why respect should be shown. I will show how the Pāli canon does indeed contain passages in which disrespect is a hindrance on the Buddhist path. This is why I think there is a valid argument for comparing episodes in the Pāli canon to incidents in modern Burma, and to draw from these certain conclusions about engaged Buddhism.

An analysis of 'Blasphemy' in the Pāli canon

In his book, *Blasphemy in the Christian World: A History* (2007), David Nash has suggested that blasphemy is simultaneously four things:

> Blasphemy is a manifestation of what people think about their God and the sacred. It is also a display of power, a crime, and a species of flawed social interaction transgressing norms of manners and acceptable behavior. (6–7)

Nash's description explains blasphemy in terms of social, cultural and religious identities and in terms of social behaviour. In this context we might better understand how there can be notions of blasphemy in Buddhist societies. We will not find an abundance of descriptions of blasphemy and related ideas in the Pāli canon, precisely because this body of texts is rarely concerned with these issues. The Pāli canon (and there are a few notable exceptions) is on the whole concerned with descriptions of an ascetic path which leads to liberation; however, some scholars have recently suggested passages where political ideas are present, and these have been considered in Chapter 4. Though not prominent, there are certain key passages in which central objects of Buddhist devotion are seen as needing protection against disrespect, dishonour and slander. As I have said, these passages are not necessarily used by modern

Burmese engaged Buddhists to justify the idea of blasphemy in Buddhism but they could be used to make legitimate claims that the Pāli canon could justify such forms of behaviour.

There are a number of terms in the Pāli canon that refer to ideas of disrespect being shown towards venerated objects and people. The first term I will consider appears in a group of seven (or alternatively six) types of 'disrespect' (agārava) to sacred objects. The list of seven is found at A IV 84 where the Buddha is questioned by the Venerable Kimbila:

> What is the cause and reason why, Bhante [a very polite form of address], the good Dhamma does not continue long after the Tathāgata [the Buddha] has attained final nibbāna [Nirvāna]?
>
> Here, Kimbila, after a Tathāgata (a Buddha) has attained final nibbāna, (1) the bhikkhus, bhikkhunīs [monks and nuns], male lay followers, and female lay followers dwell without reverence (agārava) and deference toward the Teacher. (2) They dwell without reverence and deference toward the Dhamma. (3) They dwell without reverence and deference toward the Saṅgha. (4) They dwell without reverence and deference toward the training. (5) They dwell without reverence and deference toward concentration. (6) They dwell without reverence and deference toward heedfulness. (7) They dwell without reverence and deference toward hospitality. This is the cause and reason why the good Dhamma does not continue long after the Tathāgata has attained final nibbāna. (A IV 84)

However, if there is reverence and respect paid towards these seven, then the Dhamma will last long after the Tathāgata has attained final Nibbāna.[8] These passages suggest that there is a clear idea that disrespect should not be shown to the Buddha, Dhamma, the Saṅgha and other sacred Buddhist objects and ideas. There is a sacred physical, ideational and material culture that should be treated respectfully which these passages describe. These texts could also give validity to episodes in modern Burmese engaged Buddhism, for, although not frequent, texts like these suggest ideas that come close to a notion of blasphemy. At the very least the actions described in these passages overlap with David Nash's description of blasphemy 'transgressing norms of manners and acceptable behaviour' (Nash, 2007: 6–7). They are also suggestive of the idea that if contempt and disrespect are shown to the sacred objects of Buddhism, then this will hasten the decline of the Dhamma (of Buddhism), as I discussed in the previous chapter.

As Nash notes, historically there has been an inability to establish the 'genuine intention' of those behaving with disrespect, thus leading to the action to be labelled as 'blasphemy'. This has 'plagued legal practice around blasphemy until this day' (Nash, 2007: 54). The matter of intention is partly taken-up in the *Kathāvatthu* (Kvu 472), an important text in Theravāda Buddhism, where a particular point is debated regarding 'views' (*diṭṭhi*) and murder. The point of the passage is to debate the following: 'That a person who is accomplished in view (*diṭṭhi-sampanna*) may yet deliberately commit murder.' The idea of the debate is fundamentally discussing if an advanced practitioner on the Buddhist path can commit a serious offence.

The *Kathāvatthu* suggests that the person who is advanced on the Buddhist path cannot deliberately kill another living being, and certainly not commit even the worst type of murder, namely the murder of one's mother, father or an Arahant. It is also impossible that such a person

> May defile (*ohadeyya*) Buddha shrines, desecrate them (*omutteti*: Literally urinate on them), spit on them (*niṭṭhubhi*), behave disrespectfully in the presence of them (*apabyamāta*). (Kvu 472)

The text concludes that the person advanced on the Buddhist path may not perform any of these deeds. This debate in the *Kathāvatthu* is arguably describing actions that might easily be explained as blasphemous, such as 'defiling Buddhist shrines', 'desecrating them', 'spitting on them', etc. One could clearly argue that an idea of blasphemy is suggested by these episodes.[9]

Disrespect and misrepresentations of Buddhist images are primarily offensive because acts of disrespect are seen as dangerous and inauspicious. There is a complex mix of ideas. Sacred objects often form part of national and cultural identity. In this context there is a dangerous alliance of religious and cultural identities. Not only is the mistreatment of sacred objects inauspicious for the individual, but also for the preservation of the culture and the nation. The key here is that, as was shown in the examples from the Pāli canon, performing acts of irreverence and disrespect towards the material culture of Buddhism was considered a major offence. A similar mindset seems to be central to episodes in modern Burma where performing acts of irreverence and disrespect is central to the enactment of violent behaviour. I would suggest that there is a basic premise in the Pāli canon similar to the idea of blasphemy which can also be clearly seen in these incidents.

As I suggested earlier, modern secular forms of Buddhism emphasize those parts of the Buddha's teachings that focus upon notions such as freeing the mind of all forms of attachment, including attachment to sacred objects. It is for this reason, among many, that it is often assumed that there is no notion of blasphemy in Buddhism. This perspective often misses other important aspects of Buddhism which emphasize the protective power of the Buddha, Dhamma and the Saṅgha.

The power of images of the Buddha in Myanmar and the DJing Buddha

In traditional forms of Buddhism the stress is often on protective and auspicious acts. Images, texts and chanting are partly concerned with averting danger. Primarily it is the Buddha (and images of him), because of his great meritorious and ethical deeds, who accomplishes this. Reciting a Pāli text can also be used to avert danger. In this context blasphemy is a perfectly coherent idea.

In late 2014 a New Zealand citizen, Philip Blackwood, caused outrage among a group of hardline Buddhist monks in Myanmar by using an image of the Buddha wearing headphones and being portrayed as a DJ in a trance-like state. This image was used as part of a promotion for a bar in Yangon, the former capital of Myanmar. Two Burmese citizens, Tun Thurein and Htut Ko Ko Lwin, were also charged.[10] They were charged under articles 295 and 295(a) of the Myanmar Penal Code, which reads:

> 295. Injuring or defiling place of worship, with intent to insult the religion of any class.
>
> 295 (a). Deliberate and malicious acts intended to outrage religious feelings of any class by insulting its religion or religious beliefs. ('Myanmar Penal Code')

It was under these laws that the three accused were charged and given two-and-a-half year prison sentences. Monks from the MaBaTha movement (which were described in the previous chapter), a Burmese acronym for the 'The Organisation for the Protection of Race and Religion'), expressed outrage at what they perceived to be the misuse of an image of the Buddha. The MaBaTha monks, as far as I am aware, did not quote from a specific text from the Pāli canon, or use any textual resources to justify their outrage. However, MaBaTha monks have used language reminiscent of the Pāli texts. Between 19 and 21 June 2015, MaBaTha held their annual conference at Insein's Ywarma Monastery on the outskirts of Yangon. A 12-point statement was released.[11] Point 7 argues the following:

> We urge that vicious and blasphemous attacks on Venerable monks [. . .] using improper literature and images which affect our national culture and the image of Buddhist culture must be completely stopped.[12]

As I have indicated earlier, texts from the Pāli canon could be used to give legitimacy to their actions, and statements like this are similar to the passages from the Pāli canon which I cited above. Statements like these from the MaBaTha movement suggest that the Pāli canon foreshadows recent Buddhist thinking about blasphemy. They are also engaging in the culture and society of modern Myanmar – they are engaged Buddhists.

Some of the confusion in the reporting of this story is that, as described in this chapter, blasphemy is not an idea usually associated with Buddhism. However, once we consider the idea of blasphemy to be a credible and even prevalent notion in Buddhist culture, our understanding of this issue might be clearer. I am clearly not suggesting that the treatment of Philip Blackwood, Tun Thurein and Htut Ko Ko Lwin is in any way justified. However, it is worth considering some possible reasons that they were thought to cause such offence.

It could be assumed in modern manifestations of Buddhism that the sanctity and holiness of the image of the Buddha is a cultural accretion and one that is not essential to the practice of Buddhism. However, I have suggested that in the Pāli canon there is the idea that one should not disrespect images of the Buddha and other sacred objects of Buddhism and that the actions of the prosecutors of blasphemy could be considered legitimate parts of Pāli Buddhist patterns of behaviour.

The idea that blasphemy has no place in Buddhism

In the more popular understanding of Buddhism, nothing should become an object of attachment. One cannot, in a sense, insult a Buddhist because the material culture and religious objects of Buddhism have no real sacred value. The well-known Simile of the Raft is often used to justify this understanding. If the material culture and the ideas and truths of Buddhism become an object of attachment, then they would be classified as a manifestation of greed and attachment. One cannot, in effect, insult Buddhism. On a certain level such an understanding is perfectly reasonable and can, as I have said, be justified. A notable textual basis for such an understanding is a famous passage from the *Brahmajāla-sutta* (D I 1–46) where the following is stated:

> Monks, if anyone should speak in disparagement of me, the Dhamma or of the Saṅgha, you should not be angry, resentful or upset on that account. If you were to be angry or displeased at such disparagement, that would only be a hindrance to you. For if others disparage me, the Dhamma or the Saṅgha, and you are angry or displeased, can you recognise whether what they say is right or wrong? 'No, Lord.' 'If others disparage me, the Dhamma

or the Saṅgha, then you must explain what is incorrect as being incorrect, saying: "That is incorrect, that is false, that is not our way, that is not found among us."' (D I 2–3)

There appears to be a relatively clear (though not unambiguous) message here. To become angry at misrepresentations or insults directed at the Buddha, the Dhamma, and the Saṅgha would be an obstacle for those who take offence. Anger would distort the minds of those offended, and this is far worse than the situation causing offence.

This idea is enforced in the *Alagaddūpama-sutta* (M I 130–42) in which the Buddha emphasizes that

If others abuse, revile, scold and harass you, on that account you should not entertain any annoyance, bitterness, or dejection of the heart. (M I 140)

In both the *Brahmajāla-sutta* and the *Alagaddūpama-sutta*, the Buddha is very clear in his condemnation. His criticism is not aimed at those who *cause* offence, but at the negative and unwholesome states of mind in those who *take* offence. The message that is repeated throughout the Buddha's teachings is that they are concerned with the overcoming of suffering. A major obstacle to this is not in external factors, in others' praise or disparagement, but in controlling feelings of anger and resentment.

In this understanding the Buddha certainly did teach a moderate path in which greed, hatred and delusion are the real obstacles. Those offending the sacred objects of Buddhism, such as images of the Buddha, should not cause anger to arise. However, Buddhism is far more culturally complex than is often appreciated.

That the image of the Buddha is sacred and has very real power to practitioners of Buddhism appears to be unknown to those who only acknowledge the form of Buddhism practised in modern, urban Asian and Western cultures. The power of Buddhist sacred objects is part of what has been termed 'apotropaic Buddhism' (Spiro, 1982).[13] The term apotropaic refers to objects, texts and teachings that are regarded as having protective and often magical qualities. An image of the Buddha (which, as Donald K. Swearer has suggested, is not simply an image, but 'is' the Buddha, a surrogate Buddha, as it were) has the power to protect and avert danger (Swearer, 2004).

It is in this context that the offence caused by the DJing trance-like Buddha image is lost on those producing such an image. The images are not only offensive to certain sensibilities but primarily dangerous and inauspicious. As I have said, modern Buddhist practice might emphasize those parts of the Buddha's teaching that focus upon notions of freeing the mind from all forms of attachment, including attachment to sacred objects, but this is to miss other important aspects of Buddhism that emphasize the protective power of the Buddha, Dhamma and the Saṅgha. Neither side can claim to be correct in their emphasis upon these two aspects of the Buddha's teachings. There clearly needs to be sensitivity on both sides.

One could say these are two distinctive forms of Buddhism. It does seem clear that in modern manifestations of Buddhism, only the rational and empirical aspects of Buddhism are given prominence.[14] As I described in Chapter 3, the idea of modern Buddhism is based upon this idea. Other practices common to Buddhist culture where power, protection and auspiciousness are prominent go unacknowledged and ignored (Davis, 2016). By this I simply mean that where notions of blasphemy in Buddhism are discounted, the reason for this is often prejudice – there is no understanding of what authentic Buddhism is. Authenticity is denied to those practices in which Buddhists do indeed view their religious artefacts as removed from the secular world. Those using an image of the Buddha in a commercial way stress part of the teachings of Buddhism in which 'letting go' and 'non-attachment' are the central focus. In turn there is the assumption that the use of an image will not be offensive because the Buddhist is not attached to such things.

Most Buddhists, one would imagine until very recent times, do not practice in this way. For them the stress is on protective and auspicious acts. Images, texts and chanting are crucially concerned with averting danger. Primarily it is the Buddha (and images of him), because of his great meritorious and ethical deeds, who accomplishes this.

Therefore, on the one hand, the manipulation of the Buddha image is harmless and surely the Buddha of the popular imagination, being free from all attachment, would not have taken any offence. In another sense, a Buddha was not simply an ordinary person but someone who had strived for thousands of lifetimes generating ethical actions so that one day he could become a Buddha (Gethin, 1998: 27–30). From an early point in Buddhist history, his ethical actions were considered to have generated power, and it is this aspect of Buddhism which needs to be appreciated when considering the reaction to the use of the image of the Buddha in what is considered to be an inappropriate way. At the same time, those taking offence might also be prompted to reflect on the centrality of the idea of non-attachment and to understand that their resentment is a hindrance upon the Buddhist path.

Conclusion

I have argued that, from a textual perspective, there are certain Pāli terms that convey the idea of 'disrespect' towards Buddhism. Some passages clearly have the idea that insults can be directed against Buddhism and that these are serious offences. When these ideas are seen from the perspective of modern culture, then the seemingly innocent uses of sacred Buddhist objects and images is deemed to be an offence against the sanctity of Buddhism. Whether or not this is in the spirit of Buddhism is another matter.[15] Notions of non-attachment and the idea that a Buddhist should be more focused upon mental calm and purity is radically at odds with the idea of Buddhism and blasphemy, though clearly I am making no attempt to locate an authentic form of Buddhism, and one need not rehearse ideas of what authentic Buddhism is.

It can readily be argued, with the use of the *Brahmajāla-sutta*, for example, that blasphemy has no place in Buddhism.[16] Yet there are terms used in the Pāli canon, which I have analysed in this chapter, and episodes in modern Burma/Myanmar that suggest that Buddhism does use a concept comparable to the idea of blasphemy as understood in other religious traditions. The passages from the Pāli canon are not cited by modern Burmese monks who are using ideas of blasphemy and disrespect in the modern context. However, passages from the Pāli canon can be found that lend legitimacy to their actions, even though one might strongly disagree with them. One of the main points of this chapter has been to suggest that episodes in modern Burma are not necessarily a departure or deviation from the Buddhism described in the Pāli canon. Although Burmese monks have recently reacted violently against individuals who it claims are betraying and destroying Buddhism, in considering the Pāli canon there are textual resources to justify their behaviour. Without acknowledging the Pāli canonical texts which anticipate this modern discourse, we could be prone to misunderstand the idea of blasphemy in the Pāli canon and modern Burma.

This is precisely where protectionist engaged Buddhism takes its place. In many ways it is an engaged Buddhist movement which takes its message from a different aspect of Buddhist history than is usual for engaged Buddhist groups. Another way of stating this is to suggest that ethnocentric and protectionist engaged Buddhism has different concerns to more progressive engaged Buddhist movements. Its ideology is completely different from the engaged Buddhism often envisaged as genuine and close to the original message of Buddhism. These new and emerging patterns in engaged Buddhism have a different rhetoric, radical forms of expression, and are engaged in society with the aim of using Buddhism politically, as a force to counter threats to the survival of Buddhism. As I argued in the opening of this chapter, in understanding ethnocentric and protectionist engaged Buddhism the idea that engaged Buddhism is evaluated on its virtuous message needs to be downplayed for us to understand these new forms of Buddhism. They are heavily involved in culture, they are local, and they express the interests of the societies they are part of. The engaged Buddhist movements I have outlined in this and the previous chapter have to be included in our studies of engaged Buddhism. The category of engaged Buddhism needs to be extended so that local and universal expressions of Buddhism can explained.

Discussion questions

1. Does the category of 'blasphemy' fit into the conceptual framework of Buddhism?

2. Can Buddhism be insulted?

3. What is insulting, if anything, about the DJing Buddha?

Suggestions for further reading

Frydenlund, Iselin. 2019. 'The Rise of Religious Offence in Transitional Myanmar'. In *Outrage: The Rise of Religious Offence in Contemporary South Asia*, ed. Paul Rollier, Kathinka Frøystad, and Arild Engelsen Ruud, 77–102. London: UCL Press.

Fuller, Paul. 2016. 'The Idea of "Blasphemy" in the Pāli Canon and Modern Myanmar'. *Journal of Religion and Violence* 4 (2): 159–81.

Jerryson, Michael. 2016b. 'Introduction: Buddhism, Blasphemy, and Violence'. *Journal of Religion and Violence* 4 (2): 119–28.

Nash, David. 2007. *Blasphemy in the Christian World: A History*. New York: Oxford University Press.

Shields, James Mark. 2010. 'Sexuality, Exoticism and Iconoclasm in the Media Age: The Strange Case of the Buddha Bikini'. In *God in the Details: American Religion in Popular Culture*, revised 2nd edn, ed. Eric M. Mazur and Kate McCarthy, 80–101. London: Routledge.

Walton, Matthew J. and Susan Hayward. 2014. 'Contesting Buddhist Narratives: Democratization, Nationalism, and Communal Violence in Myanmar'. *Policy Studies* 71. Honolulu: East-West Center.

10

Conclusion

All Buddhism is engaged?

In this book I have explained that engaged Buddhism can be distinguished from other types of Buddhism by its explanation of suffering. Suffering is the central impediment to be overcome in all Buddhist traditions. It is most often explained that it originates in the mind and is overcome by ethical actions, meditation and an insight into the true nature of reality – by calm and insight. In engaged Buddhism, the discussion of suffering is widened and its causes include the ecological crises, political oppression, gender discrimination, sexuality and wider issues related to identity and racism.

In the process of redefining suffering, many of the conceptual and metaphysical ideas around which Buddhist teachings are explained are adapted, changed and, occasionally, redefined. Rebirth and awakening are given a radically different interpretation in engaged Buddhism. The idea that the actions performed in the present life will result in a specific rebirth in the future is often neglected in engaged Buddhism. Attention is turned to the current life, and engaged Buddhists focus the teachings on solving problems encountered in an individual's life, in the community, society or nation. This is why Thich Nhat Hanh described this emerging style of religious practice as 'Buddhism entering into life'.

There are traditions of social service in Buddhism including making regular offerings to orphanages and care for the elderly. However, charitable works are often based upon the idea of averting misfortune in the present life or in expediating an auspicious future rebirth. There is a karmic exchange in which wholesome beneficial actions are later rewarded. In many ways, engaged Buddhism removes the karmic motivations of social engagement and offers a

Buddhist solution to ecological, political and social problems without the idea of being granted a better rebirth.

It is for these reasons that engaged Buddhism is a this-worldly, outward-facing Buddhist movement. Its central teaching is interdependence. Rather than understanding this idea as a key teaching of the earlier Buddhist traditions, I have suggested that interdependence is in fact a hybrid Buddhist idea which embraces a number of Buddhist doctrines. In many ways, this is a process that we can see throughout Buddhist history, from the innovations in interpreting the ideas of the Buddha in the earliest centuries of Buddhism, to the emergence of so-called Mahāyāna Buddhism and its re-evaluation of the path to awakening and modern Buddhist encounters with non-Buddhist ideas around Asia and the West. Interdependence is the key idea of engaged Buddhism in a similar way that emptiness became the focus of Mahāyāna Buddhism and impermanence was the focus in the earlier traditions.

Much of engaged Buddhism tackles human problems by utilizing Buddhism in a positive and life-affirming fashion. Buddhism has an abundance of ideas that can be deployed in this way. The key ideas of compassion, loving-kindness, mindfulness, tolerance and non-discrimination can be used to counter intolerance, discrimination, prejudice and racism. Engaged Buddhism emphasizes the idea that to act in the world the Buddhist should not be attached to fixed views and opinions. With its emphasis on the dangers of attachment to fixed views, opinions and beliefs, engaged Buddhism should use its political voice in a way that avoids partisan attitudes. Philosophically it has teachings to counter discrimination on the grounds of gender and sexuality. In all of these settings engaged Buddhism is often understood as a moral category – it is a force for good in the world.

However, I have also spent some time describing how engaged Buddhists are also motivated by defending Buddhism. There are localized expressions of engaged Buddhism which aim to protect Buddhism. I have termed these ethnocentric engaged Buddhism and protectionist engaged Buddhism. Buddhists will often be aligned to specific nations, cultures and ethnicities. Buddhist ideas can be used in aggressive ways, to do precisely what they shouldn't – to promote discrimination, intolerance, racism and violence. Engaged Buddhism can include practices that might not be considered ethical or that many Buddhists would not support. Acting to protect Buddhism is an expression of engaged Buddhism; defending one's Buddhist identity is engaged Buddhism; using violence to defend Buddhist culture is engaged Buddhism. It might not be a terribly attractive brand of engaged Buddhism, but that should not exclude ethnocentric engaged Buddhism from our study.

It is then worthwhile to consider if there are Buddhist teachings that can be used to support violence. There are teachings to support protest against the eco-crises, such as interdependence, and alternative sexualities, such as non-duality. There are also ideas which can be used to justify violence, such as the defence and protection of Buddhism. In my analysis this is part of the phenomenon of engaged Buddhism. The teachings of Buddhism display passive and aggressive temperaments.

By way of conclusion and summary, it is worth reflecting on some of the central themes of engaged Buddhism. The American Theravāda Buddhist monk Bhikkhu Bodhi spent a number of decades translating Buddhist texts. He is one of the greatest modern translators of the Pāli canon. As I mentioned in Chapter 1, in the 1980s he founded the engaged Buddhist organization 'Buddhist Global Relief' which has the aim of alleviating global suffering. He has explained why Buddhists must be engaged in tackling suffering:

> For billions of people around the world the principal causes of the real suffering they face on a daily basis are endemic poverty, social oppression and environmental devastation. If Buddhism is to live up to its moral potential, its followers must make a stronger commitment to peace, justice and social transformation. Inspired by the ideals of lovingkindness and compassion, they must be ready to stand up on behalf of those who cannot speak for themselves, for those burdened by harsh and exploitive social structures. For all its unsavoriness, politics has become the stage where the critical ethical struggles of our time are being waged. Any spiritual system that spurns social engagement to safeguard its purity risks reneging on its moral obligations. Its contemplative practices may then turn into the intellectual plaything of an upper-middle-class elite or a cushion to soften the impact of the real world. (Bodhi, 2015)

In this statement Bhikkhu Bodhi is describing many of the motivations of engaged Buddhism. Primarily, engaged Buddhism is a reaction to suffering which uses Buddhist ideas to counter suffering. Historically, Buddhism has addressed the suffering caused by craving, impermanence and attachment, which can be overcome by a rigorous discipline of solitary meditation. In principle, the best way to achieve this is within a monastic community, freed from the burden of family, society and politics. Engaged Buddhism is a departure from this path to alleviate personal suffering. As described by Bhikkhu Bodhi, engaged Buddhism focuses Buddhism on the essential idea of compassion and on reacting to suffering experienced within society. This is the central feature of engaged Buddhism.

Engaged Buddhism is involved in life; it focuses upon a wider spectrum of suffering than has traditionally been the case. Engaged Buddhist philosophy is based upon alleviating attachment to fixed views and opinions. Its key doctrine is interdependence which encapsulates a number of central Buddhist ideas. Engaged Buddhism adapts some of the key metaphysical ideas of Buddhism and, as a result, has less concern with rebirth. It refocuses the idea of karma and changes its emphasis from rebirth to focus it on the nature of immediate actions and experiences. Karma is something we do now to change our current life, not something we do to change our future life. Engaged Buddhist karma is a focus on the present moment. It is a Buddhism which is concerned with gender, sexuality and identity, and how suffering can be removed which is caused by these set categories. It uses Buddhist ideas, such as not-self and non-duality, to eradicate strict ideas about various personal and social identities. It has a focus upon the suffering caused by all aspects of the climate crises, from climate change, deforestation and the destruction of species, caused by ecological exploitation. Engaged Buddhism has a focus on politics. Political involvement can alleviate suffering and a Buddhist can act politically without destroying the purity of the Buddhist tradition. It is involved in the mundane and supramundane worlds – the religious life enters the social life. Engaged Buddhism can be involved in ethnic and local identities and in these situations can support violence and aggression. Finally, it can also be involved in defending the sanctity of Buddhist material culture. These are all central features of engaged Buddhism. As many engaged Buddhists have suggested, engaged Buddhism is simply Buddhism when practised to alleviate suffering – in this understanding, all Buddhism is engaged.

Discussion questions

1. What are the central features of engaged Buddhism?

2. Is engaged Buddhism a radical departure from earlier types of Buddhism?

3. Are some ideas so central to Buddhism that they cannot be discarded?

Suggestions for further reading

Bodhi, Bhikkhu. 2018. 'A Call to Conscience'. *Tricycle*. Fall 2018.
Clayton, Barbra R. 2018. 'The Changing Way of the Bodhisattva: Superheroes, Saints, and Social Workers'. In *The Oxford Handbook of Buddhist Ethics,* ed. Daniel Cozort and James Mark Shield, 135–60. Oxford: Oxford University Press.

Hunt-Perry, Patricia and Lyne Fine. 2000. 'All Buddhism Is Engaged: Thich Nhat Hanh and the Order of Interbeing'. In *Engaged Buddhism in the West,* ed. Christopher S. Queen and Sallie B. King, 35–66. Somerville, MA: Wisdom Publications.

Victoria, Brian Daizen. 2001. 'Engaged Buddhism: A Skeleton in the Closet?' *Journal of Global Buddhism* 2: 72–91.

Notes

Chapter 1

1 As Donald Rothberg has explained, engaged Buddhism embraces the idea that 'Buddhist teachings and practices can be directly applied to participation in the social, political, economic and ecological affairs of the nonmonastic world' (Rothberg, 1998: 117). Donald Rothberg maintains an excellent website with a large number of resources for the study of engaged Buddhism: www.donaldrothberg.com

2 See Smith, Nixon, and Pearce (2018), who have convincingly argued that there is a tendency to evaluate true religion as compassionate and to be based upon ethically sound principles, essentially 'loving and peaceful' whereas violent religion is regarded as 'false religion' (2018: 361). In an essentialist understanding, religion is, in essence, peaceful, loving and good. This book, while primarily concerned with forms of engaged Buddhism which are based upon compassion and are primarily peaceful, will also describe forms of Buddhism that are far from peaceful. However, they will still be regarded as Buddhist.

3 See Main and Lai (2013) for a similar method in analysing engaged Buddhism.

4 For example, the entry for 'engaged Buddhism' in Damien Keown's *A Dictionary of Buddhism* states simply that the term engaged Buddhism was coined by Thich Nhat Hanh in 1963, without offering any reference (Keown, 2003). Phil Henry discusses the origins of the term (2013: 9–10) and cites Yarnall (2003: 286). Yarnall in turn simply states that Thich Nhat Hanh was credited with coining the term (2003: 286). Matthew Moore also suggests that Thich Nhat Hanh coined the term engaged Buddhism, and cites a large selection of references, none referring to a specific book written by, or attributed to, Thich Nhat Hanh (Moore, 2016: 275). These references can be compared to similar remarks by Kraft (1992: 18), Hunt-Perry and Fin (2000: 38) and DeVido (2007: 251). Phil Henry also considers Stephen Batchelor's ideas about the origins of engaged Buddhism (Batchelor, 1994). This discussion traces engaged Buddhism to periods of conflict in Vietnam in the 1930s and 1940s. Batchelor argues that the idea of social engagement was developed by Vietnamese Buddhists in the 1930s during colonial conflicts (Batchelor, 1994: 360. I am not clear about the use and translation of some of the terms in Vietnamese used by both Henry and Batchelor, and these should be treated with caution.). As Hunt-Perry and Fine state: 'The development of engaged Buddhist practice in Vietnam and the West by

Thich Nhat Hanh and others is rooted in Vietnamese history and Vietnamese Buddhist traditions' (Hunt-Perry and Fine, 2000: 36).

5 Thanks to Dana Healy from SOAS University of London, for help with the translation of this term: *Dao Phat* (Buddhism) *di vao* (to enter) *cuoc doi* (life). With diacritics: *Đạo Phật Đi Vào Cuộc Đời*. As Elise DeVido points out, Thich Nhat Hanh developed his ideas of engaged Buddhism in three books written in Vietnamese in the early 1960s, all published in Saigon: 1964. *Dao Phat Di Vao Cuoc Doi* [Engaged Buddhism], 1965b. *Dao phat ngay* nay [Buddhism Today] and 1965c. *Dao phat hien dai hoa* [Modernization of Buddhism]. See DeVido, 2009: 447, note 31.

6 *Đạo Phật Đi Vào Cuộc Đời* (the title with the Vietnamese diacritics).

7 I am extremely grateful to Elise DeVido for help in finding the English translation and for discussing some of the ideas about the translation. See DeVido, 2009: 437, 449. I am also very grateful to Carole Atkinson and her colleagues at Cornell University library for their help. The fact that the English manuscript is only found in Cornell University library suggests that Trinh Van Du was resident in this area in the early 1960s (or deposited the manuscript at a later point) and was a friend or acquaintance of Thich Nhat Hanh, perhaps with better English skills than the latter at this time. The manuscript itself is hand-typed (or typewritten) on thin paper with corrections in pen. On its final page it is stated that it is a verbatim translation by Trinh Van Du, who is a graduate of the Faculty of Pedagogy, Saigon. It gives his address and is dated, by hand, 15 October 1965, and signed by Trinh Van Du (Nhat Hanh, 1965: 93). The title page of the manuscript reads 'Engaged Buddhism (with other essays), by Nhat Hanh, Saigon, 1964'. I am following Elise DeVido in using the 1965 date, but I am not clear if it should be 1964.

8 The suggestion has been made by Elise DeVido that the term engaged Buddhism is influenced by the French term *engagé*, the politically engaged intellectual, associated with the existentialist novelist and philosopher, Jean Paul Sartre. If this is the case then the 'engaged' of engaged Buddhism was originally inspired by the *engagé* of the French intellectuals of the 1950s and 1960s, who suggested that the writer or philosopher should go out into society and be a politically engaged intellectual. This is quite possible considering the time period involved. See DiVido, 2009: 436–7. As DeVido suggests, French existential ideas were very much discussed in Vietnamese Buddhist circles in the late 1950s and early 1960s (DeVido, 2009: 447, note 33). Perhaps the translator Trinh Van Du had some connection with a group of Vietnamese expats around Cornell University.

9 Of course, there are valid arguments to suggest that meditation has not been a central practice of Buddhism, except for a small elite group, until modern times. I would accept these arguments and suggest that Buddhism has historically been involved in society, and other forms of Buddhist practice have been far more prevalent, such as rituals protecting Buddhists and their culture, concerns with politics and the accumulation of wealth and prestige, in the maintenance and preserving of the Buddhist Saṅgha.

10 http://inebnetwork.org/about/. See Darlington (2018) on placing INEB in the wider context of international eco-Buddhism.

11 http://inebnetwork.org/activity-covid-19-emergency-relief-fund. Accessed 28/04/2020.

12 Thanks to Chien-Ya Sun for clarifying some of these points.

13 See also Weiner (2003) and Skidmore (1996). Darlington (2018) has an excellent discussion of some of these Southeast Asian movements. See particularly 85–90.

14 www.buddhistpeacefellowship.org.

15 See Queen, 2013: 527. For the appearance of engaged Buddhism in recent East Asian history see the special issue of *The Journal of Global Buddhism,* 2009: 'Buddhist Activism and Chinese Modernity'. Of particular interest are Ip, 2009, Jones, 2009 and Tsomo, 2009.

16 The ideological Buddhist groups I am introducing at this point will themselves be described as forms of engaged Buddhism in Chapter 8. A connection can clearly be made between Buddhist punk movements in Asia and Noah Levine's *Dharma Punx* (Levine, 2004).

17 Richard King has argued that there could be a historical and colonial legacy in seeking distinct canons of authoritative texts (King, 1999: 146). This could be occurring in my description. However, it is still useful to describe some text historically prominent for engaged Buddhism.

18 Anyone working on engaged Buddhism owes a massive debt to both Christopher Queen and Sallie King. Though the current book might depart from some of their key ideas, it is often based upon some of their outstanding scholarship.

19 Some of the underlying themes discussing the origins of engaged Buddhism are discussed by Yarnall (2000).

20 Attributed by Jones to Thich Nhat Hanh from a 1983 *Buddhist Peace Fellowship Newsletter.*

21 See Lele, 2019: 240, note 3 for a discussion of the quote that 'Buddhism is already engaged, if it is not, it is not Buddhism' (Hunt-Perry and Fine, 2000: 36). This is attributed to Thich Nhat Hanh from *Love in Action: Writings on Nonviolent Social Change* (Nhat Hanh, 1993). I have not been able to find this reference and agree with Amod Lele that that particular wording has been wrongly attributed. Thanks to Amod for some kind and informative correspondence on this point. Very similar sentiments are found in a talk by Thich Nhat Hanh originally from 2012 (Parallax Press, 2019: 383).

22 Nhat Hanh, 2010. Unpublished lecture given by Thich Nhat Hanh at the European Institute of Applied Buddhism, Germany, 11 June 2010. Thanks to Plum Village for help with this document.

23 See Queen, 1996a: 17–18.

24 For examples of social engagement in the Pāli canon, see Bodhi, 2016.

25 On the topic of early Buddhism and racism see Anālayo, 2020.

26 www.buddhistglobalrelief.org/index.php/en/about-us-en/guideposts. Accessed 30/11/2019.

27 I would strongly recommend the collection of articles edited by Jessica L. Main and Rongdao Lai appearing in *The Eastern Buddhist* (2013: 44/2), with

an emphasis on Chinese material. The introductory article (Main and Lai, 2013: 1–34) is an outstanding summary, coming to conclusions similar to some of those in this book.

Chapter 2

1 When texts are cited, abbreviations will often be used. See the list of abbreviations for the text being cited. With Pāli texts, the volume, and page number of the Pāli text society editions are being referred to.

2 See Ives (2008) for a discussion of the possible wider uses of the four noble truths by engaged Buddhists, particularly 34–8. Ives 2013: 553–4 also has a brief discussion. As an example of Buddhist involvement in international relief work at various locations around Asia see Kawanami and Samuel 2013.

3 For a modern discussion see Walton 2017a: 53–8. I will return to a discussion of these categories in Chapter 5: 87–9.

4 On the face of it the arguments made here, that we can find a dichotomy in early Buddhism about a mundane and supramundane path, and those made in the Introduction, suggesting that Buddhism has always been engaged, appear contradictory. I think in some senses these ideas do not sit easily together. However, I would suggest that the complexity of Buddhism does not allow for consistency; it can be one thing sometimes, but, looked at differently, something else. For example, the textual tension proposed by the mundane/supramundane paths might suggest a lack of historical engagement. Conversely, if we propose that the central idea of Buddhism is to overcome all suffering, whether mundane or spiritual, then the dichotomy is collapsed by engaged Buddhists.

5 Sallie B. King in *Buddhism in the Modern World*, edited by David L. McMahan, Routledge 2012, p. 207.

6 A II 48.

7 See Goldberg (2013: 110–11) for a description of how Buddhist meditation, particularly the so-called divine abidings, or *brahma-vihāras* are used as a tool for social engagement. Thus, the practice of solitary meditation is used as a tool for compassionate action in the world.

8 At A IV 247, as part of a larger list of eight it states that each of the precepts, if broken, leads to 'hell, to the animal realm, and to the sphere of afflicted spirits'. It then gives the repercussions in this life: (1) taking life leads to a short life; (2) stealing leads to a loss of wealth; (3) sexual misconduct leads to enmity and rivalry; (4) false speech leads to false accusations; (5) drinking alcohol leads to madness (A IV 247-8). I have omitted divisive speech, harsh speech and idle chatter. In the context of lay and monastic discipline, lists of five, eight and ten occur, for example ten at Vin I 82-4, and are in the context of training rules for Buddhist monastics (Gethin, 1998: 87, 110, 170–2). A slightly different ten occur at S IV 342; A II 253-5; A V 260-1; D I 4-5. These have variations in their content, though the basic five are usually present, with the exception of drinking alcohol which is not always included (A V 260-1). For details see PED under the entry for '*sīla*'.

Chapter 3

1 I am taking views, opinions and beliefs to be overlapping notions. See Muller, 2018: 1.

2 See Edelglass, 2009a: 421.

3 Nhat Hanh, 1998. Previous editions appeared in 1987, 1993.

4 See for example Stephen Batchelor's thesis that modern Buddhism needs to be a Buddhism without beliefs (Batchelor, 1997). Some of this debate is based upon the idea that there is a secular Buddhism and a religious Buddhism. The latter entails belief in a number of metaphysical assumptions, including certain interpretations of karma and rebirth. For a popular description see Batchelor 2017. See also Lopez, 1998b for a critical evaluation of belief in the study of religion.

5 For a very detailed study of views, see Fuller, 2004.

6 I would not agree with Christopher Queen who equates both no-views, and Thich Nhat Hanh's first and third precepts of engaged Buddhism with a form of agnosticism (Queen, 2002: 330).

7 Of course, a criticism could be made of the interpretation of the texts being taken here. This would suggest that the early texts are not really advocating engaged Buddhism. The texts are simply explaining that the nature of the mind needs to be understood and adapted. This is certainly a valid argument. However, a more positive and creative interpretation is that the texts are proposing that mental transformation leads to social transformation.

Chapter 4

1 This entire period is usefully described by Mitchell (2016: 31–48).

2 Almond, 1988, Fields, 1992, Batchelor, 1994, Silk, 1994, Lopez, 1995, King, 1999, Coleman, 2001, Prebish and Baumann, 2002, Elverskog, 2020.

3 For an overview of modern Buddhism, see David McMahan's ground-breaking *The Making of Buddhist Modernism*, 2008. See also his excellent edited volume, *Buddhism in the Modern World*, 2012. See Bechert, 1973: 89–92 for a discussion about the historical formation of modern Buddhism.

4 See Fuller, 2004: 201 note 144.

5 Other modern Thai Buddhists also argue that Nirvāna is a universal attainment that can be achieved by lay people and monastics (MacKenzie, 2007: 174).

6 For an overview of the movement in the context of Buddhist economics, see Harvey, 2000: 225–34.

7 For an analysis of the place of rebirth in Buddhism see Anālayo, 2018. For further context see Westerhoff, 2017.

8 Criticisms of the modern Dhammakāya movement in Thailand is based upon similar reasoning. Merit is central to Dhammakāya practice. However, it has come in for a degree of criticism because of a 'commodifying approach to merit making' (MacKenzie, 2007: 63) in which the accumulation of merit has definite rewards in this life and the next. Donors are offered rewards in this life and the next by making a monthly contribution to the temple (MacKenzie, 2007: 59). See Scott, 2009, for a comprehensive study of the *Dhammakāya* movement.

9 For an accessible and popular critique of the centrality of the notion of rebirth in Buddhism, see Stephen Batchelor's chapter in his book *Buddhism Without Beliefs*, 1997: 34–8.

10 McMahan (2009: 153) mentions the hybrid nature of the concept of interdependence. In the current analysis I will concentrate on the hybridity of the idea from a Buddhist perspective. I will mention some of McMahan's wider themes, which are extremely useful.

11 The original text is likely to have circulated as a group of separate texts, perhaps going back to the early years of the Common Era. It was subsequently translated into Chinese from around the third century CE (Williams, 2009: 132–3).

12 For an excellent overview of some of the colonial and orientalist interpretations of Buddhism, see King, 1999: 143–60.

13 See Wright, 2017, and Thompson, 2020, for two popular discussions of this theme of Buddhism and science.

14 Lopez convincingly argues against this compatibility (Lopez, 2008: Xii–Xiii). Peter Jackson, in his study of Buddhadāsa's ideas on Buddhism and science, suggests similar sentiments to Lopez: 'The idealized view of science found in many recent Buddhist works suggests that the actual relation between science and Buddhism is not the real issue. Rather, modernist Buddhist scholars appear to be attempting to construct a justification or apologetic for Buddhist teachings which appeals to science because of its assumed authority' Jackson, 2003: 44.

Chapter 5

1 I am grateful to Melvin McLeod for prompting this idea (McLeod, 2006: 8).

2 In this chapter I am using the term 'state' rather loosely to simply refer to a location with a defined population and a set of institutions. At one point I will refer to a nation state to distinguish it from similar terms. A nation state shares a common culture.

3 In this book I am giving these different arguments. I am not arguing for one position or the other.

4 Ian Charles Harris has suggested a sixfold typology in which the interaction of Buddhism and politics might be understood. (A) Institutional Framework: (1) Buddhist authority over the political; (2) Fusion of Buddhism and the

political; (3) Authority of political power over Buddhism. And (B) Tactical Positions: (1) Complete withdrawal; (2) Antagonistic symbiosis; (3) Buddhism in conflict with the political. Harris attempts to describe different societal and practical ways in which Buddhism might interact with the culture in which it is found (Harris, 2016: 1–10). The following owes a massive debt to Harris's model, but I have adapted it, while incorporating many of its elements.

5   For a study of the idea of Gross National Happiness, see Long, 2019: 113–17.

6   See the *Pattanikkujjana-sutta*. 'Monks, the Saṅgha (the Buddhist monastic community) may, if it wishes, turn the bowl upside down for a lay follower on eight grounds. What eight? They try to prevent the mendicants from getting material possessions. They try to harm mendicants. They try to drive mendicants from a monastery. They insult and abuse mendicants. They divide mendicants against each other. They criticize the Buddha, the teaching, and the Saṅgha. The Saṅgha may, if it wishes, turn the bowl upside down for a lay follower on these eight grounds' (A IV 344–5).

7   If we accept the idea that there is a sharp distinction between politics and religion.

8   For those seeking a more democratic form of Buddhist politics, the ideas of Sulak Sivaraksa, A.T. Ariyaratne's Sarvodaya Shramadana movement in Sri Lanka, the Dalai Lama or the earlier Aung San Suu Kyi offer a liberal and palatable interaction of Buddhism and politics (Sivaraksa, 2005; Swearer, 1996; Bond, 1996; Cabezón, 1996; Silverstein, 1996).

9   There are a number of texts in the Pāli Canon where political ideas are discussed in a comprehensive fashion (Moore, 2015: 37–8). These are the *Cakkavatti-Sīhanāda-sutta*, 'The Lion's Roar on the Turning of the Wheel' (D III 58–79), the *Mahāsudassana-sutta* 'The Great Splendour: A King's Renunciation' (D II 169–99), the *Aggañña-sutta*, 'On knowledge of beginnings' (D III 80–98) and the beginning of the *Mahāparinibbāna-sutta*, 'The Great Passing: The Buddha's Last Days' (D II 72–168).

10 For some related ideas see Collins, 1998: 63–72.

11 Collins, 1998: 473. For a summary of the Buddhist symbol of the wheel see Karunaratne (1969).

12 For an excellent study of the role of a king, see Zimmerman (2006).

13 However, it should be pointed out that historically, it is not clear that the Aśoka found in his inscriptions in the nineteenth and twentieth centuries is not the one known by Buddhist rulers in the previous centuries (Bechert, 1973: 88–9).

14 These seven treasures are described in detail in the *Mahāsudassana-sutta* (D II 169–99). They are the Wheel treasure, the Elephant Treasure, the Horse Treasure, the Jewel Treasure, the Woman Treasure, the Householder Treasure and the Counsellor Treasure. An individual becomes a wheel-turning monarch through moral purity and maintains his status through the possession of the seven treasures, which appear to the King on an auspicious day. The Wheel treasure (*cakkaratana*) is the mark of a wheel-turning monarch's status and appears before a king when he becomes a wheel-turning monarch. The treasures indicate power and auspiciousness. They are symbols of royalty. Both a Buddha and a Wheel-turning monarch display thirty-two auspicious

marks on their bodies. The treasures seem appear to be an extension of these. The monarch is also handsome, long-lived, free from illness and popular. These are the wheel-turning monarch's four properties or qualities (D II 177–8).

15 The process depicted is what is known as the 'ten unwholesome courses of action' (*dasa akusalakammapathā*) appearing and the 'ten courses of wholesome action' *dasa kusalakammapathā*), disappearing. The Sutta mentions these but does not list them. The ten courses of wholesome action are the following: 'Abandoning the killing of living beings, abstaining therefrom; abandoning the taking of what is not given, abstaining therefrom; abandoning misconduct in sensual pleasure [. . .] abandoning false speech [. . .] malicious speech [. . .] harsh speech [. . .] gossip, abstaining therefrom. Abandoning covetousness, he is no more covetous. Abandoning malevolence and hatred, his heart becomes free from ill will. Abandoning wrong-view, he becomes one of right-view' S IV 350–1 (Fuller, 2004: 125). Killing living beings, taking what is not given, misconduct in sensual pleasure, false speech, malicious speech, harsh speech, covetousness, malevolence and hatred, and wrong-view are the ten courses of unwholesome action (Fuller, 2004: 50–3).

16 This is the lowest point in human history. See Walshe (1995) note 798: 602–3.

17 This refrain is repeated several times throughout the *Aggañña-sutta*: *Dhammo hi seṭṭho jane tasmiṃ diṭṭhe ceva dhamme abhisamparāyeca*.

18 In the texts, various vocations are given as the original meaning of the class (*varṇa*) system.

19 Adapted from Ian Harris, 2016: 3. See Shaw, 2006: 122–8. A Buddhist king also directs loving-kindness (*mettā*), compassion (*karuna*), sympathetic joy (*muditā*) and equanimity (*upekkhā*) towards all sentient beings (D II 196, III 223).

20 For details see Moore, 2015: 41.

21 For a discussion of these themes in the Burmese Buddhist context see Walton, 2017a: 53–8.

22 Melvin McLeod's *Mindful Politics: A Buddhist Guide for Making the World a Better Place* (McLeod 2006) is another book with a similar emphasis (though it consists of an anthology of articles and essays). See Moore, 2016b: 277–8 for a further discussion of these themes.

23 Moore traces the interest in mindfulness in the 1980s. Jon-Kabat Zinn, an American Buddhist, popularized the term 'mindfulness' in his idea of Mindfulness-Based Stress Reduction. This method used mindfulness as a therapeutic tool to cope with pain and illness. His most popular book is *Coming to Our Senses: Healing Ourselves and the World Through Mindfulness* (Kabat-Zinn, 2005; Moore, 2016b: 277).

Chapter 6

1 See, for example, the Ecodharma organization based in Catalonia, Spain: www.ecodharma.com.

2 One should also note two works produced in Thailand in the 1980s, Davies (1987), and Kabilsingh (1987). See Darlington (2018) for a discussion of these books.

3 See also her essay 'The Ecological Self', a version of which appears in Edelglass and Garfield, 2009: 428–36.

4 For a popular description see Kaza, 2006. In a slightly different context see Ethan Nichtern's *One City: A Declaration of Interdependence*, which has a pop-culture narrative entwined with what might best be described as popular Buddhist wisdom (Nichtern, 2007).

5 There are also clear affinities in this line of thinking with Arne Naess, who formulated the idea of Deep Ecology (Macy, 1990: 61–2; Naess, 1973, Henning, 2002; Keller, 2009). Deep Ecology proposes that there should be an equality in the value given to different parts of the ecosystem, a reorientation in the way we use and understand the environment (Keller, 2009: 206). Both human and non-human life has intrinsic value (Naess, 1986: 14. See Keller, 2009: 210). Studies of engaged Buddhism will sometimes propose this affinity between eco-engaged Buddhism and deep ecology. This entails a further link with the idea of interdependence. See Elverskog, 2020, for a recent and, at times, very strong criticism of the environmental credentials of Buddhism.

6 See also her chapter on Buddhism and ecology (King, 2009: 118–36).

7 Clippard cites Sulak Sivaraksa and Chatsumarn Kabilsingh as two prominent Thai Buddhists who interpret dependent-origination as meaning interdependence (2011: 218; King, 2009: 121).

8 A recent article using the dependent-origination/interdependence model is Cummiskey and Hamilton, 2017.

9 This is another of Gary Snyder's terms (the writer of Smokey the Bear Sutra). See Johnston, 2006: 74.

10 Schmithausen translates *paṭiccasamuppāda* as 'Origination in Dependence'. 1997: 12.

11 Other scholars have also strongly argued against the use of the 'dependent-origination/interdependence' model, notably Harris (1991; 1994a; 1994b; 1995a; 1995b; 1997) and Ives (2009a, 2013). Anālayo has argued that from the perspective of early Buddhism the aim of the Buddhist path is liberation (Anālayo, 2019: 18). However, he also offers a very nuanced interpretation of the value of eco-Buddhism.

12 Something like this has been proposed by Joanna Macy with her idea of the 'greening of the self'. See Hunt-Badiner, 1990: 53–63. See also Macy's idea of the 'ecological self' in Edelglass, 2009b.

13 The scholar who has done the most work on the Thai tree ordination is Susan Darlington. Her main work on this topic is *The Ordination of a Tree: The Thai Buddhist Environmental Movement* (Darlington, 2012). I am relying on her wider body of work in much of what I will say in the following paragraphs. Susan also kindly supplied a photo for inclusion in this book, for which, many thanks.

14 For a comprehensive study of the idea of development monks, see Suksamran, 1988.

15 These are the questions posed by Clippard, 2011.

Chapter 7

1 For a pioneering discussion of gender, see West and Zimmerman, 1987. See also Fenstermaker and West, 2002. I appreciate that this chapter is longer than the others in this book. I have considered splitting the material into two chapters. However, the material is linked in a conceptual way which would make it a rather artificial exercise.

2 Cabezón's book has attracted considerable attention, for example Powers, 2019 (along with a number of other review articles appearing in a special edition of *Religion* 2017, volume 49, no. 4).

3 I am using the accepted nomenclature LGBTIAQ+: Lesbian, gay, bisexual, transsexual, intersex. 'A' is for 'asexual'. The plus sign '+' is important for leaving the acronym ever open to future possibilities, that is inclusive, rather than being closed off or final. This is also why it is 'Q+', that is, 'Q' at the end before the '+', as 'Queer' also implies this openness or 'non-pin-down-able-ness' or perhaps (inherent) irreducibility. Thanks to Leah McGarrity of the University of New South Wales, Australia, for help with this point and for her careful, helpful and insightful reading of the current chapter. Let me use a quote from the Intersex Society of North America to explain the term intersex. Intersex is described in the following terms:

> Intersex is a general term used for a variety of conditions in which a person is born with a reproductive or sexual anatomy that doesn't seem to fit the typical definitions of female or male. For example, a person might be born appearing to be female on the outside, but having mostly male-typical anatomy on the inside. Or a person may be born with genitals that seem to be in-between the usual male and female types – for example, a girl may be born with a noticeably large clitoris, or lacking a vaginal opening, or a boy may be born with a notably small penis, or with a scrotum that is divided so that it has formed more like labia. Or a person may be born with mosaic genetics, so that some of her cells have XX chromosomes and some of them have XY.

See the 'Intersex Society of North America' (https://isna.org/faq/what_is _intersex/). Accessed 15 October 2019. I will use LGBTIAQ+ even when the work under discussion simply uses LGBT.

4 Translation adapted from K. R. Norman's translation. Norman, 2001: 103. There are some important linguistic nuances in these texts between different terms for craving, lust and desire, which are being used. However, the general point is that forms of craving, desire and lust are negative.

5 For a scholarly discussion of the third precept see Collins, 2007.

6   There is clearly a bias in the descriptions of how a man can break the precept. See, for example, this passage; 'He misconducts himself in sensual pleasures (*kāmesumicchācārī*); he has intercourse with women who are protected by their mother, father, mother and father, brother, sister, or relatives, who have a husband, who are protected by law, and even those who are garlanded in token of betrothal' (M I 286). This is described as conduct not in accordance with the Dharma, and unrighteous conduct. See Pandita, 2019, for a further discussion of the precepts and their relationship to females.

7   Adapted from Harvey, 2000: 73. According to Peter Harvey some Tibetan accounts add 'in a generally improper way, i.e. by coercion, or with a man' (this appears to be a man with a man). Other historical accounts include visiting brothels and masturbation (Harvey, 2000: 73). Cabezón (2017: 453–528), expands upon many of these descriptions as preserved in Indian and Tibetan Buddhist traditions. See Vasubandhu's fourth century *Abhidharmakośabhāṣyam* (Vasubandhu, 1988, volume 2, 604). See also Langenberg, 2018: 584 for the *Abhidharmakośabhāṣyam* reference.

8   I would particularly recommend Gyatso (2005) for an overview of the topic of 'sex'. Her article is particularly helpful on the Buddhist discussion of the monastic view of sex in the Vinaya. The Vinaya is that portion of Buddhist textual traditions that deals with the regulations and rules of the Buddhist monastic community.

9   For an overview of some of the key themes related to Buddhism, feminism and gender see Gross, 2014: 472–3. For an engaged Buddhist reevaluation of these themes see Hu, 2011.

10 See Ohnuma, 2006 and Gyatso, 2003, for excellent discussions of this passage. The passage occurs in the *Vinya* (Vin II 253–6) and in the *Aṅguttara Nikaya* (A IV 274–9). On the idea of a pervasive and 'institutional androcentrism' see Sponberg, 1992: 13–18.

11 See Collett, 2018: 555 for a useful list of other passages.

12 See Ohnuma, 2000: 126.

13 However, and this is an important but often overlooked point, in early Buddhist traditions there is what Appleton describes as a 'soteriological equality of men and women' (Appleton, 2011: 44). So, though a woman cannot be a Buddha, a woman can achieve Nirvāna, and so become very advanced on the religious path of Buddhism. See also Anālayo (2009) who suggests that the idea that women cannot attain the higher states of the Buddhist path might have been a later addition to the original text.

14 See Derris (2008) and Ohnuma (2000) on the question in the Theravāda tradition of the Buddha being a woman in his previous births, namely, when he was a Bodhisattva striving for awakening. See also Collett and Anālayo (2014) for the similar question of whether women can become Arahants.

15 *mātugāmo, issukī ānanda mātugāmo, maccharī ānanda mātugāmo, duppañño* [. . .] *mātugāmo*, A II 82–3. Alice Collett helpfully lists the other misogynistic pronouncements from the Jātakas: women are naturally wicked and . . . plot evil against you. (Jat 6, I. 128); women are lustful, heedless, vile and debase . . . (Jat 61, I.285); given the opportunity, all women become

wicked. (Jat 62, I.289); women are ungrateful and deceitful . . . (Jat 63, I.295); women are feckless and immoral . . . (Jat 64, I.300); women are common to all [referring to sexual infidelity], this immorality defines them . . . (Jat 65, I.301–302); women have insatiable sexual appetites . . . (Jat 120, I.440). (Collett, 2018: 555).

16 A I 1, where the same is said of men for women.

17 A II 8 is a prominent example of a positive evaluation.

18 I am using Alice Collett's work as representative of those scholars who have also attempted a kind of academic apologetic for the misogyny of some early Buddhist textual material. One of the leading pioneers of this approach was the late Rita Gross. Her *Buddhism After Patriarchy: A Feminist History, Analysis, and Reconstruction of Buddhism* (Gross, 1993) was, at the time a seminal study, and remains of interest to those seeking to counter arguments about the early Buddhist negative view of female gender. It could be suggested that the approach I am taking to gender and sexuality in this chapter is different to that taken, for example, on notions of ethnicity, race and discrimination in Chapters 8 and 9. In those chapters I have not given a Buddhist response to uncomfortable questions of discrimination by Buddhist communities. It could be suggested quite categorically, and for similar reasons, that Buddhists should not be misogynistic or racist. They are, on occasions, both, and there are ideas in the Buddhist traditions that support and counter gender, sexuality and racial discrimination.

19 For a brief summary of their activities see Gross, 2014: 475–8. See also Tsomo, 2004, 2012. See Langenberg 2019 and 2020 for recent studies.

20 There are very few references to lesbianism in the Buddhist tradition. A detailed account is given by Rylance (2011).

21 An explanation of this terms as used in modern LGBTIAQ+ Buddhist discourse is the following:

> By 'queer' I mean anyone whose sexuality does not fit the accepted social model – lesbian, gays, bisexual, transgendered persons, and heterosexuals who enjoy non-normative sexual activities such as bondage, sadomasochism, and fetishism. What all these persons have in common is their indifference, or even opposition to heterosexual activity in the missionary position. By their very existence they proclaim the absence of an intrinsic maleness or femaleness, and since most queers engage in non-reproductive sex they demonstrate that sexual love in humans is more about relationship than about reproduction Corless, 2004: 237.

22 As an example see Corless, 2000, for a summary of the ideas of the Gay Buddhist Fellowship.

23 This general theme is also suggested by Venerable Sujato: 'The Suttas essentially ignore any issues around homosexuality. Now, arguments from absence are always difficult. But the presence of thousands of discourses detailing lists of many kinds of ethical violations, strongly suggests that the Buddha tried to be reasonably comprehensive in addressing ethical concerns, and homosexuality was not one of them' Sujato, 2012: n.p.

24 Though there are clear and notable exceptions to this general rule. Harvey, citing Faure (1991: 249), suggests that Japanese Buddhism is more accepting of homosexuality (Harvey, 2000: 428).

25 Though the Conkin article suggests that the Dalai Lama did later qualify many of his comments. See especially Conkin, 1998: 354.

26 This is from the commentary to the *Cakkavatti-Sīhanāda-sutta*, 'The Lion's Roar on the Turning of the Wheel' (D III 58–79), at D III 70. It is found at D.A. 853. As Venerable Sujato suggests, the commentary was several centuries later than the text, and there is little evidence that this interpretation was supported at an earlier point in Buddhist history (Sujato, 2012: n.p.).

27 Fo Guang Shan is a Taiwanese engaged Buddhist movement known for their idea of 'Humanistic Buddhism'. This is a form of Buddhism that promotes a return to an original form of Buddhism, centred on the individual. See also Wilson (2012) for comparable arguments from a particular Buddhist tradition in favour of marriage equality.

28 For a very brief overview of 'tantric sex' see Gross, 2014: 471.

29 Corless uses the philosophy of Yogācāra to explain how what he calls 'queer consciousness' is more compatible with fundamental Buddhist ideas than a patriarchal view of the world. In a patriarchal understanding of culture and society, the male subject is always superior to the female object. It is privileged culturally, socially and in the thinking of individuals. In history, philosophy and politics the male is superior to the female (Corless, 2004: 238). A contemporary trans-Buddhist interpretation, focussing upon the doctrine of not-self, is given by Euw, 2019.

30 However, as Ohnuma suggests, the fact is that, in many of these episodes, even those in which the larger philosophical point is being made, there remains the idea that the adaptation from female to male is making a larger point about male superiority and carry some significance. In Ohnuma's understanding, the texts are only pretending to be gender-neutral, when in fact they are making a different point about the reality of male superiority (Ohnuma, 2000: 131). Men are more spiritually advanced, and the tradition as a whole, even in these philosophical moments, is still supportive of this understanding. In Ohnuma's terms, the transformation from female to male is not to show the ultimate non-existence of the genders, but the move from bondage (female) to freedom (male), from suffering to awakening (Ohnuma, 2000: 131).

31 Williams, 2009: 103–28.

32 Gethin, 1998: 145–6.

33 See Gross, 2015: 244, for the idea of suffering caused by the related issue of androcentrism, the placing of the male gender at the centre of, for example, culture and society.

34 Chinese: Guanyin; Vietnamese: Quan Am; Korean: Kwan Um; Japanese: Kannon; Tibetan: Chenrezig. Hu, 2016: 663.

35 The possible reason is that the character and iconographical and religious detail of Avalokiteśvara was superimposed upon a local female Chinese deity. I have some vague memory that Guan Yin might be based on the 'Heavenly Mother from the West' deity.

36 Williams, 2009: 57–8. See also Buckner, 2017.

37 The motif of change of sex is found in a number of studies. The following is not exhaustive, but represents some of the major studies and important comments: Appleton, 2011: 43–7; Balkwill, 2018; Gyatso, 2003; Ohnuma, 2000; Paul, 1985: 166–99; Powers, 2009: 134–40; Scherer, 2006. For a more complete list see Anālayo, 2014: 111, note 8.

38 See Zwilling, 1998: 51.

39 Found in the commentary to the *Dhammapada* (Burlingarme, 1921: 23–8). See also Anālayo, 2014: 111; Harvey, 2000: 412; Powers, 2009: 137–8.

40 See Harvey, 2000: 412. See also *Milandapañha* (267): 'men who have turned into women. women who have turned turn into men'. It is stated that these things are found in the world, that they exist in the world.

41 There are nuances in the tradition, suggested by Anālayo, in that any gender change is the result of unwholesome or negative karma, although male to female is the result of stronger unwholesome karma, and female to male of more wholesome karma (Anālayo, 2014: 113, note 14). See also Faure, 2003: 100; Powers, 2009: 137; Ohnuma, 2000: 124–5; Mrozik, 2002: 5.

42 A recent collection of non-academic articles has appeared edited by Kevin Manders and Elizabeth Manders, *Transcending: Trans Buddhist Voices* (Manders and Marston, 2019). Most of the articles in the collection describe the trans-Buddhist experience.

43 See for example Dale S. Wright's idea of 'naturalized karma', which lessens the emphasis on supernatural elements related to the idea of karma (Wright, 2004). See also Loy, 2008: 53–64.

44 A useful collection of essays, sometimes touching on similar themes to those being described here outlining contemporary approaches to gay Buddhist issues can be found in Leyland, 1998: 299–358. A more recent collection is Harrold, 2019. The sense of suffering caused by LGBTIAQ+ identities is also noted by Ken Jones: 'A sense of gay community has resulted in a deepening awareness of a personal and group woundedness, amounting in extreme cases to guilt and even self-hatred. Here, then, is a specific form of suffering previously barely acknowledged. How is the Dharma to be understood, practiced and internalized as a liberation from this suffering? A variety of gay Buddhist groups have come into being to work through these questions together' (Jones, 2003: 204. Cited by Alexander and Yescavage, 2010: 157–8).

45 Translation adapted from the Amaravati Saṅgha translation available at: https://www.accesstoinsight.org/tipitaka/kn/snp/snp.1.08.amar.html. Accessed 1-06.19. It is found at Sn 143-152.

46 For a brief and informative overview of the #MeToo movement see Pellegrini, 2018.

47 For an analysis of the phenomenon of what has been termed 'clergy sexual misconduct' (Monson, 2018) in the wider practice of non-Buddhist context of Yoga see Remski, 2019. It has a conceptual consideration of abuse in guru/teacher-centred movements. For a wider general discussion of the contemporary Buddhist sex scandals see Gleig, 2019: 84–110.

48 See Anders, 2019, for an outline of how various types of abuse and trauma can become problematic in modern Vajrayāna Buddhist groups.

49 Newman, 2018.

50 *The Guardian,* 5 March 2018. For an overview of some of the accounts of sexual misconduct in Buddhist groups in America, see Lama Willa B. Miller, 'Breaking the Silence on Sexual Misconduct', *Lion's Roar*, May 2018. For an overview of Shambhala, written before the allegations, see Mitchell, 2016: 149–51.

51 There are three reports against the wider organization found here: http://andreamwinn.com/offerings/bps-welcome-page/ (accessed 7/10/19).

52 For the Chinese example, see *The Guardian.* (2018) and *New York Post* (2018). For a critical account of Sogyal Rinpoche see Finnigan and Hogendoorn, 2019 and Newland, 2019. See also Gleig, 2019: 84–110. For an overview of the recent problems in Western Tibetan Buddhism, see Stuart Lachs (N.D), *Tibetan Buddhism Enters the 21st Century: Trouble in Shangri-la*. Finally, for a personal account of abuse in a Buddhist community, see Miller (2018).

53 Jacoby, 2018: 5. Thanks to Ray Buckner for help with this reference.

54 Some relevant recent articles, post #MeToo, can be found in Sakyadhita, 2019.

55 See Lopon Monson, 2018.

Chapter 8

1 Johan Elverskog mentions that the idea that Buddhism is primarily pacifist and peace loving is challenged by the ethnic cleansing of Hindu Tamils in Sri Lanka and Muslim Rohingya in Myanmar (2020: xii). As Elverskog notes, Buddhist history has been as violent as any other religious tradition.

2 An earlier version of this chapter appeared in *The Journal of the British Association of Religious Studies*, Fuller (2018). Many thanks to the JBRS for permission to include parts of that article.

3 In Myanmar it could be argued that ethnocentric Buddhism has its roots in the 1950s and U Nu's attempt to establish Buddhism as the national religion. For details of U Nu, who was the first prime minister of what was then an independent Burma from 1948 to 1958, and from 1960 to 1962, see Kawanami, 2016b.

4 The basic formula is found in the *Khuddakapāṭha*, an ancient text found in the Pāli canon (Khp I 01). Rupert Gethin suggests that going for refuge loosely defines an individual as a Buddhist (1998: 107–8). As a historical way of describing Buddhist identity and affiliation, the taking of refuge is a useful identifying formula. When occurring in the Pāli Canon, the request in the presence of the Buddha to take refuge is often found in the following form: 'I go for refuge to the Lord Gotama, the Dhamma and the Saṅgha. May the

Reverend Gotama accept me as a lay-follower who has taken refuge from this day forth for as long as life shall last!' (D I 234).

5   The Burmese digits of the numbers 969 are intended to symbolize the virtues of the Buddha, the Dhamma and the Saṅgha (the nine special attributes of the Buddha, the six special attributes of the Saṅgha and the nine special attributes of the Saṅgha). They are linked to ideas of identity.

6   Bookbinder, 2014. See also Walton and Hayward, 2014: 14.

7   This form of identity would be at odds with a more international Theravāda Buddhist identity based upon the Pāli Canon together with a shared and interacting monastic lineage. This international understanding of Theravāda Buddhist history would be one in which ethnic, racial and national identity is unimportant. See Borchert, 2014: 603.

8   For a good overview of the agendas of the 969 movement and MaBaTha see Schonthal and Walton, 2016: 84–9.

9   Thomas Linehan has stated the following about Islamophobia in modern Britain and many of his points could also be applied to parts of Buddhist Asia:

> [R]eligious Islamophobia in contemporary Britain, as with earlier religious antisemitism, is fuelled by ethnocentric conspiratorial attitudes whereby Muslim religious rites and practices, the dress that indicates Muslim religious affiliation, and all other signifiers of Muslim and Islamic religious difference, are seen to represent a danger to Britain's traditionally cohesive national identity based on a long-standing Christian heritage. (Linehan, 2012: 380)

10   See also Keyes, 2016: 1.

11   For a summary of the history of the term 'ethnocentic' see Bizumic, 2014.

12   As In 'MaBaTha', *amyo-barthar-tharthanar*. Its full name in Burmese is *myo barthar tharthanar saun shauk ye a-pwe*. See Walton and Hayward, 2014: 14. Elsewhere Walton compares the dialogue about ethnicity in Myanmar and the notion of Burman-ness and suggests that it can be seen as a similar category to 'whiteness', denoting privilege, particularly that of Burmans:

> The initial challenge in seeking to explain ethnic dominance in Myanmar in terms of Whiteness is in equating race and ethnicity. While the dominant criterion of comparison and categorization in the West has been race (and in America, the black/ white racial distinction), in Southeast Asia individuals and groups more frequently identify themselves in other ways. Ethnic categories are prominent markers of identity in Southeast Asia, although ethnicity itself is a more recent construct and reflects a contemporary solidification of historically malleable identity markers.

13   See Schober, 2017: 159. One of the many things that Schober highlights in her article is the use of what she terms 'digital technologies' in the formation of different 'realities' and forms of identity. Social media thus plays a significant role in the formation of Buddhist nationalism and more specifically ideas of belonging.

14 An argument could also be made for certain key ethical ideas as being foundational in the formulation of Buddhist identity. Susan Hayward suggests that the very popular *Mangala-sutta* (Sn 2.4) serves this purpose and constitutes the ethical foundation of being Burmese, and therefore Buddhist (Hayward, 2015: 31).

15 In commenting upon religious discourse in modern Myanmar and the interplay of MaBaTha rhetoric and ideas of human rights she comments: 'A close analysis of Buddhist protectionist ideology and MaBaTha material shows that the language of anxiety, deracination and protection is far more prevalent than religious freedom advocacy' (Frydenlund, 2017: 3). See also Foxeus, 2019.

16 See also Schissler, Walton and Thi, 2017: 376–95; Cheesman, 2017: 335–52; Klinken and Aung, 2017: 353–75.

17 Similar laws are being discussed in Sri Lanka.

18 McCarthy and Menager, 2017, describe the long history (originating in the colonial era) of legislation regulating the marriage of Buddhist women to non-Buddhist men. See also Walton, McKay and Kyi, 2015.

Chapter 9

1 An earlier version of this chapter appeared in the *Journal of Religion and Violence* (Fuller, 2016). I am grateful to the editors of that journal for permission to use the material. Particular thanks to Michael Jerryson for much helpful advice while writing the article. My article appeared alongside some excellent contributions in a special issue titled 'Buddhism, Blasphemy and Violence' (*Journal of Religion and Violence*, volume 4, issue 2, 2016).

2 I am basing this assumption upon the idea that the central focus of Buddhism is non-attachment. Therefore, the idea that Buddhism has an idea similar to blasphemy is often dismissed. A recent discussion on H-Buddhism showed a variety of scholarly opinions with some leading scholars dismissing the notion that blasphemy has any place within Buddhism.

3 My description of the Pāli material has the intention of showing how the recent incidents are foreshadowed by the textual tradition and could be used to validate them. Thanks to Leah McGarrity of the University of New South Wales, Australia, for helping me to clarify my thinking on this point.

4 By modern Burmese Buddhism I am simply referring to the form of Buddhism practised in twenty-first-century Burma/Myanmar. I appreciate that these are not perfect categories and that their complexity deserves greater analysis.

5 A possible means of influence of the Pāli Canon directly upon Burmese monks is in the popularly used Burmese *nissaya* glosses. These are texts in which a Pāli word is given with its Burmese equivalent. Thanks to Professor Rupert Gethin of the University of Bristol, UK, for suggesting to me this possible way in which the Pāli Canon influences modern Buddhist monastic culture.

6 While suggesting that non-attachment is the central attitude in Buddhism I appreciate that other attitudes, teachings and ideas could also claim

centrality in Buddhist history. By making such statements I am trying to find a workable idea about key Buddhist teachings. From this point I hope we can begin to evaluate the place of blasphemy in Buddhist culture, its texts and its philosophy.

7 See Gombrich (2006: 171–95) on the idea of 'Protestant Buddhism' to which many of these ideas of secular Buddhism relate. Figures like Anagārika Dharmapāla (1864–1933) in Sri Lanka are prominent in this new, political, secular form of Buddhism ,which has shaped the modern understanding of Buddhism to such an extent that it is now often held to be the most authentic example of Buddhism. Clearly though, Dharmapāla's legacy has ultimately been one in which Buddhism is intimately bound with cultural and national identity within Sri Lanka. There are two ways of looking at these phenomena – the first in which a modern secular form of Buddhism is prominent, the second in which a form of Buddhism emerges with a stress upon cultural and national identity. For a brief summary of Dharmapāla and this particular point in Sri Lankan history see Mitchell, 2016: 38–41.

8 A list of six types of 'disrespect' (agārava) is found at D III 244 with 'concentration' omitted:

'Six kinds of disrespect (agārava): Here, a monk behaves disrespectfully and discourteously towards the Teacher, the Dhamma, the Saṅgha, the training, in respect of earnestness/heedfulness (appamide), of hospitality (patisanthire)'. These are contrasted with 'six kinds of respect (gārava), where a monk behaves respectfully towards all six.' (D III 244)

9 For more examples see Fuller, 2016.

10 We sadly know very little about the views of Tun Thurein and Htut Ko Ko Lwin. This is unfortunate as the context of the production of the image is not known. Did Tun Thurein and Htut Ko Ko Lwin realize that the image would cause such a reaction?

11 Myanmar Times, 23 June 2015. I was given this document by a journalist who was present. The documents were in Burmese and have been translated.

12 Similar incidents continue to take place in Myanmar. In April 2020 a Burmese street artist was charged with blasphemy for the depiction of the lord of death which, it was claimed, resembled a Buddhis monk.

13 More recently see Wynne (2015: 65–6).

14 See for example Lopez (2012, 2013).

15 I am, of course, working with general notions about Buddhism and do not claim that there is a definite 'spirit of Buddhism' or that Buddhism is fixed and describable in historical or philosophical terms. However, I would hold that there are certain tendencies in the Buddha's teachings around which we can begin to discuss ideas like blasphemy and their place within Buddhist culture.

16 I am clearly not saying that it does not have a place. I am arguing that if we select certain passages, like the Brahmajāla-sutta, then we might come to the conclusion that blasphemy has no place in Buddhism.

Bibliography

Abeysekara, Ananda. 2002. *Colors of the Robe: Religion, Identity, and Difference*. Columbia, SC: The University of South Carolina Press.

Alexander, Jonathan and Karen Yescavage. 2010. 'Bi, Buddhist, Activist: Refusing Intolerance, But Not Refusing Each Other'. *Journal of Bisexuality* 10 (1–2): 154–65.

Almond, Philip. 1988. *The British Discovery of Buddhism*. Cambridge: Cambridge University Press.

Ambedkar, Bhimrao Ramji. 1984. *The Buddha and His Dhamma*. Bombay: Siddharth.

Anālayo, Bhikkhu. 2009. 'The Bahudhātuka–sutta and Its Parallels on Women's Inabilities'. *Journal of Buddhist Ethics* 16: 137–90.

Anālayo, Bhikkhu. 2014. 'Karma and Female Birth'. *Journal of Buddhist Ethics* 21: 109–53.

Anālayo, Bhikkhu. 2018. *Rebirth in Early Buddhism and Current Research*. Boston: Wisdom Publications.

Anālayo, Bhikkhu. 2019. *Mindfully Facing Climate Change*. Barre, MA: Barre Center for Buddhist Studies.

Anālayo, Bhikkhu. 2020. 'Confronting Racism with Mindfulness'. *Mindfulness* 11: 1–15.

Anders, Ann Iris Miriam. 2019. 'Silencing and Oblivion of Psychological Trauma, Its Unconscious Aspects, and Their Impact on the Inflation of Vajrayāna. An Analysis of Cross-Group Dynamics and Recent Developments in Buddhist Groups Based on Qualitative Data'. *Religions* 10 (11): 1–23.

Anderson, Benedict. 2006. *Imagined Communities: Reflections on the Origin and Spread of Nationalism*. London: Verso.

Anderson, Carol. 2017. 'Changing Sex or Changing Gender in Pāli Buddhist Literature'. *The Scholar and Feminist Online* 14 (2): 231–51.

Appleton, Naomi. 2011. 'In the Footsteps of the Buddha? Women and the Bodhisatta Path in Theravāda Buddhism'. *Journal of Feminist Studies in Religion* 27 (1): 33–51.

Appleton, Naomi. 2014. 'Buddhist Scriptures: An Overview'. *The Expository Times* 125 (12): 573–82.

Ariyaratne, Ahangamage T. 1980. 'The Role of Buddhist Monks in Development'. *World Development* 8: 587–9.

Ashin, Janaka and Kate Crosby. 2017. 'Heresy and Monastic Malpractice in the Buddhist Court Cases (Vinicchaya) of Modern Burma (Myanmar)'. *Contemporary Buddhism* 18 (1): 199–261.

Bailey, Cathryn. 2009. 'Embracing the Icon: The Feminist Potential of the Trans Bodhisattva, Kuan Yin'. *Hypatia* 24 (3): 178–96.

Balkwill, Stephanie. 2018. 'Why Does a Woman Need to Become a Man in Order to Become a Buddha? Past investigations, New Leads'. *Religion Compass*.

Baranov, David and Kevin A. Yelvington. 2003. 'Ethnicity, Race, Class, and Nationality'. In *Understanding the Contemporary Caribbean*, ed. Richard S. Hillman and Thomas J. D'Agostino, 209–38. Boulder: Lynne Reinner.

Barnhill, David Landis. 1997. 'Great Earth Sangha: Gary Snyder's View of Nature as Community'. In *Buddhism and Ecology: The Interconnection of Dharma and Deeds*, ed. Mary Evelyn Tucker and Duncan Ryūken Williams, 187–217. Cambridge, MA: Harvard University Press.

Baroni, Helen J. 2017. 'The System Stinks: Sources of Inspiration for the Buddhist Peace Fellowship'. *Contemporary Buddhism* 18 (1): 2–20.

Bartholomeusz, Tessa J. 2002. *In Defence of Dharma: Just-War Ideology in Buddhist Sri Lanka*. Abingdon, Oxon: Routledge.

Batchelor, Stephen. 1994. *The Awakening of the West: The Encounter with Buddhism and Western Culture*. Berkeley: Parallax Press.

Batchelor, Stephen. 1997. *Buddhism Without Beliefs*. New York: Riverhead Books.

Batchelor, Stephen. 2017. *Secular Buddhism: Imagining the Dharma in an Uncertain World*. New Haven: Yale University Press.

Baumann, Martin. 2002. 'Buddhism in Europe: Past, Present, Prospects'. In *Westward Dharma: Buddhism Beyond Asia*, ed. Charles S. Prebish and Martin Baumann, 85–105. Berkeley: University of California Press.

Bechert, Heinz. 1973. 'Sangha, State, Society, "Nation": Persistence of Traditions in "Post-Traditional" Buddhist Societies'. *Daedalus* 102 (1): 85–95.

Bechert, Heinz. 1991. 'Max Weber and the Sociology of Buddhism'. *Internationales Asienforum* 22 (3–4): 181–95.

Bell, Sandra. 2000. 'A Survey of Engaged Buddhism in Britain'. In *Engaged Buddhism in the West*, ed. Christopher S. Queen, 397–422. Boston: Wisdom Publications.

Benn, James A. 2007. *Burning for the Buddha: Self-immolation in Chinese Buddhism*. Kuroda Institute Studies in East Asian Buddhism 19. Honolulu: University of Hawai'i Press.

Benn, James A. 2014. 'Self-immolation, Resistance and Millenarianism in Medieval Chinese Buddhism'. *The Medieval History Journal* 17 (2): 229–54.

Berkwitz, Stephen C. ed. 2006. *Buddhism in World Cultures: Comparative Perspectives*. Santa Barbara: ABC-CLIO.

Berkwitz, Stephen C. 2013. 'History and Gratitude in Theravāda Buddhism'. *Journal of the American Academy of Religion* 71 (3): 579–604.

Bizumic, Boris. 2014. 'Who Coined the Concept of Ethnocentrism? A Brief Report'. *Journal of Social and Political Psychology* 2 (1): 3–10.

Blackburn, Anne M. 2002. 'Buddhism, Colonialism and Modernism: A View from Sri Lanka'. *Nēthrā* 5 (3): 7–25.

Blackburn, Anne M. 2010. *Locations of Buddhism*. Chicago: University of Chicago Press.

Blum, Mark. 2009. 'The Transcendentalist Ghost in EcoBuddhism'. In *Transbuddhism: Transmission, Translation, Transformation*, ed. Nalini Bhushan, Jay L Garfield, and Abraham Zablocki, 209–38. Amherst: University of Massachusetts Press.

Bodhi, Bhikkhu. 1987. 'Foreword'. In *Buddhist Perspectives on the Ecocrisis*, ed. Klas Sandell, 5–10. The Wheel Publication No. 346/348. Kandy: Buddhist Publications Society.

Bodhi, Bhikkhu. 1995. *The Middle Length Discourses of the Buddha: A New Translation of the Majjhima Nikāya*. Boston: Wisdom Publications.

Bodhi, Bhikkhu. 2000. *The Connected Discourses of the Buddha: A New Translation of the Saṃyutta-nikāya*. Oxford: PTS.

Bodhi, Bhikkhu. 2007. 'A Challenge to Buddhists'. *Lion's Roar*. 1 September.

Bodhi, Bhikkhu. 2009. 'Socially Engaged Buddhism and the Trajectory of Buddhist Ethical Consciousness'. *Religion East & West* 9: 1–23.

Bodhi, Bhikkhu. 2015. 'Facing the Great Divide'. *Inquiring Mind* 31 (2).

Bodhi, Bhikkhu. 2016. *The Buddha's Teaching on Social and Communal Harmony: An Anthology of Discourses from the Pali Canon*. Somerville, MA: Wisdom Publications.

Bodhi, Bhikkhu. 2018. 'A Call to Conscience'. *Tricycle*. Fall 2018.

Bond, George D. 1996. 'A.T. Ariyaratne and the Sarvodaya Shramadana Movement in Sri Lanka'. In *Engaged Buddhism: Buddhist Liberation Movements in Asia*, ed. Christopher Queen and Sallie B King, 121–46. Albany: State University of New York Press.

Bond, Georg D. 2004. *Buddhism at Work: Community Development, Social Empowerment and the Sarvodaya Movement*. Bloomfield, CT: Kumarian Press.

Bookbinder, Alex. 2014. '969: The Strange Numerological Basis for Burma's Religious Violence'. *Eleven Myanmar Media*, 17 January.

Borchert, Thomas. 2007. 'Buddhism, Politics and Nationalism in the Twentieth and Twenty-First Centuries'. *Religion Compass* 1 (5): 529–46.

Borchert, Thomas. 2014. 'The Buddha's Precepts on Respecting Other Races and Religions? Thinking about the Relationship of Ethnicity and Theravāda Buddhism'. *Journal of Social Issues in Southeast Asia* 29 (3): 591–626.

Borchert, Thomas. 2016. 'On Being a Monk and a Citizen in Thailand and China'. In *Buddhism and the Political Process*, ed. Hiroko Kawanami, 11–30. Basingstoke and Hampshire: Palgrave Macmillan.

Brach, Tara. 2003. *Radical Acceptance: Awakening the Love That Heals Fear and Shame Within Us*. London: Rider.

Buckner, Ray. 2017. 'See Us Clearly: A Buddhist's View of Transgender Visibility'. *Lion's Roar*, 27 July.

Buckner, Ray. 2018. 'Our Opportunity to Include All Genders in Buddhist Communities'. *Lion's Roar*, 1 October.

Buddhadāsa, Bhikkhu. 1986a. *Natural Cure for Spiritual Disease: A Guide into Buddhist Science*. Trans. Santikaro Bhikkhu. Originally published by The Dhammadāna Foundation, 1986. Electronically published by the Buddhadāsa Indapañño Archives in collaboration with Liberation Park, 2017.

Buddhadāsa, Bhikkhu. 1986b. *Dhammic Socialism*. Trans. Donald Swearer. Bangkok: Thai Inter-Religious Commission for Development.

Buddhadāsa, Bhikkhu. 1994. *Heartwood of the Bodhi Tree: The Buddha's Teachings on Voidness*. Boston: Wisdom Publications.

Buddhadāsa, Bhikkhu. 2016. *Nibbāna for Everyone*. Trans. Santikaro Bhikkhu. Bangkok: BIA and Liberation Park with the support of the Buddhadāsa Foundation.

Burlingame, Eugene Watson. 1921. *Buddhist Legends, Translated from the Original Pali Text of the Dhammapada Commentary* (vol. 2). Cambridge, MA: Harvard University Press.

Burton, David. 1999. *Emptiness Appraised*. Oxon: RoutledgeCurzon.

Cabezón, Jose Ignacio, ed. 1992. *Buddhism, Sexuality and Gender*. New York: State University of New York Press.

Cabezón, Jose Ignacio .1996. 'Buddhist Principles in the Tibetan Liberation Movement'. In *Engaged Buddhism: Buddhist Liberation Movements in Asia*, ed. Christopher S. Queen and Sallie B. King, 295–320. Albany: State University of New York Press.

Cabezón, José. 1998. 'Buddhism and Homosexuality'. In *Queer Dharma: Voices of Gay Buddhists* (vol. 1), ed. Winston Leyland, 29–44. San Francisco: Gay Sunshine Press.

Cabezón, José Ignacio. 2003. 'Buddhism and Science: On the Nature of the Dialogue'. In *Buddhism and Science: Breaking New Ground*, ed. B. Alan Wallace, 35–70. New York: Columbia University Press.

Cabezón, José. 2017. *Sexuality in Classical South Asian Buddhism*. Somerville, MA: Wisdom Publications.

Cadge, Wendy. 2005. 'Lesbian, Gay, and Bisexual Buddhist Practitioners'. In *Gay Religion*, ed. Scott Thumma and Edward R, Gray, 139–52. Walnut Creek: Altamira Press.

Chakravarti, Uma. 1987. *The Social Dimensions of Early Buddhism*. Oxford: Oxford University Press.

Chapple, Christopher Key. 1997. 'Animals and Environment in the Buddhist Birth Stories'. In *Buddhism and Ecology: The Interconnection of Dharma and Deed*, ed. Mary Evelyn Tucker and Duncan Ryūken Williams, 131–48. Cambridge, MA: Harvard University Press.

Cheah, Joseph. 2016. 'Buddhism, Race, and Ethnicity'. In *The Oxford Handbook of Contemporary Buddhism*, ed. Michael Jerryson, 650–61. New York: Oxford University Press.

Cheesman, Nick. 2017. 'How in Myanmar "National Races" Came to Surpass Citizenship and Exclude Rohingya'. *Journal of Contemporary Asia* 47 (3): 461–83.

Cheesman, Nick. 2017. 'Introduction: Interpreting Communal Violence in Myanmar'. *Journal of Contemporary Asia* 47 (3): 335–52.

Chiovenda, Melissa Kerr. 2014. 'Sacred Blasphemy: Global and Local Views of the Destruction of the Bamyan Buddha Statues in Afghanistan'. *Journal of Muslim Minority Affairs* 34: 410–24.

Chödrön, Pema. 2007. *When Things Fall Apart: Heart Advice for Difficult Times*. Rockport, MA: Element Books.

Clayton, Barbra. 2013. 'Buddha's Maritime Nature: A Case Study in Shambhala Buddhist Environmentalism'. *Journal of Buddhist Ethics* 20: 572–90.

Clayton, Barbra R. 2018. 'The Changing Way of the Bodhisattva: Superheroes, Saints, and Social Workers'. In *The Oxford Handbook of Buddhist Ethics*, ed. Daniel Cozort and James Mark Shield. 135–60. Oxford: Oxford University Press.

Clippard, Seth Devere. 2011. 'The Lorax Wears Saffron: Toward a Buddhist Environmentalism'. *Journal of Buddhist Ethics* 18: 212–48.

Coleman, James William. 2001. *The New Buddhism: The Western Transformation of an Ancient Tradition*. Oxford: Oxford University Press.

Collett, Alice. 2006. 'Buddhism and Gender: Reframing and Refocusing the Debate'. *Journal of Feminist Studies in Religion* 22 (2): 55–84.

Collett, Alice. 2018. 'Buddhism and Women'. In *The Oxford Handbook of Buddhist Ethics*, ed. Daniel Cozort and James Mark Shields, 552–66. New York: Oxford University Press.

Collett, Alice and Bhikkhu Anālayo. 2014. 'Bhikkhave and Bhikkhu as Gender-Inclusive Terminology in Early Buddhist Texts'. *Journal of Buddhist ethics* 21: 760–97.

Collins, Steven. 1982. *Selfless Persons: Imagery and Thought in Theravāda Buddhism*. Cambridge: Cambridge University Press.

Collins, Steven. 1998. *Nirvana and other Buddhist Felicities: Utopias of the Pali Imaginaire*. Cambridge: Cambridge University Press.

Collins, Steven. 2007. 'Remarks on the Third Precept: Adultery and Prostitution in Pāli Texts'. *Journal of the Pali Text Society* 29: 263–84.

Conkin, Dennis. 1998. 'The Dalai Lama and Gay Love'. In *Queer Dharma*, ed. Winston Leyland, 351–6. San Francisco, CA: Gay Sunshine Press.

Cook, Francis H. 1977. *Hua-yen Buddhism: The Jewel Net of Indra*. Pennsylvania: Penn State University Press.

Cooper, David E. and Simon P. James. 2005. *Buddhism, Virtue, and Environment*. Aldershot: Ashgate.

Cooper, David E. and Simon P. James. 2007. 'Buddhism and the Environment'. *Contemporary Buddhism* 8 (2): 93–6.

Corless, Roger. 1998. 'Coming Out in the *Sangha*: Queer Community in American Buddhism'. In *The Faces of Buddhism in America*, ed. Charles. S. Prebish and Kenneth. K. Tanaka, 253–65. Berkeley: University of California Press.

Corless, Roger. 2000. 'Gay Buddhist Fellowship'. In *Engaged Buddhism in the West*, ed. Christopher Queen, 269–79. Boston: Wisdom Publications.

Corless, Roger. 2004. 'Towards a Queer Dharmology of Sex'. *Culture and Religion* 5 (2): 229–43.

Cummiskey, David and Alex Hamilton. 2017. 'Dependent Origination, Emptiness, and the Value of Nature'. *Journal of Buddhist Ethics* 24: 1–37.

Darlington, Susan M. 1998. 'The Ordination of a Tree: The Buddhist Ecology Movement in Thailand'. *Ethnology* 37 (1): 1–15.

Darlington, Susan M. 2007. 'The Good Buddha and the Fierce Spirits: Protecting the Northern Thai Forest'. *Contemporary Buddhism* 8 (2): 169–85.

Darlington, Susan M. 2012. *The Ordination of a Tree: The Thai Buddhist Environmental Movement*. Albany: State University of New York Press.

Darlington, Susan M. 2013. 'Sacred Protests and Buddhist Environmental Knowledge'. In *Buddhism, Modernity, and the State in Asia*, ed. John Whalen-Bridge and Pattana Kitiarsa, 245–62. New York: Palgrave Macmillan.

Darlington, Susan M. 2016. 'Contemporary Buddhism and Ecology'. In *The Oxford Handbook of Contemporary Buddhism*, ed. Michael Jerryson, 487–503. New York: Oxford University Press.

Darlington, Susan. 2018. 'Environmental Buddhism Across Borders'. *Journal of Global Buddhism* 19: 77–93.

Davies, Shann, ed. 1987. *Tree of Life: Buddhism and Protection of Nature*. Geneva, Switzerland: Buddhist Perception of Nature Project.

Davis, Erik W. 2016. *Deathpower: Buddhism's Ritual Imagination in Cambodia*. New York: Columbia University Press.

Deitrick, James E. 2003. 'Engaged Buddhist Ethics: Mistaking the Boat for the Shore'. In *Action Dharma: New Studies in Engaged Buddhism*, ed. Christopher Queen, Charles Prebish and Damien Keown, 252–69. London: Routledge Curzon.

Derris, Karen. 2008. 'When the Buddha Was a Woman: Reimagining Tradition in the Theravāda'. *Journal of Feminist Studies in Religion* 24 (2): 29–44.

DeVido, Elise Anne. 2007. 'Buddhism for This World: The Buddhist Revival in Vietnam, 1920 to 1951, and Its Legacy'. In *Modernity and Re-Enchantment: Religion in Post-Revolutionary Vietnam*, ed. Philip Taylor, 250–96. Singapore: Institute of Southeast Asian Studies.

DeVido, Elise A. 2009. 'The Influence of Chinese Master Taixu on Buddhism in Vietnam'. *Journal of Global Buddhism* 10: 413–58.

Droit, Roger-Pol. 2003. *The Cult of Nothingness: The Philosophers and the Buddha*. Chapel Hill: The University of North Carolina Press.

Eckel, Malcolm David. 1997. 'Is There a Buddhist Philosophy of Nature?' In *Buddhism and Ecology: The Interconnection of Dharma and Deed*, ed. Mary Evelyn Tucker and Duncan Ryūken Williams, 327–49. Cambridge, MA: Harvard University Press.

Edelglass, William. 2009a. 'Thich Nhat Hanh's Interbeing: Fourteen Guidelines for Engaged Buddhism'. In *Buddhist Philosophy: Essential Readings*, ed Jay Garfield and William Edelgass, 419–27. Oxford: Oxford University Press.

Edelglass, William. 2009b. 'Joanna Macy "The Ecological Self"'. In *Buddhist Philosophy: Essential Readings*, ed. William Edelglass and Jay Garfield, 428–36. New York: Oxford University Press.

Edelglass, William and Jay Garfield, ed. 2009. *Buddhist Philosophy: Essential Readings*. New York: Oxford University Press.

Edwards, David. 2001. *The Compassionate Revolution: Radical Politics and Buddhism*. New Delhi: Viveka Foundation.

Elman, Benjamin A. 1983. 'Nietzsche and Buddhism'. *Journal of the History of Ideas* 44 (4): 671–86.

Elverskog, Johan. 2020. *The Buddha's Footprint: An Environmental History of Asia*. Philadelphia: University of Pennsylvania Press.

Emmanuel, Steven. 2012. 'Buddhism: Contemporary Expressions'. In *The Wiley-Blackwell Companion to Religion and Social Justice*, ed. Michael D. Palmer and Stanley M. Burgess, 30–45. Chichester: John Wiley & Sons.

Enke, Finn. 2019. 'What Is a Body Anyway: Form, Deep Listening and Compassion on a Buddhist Trans Path'. In *Transcending: Trans Buddhist Voices*, ed. Kevin Manders and Elizabeth Marston, 5–12. Berkeley, CA: North Atlantic Books.

Eppsteiner, Fred, ed. 1988. *The Path of Compassion: Writings on Socially Engaged Buddhism*. Berkeley: Parallax Press.

Essen, Juliana M. 2005. *Right Development: The Santi Asoke Buddhist Reform Movement of Thailand*. Lanham, MD: Lexington Books.

Essen, Juliana M. 2004. 'Santi Asoke Buddhist Reform Movement: Building Individuals, Community, and (Thai) Society'. *Journal of Buddhist Ethics* 11: 1–20.

Euw, E. 2019. 'Coming Home to Themselves: The Resonance of Non-self and Impermanence for Transgender Buddhists'. In *Transcending: Trans Buddhist Voices*, ed. Kevin Manders and Elizabeth Marston, 235–50. Berkeley, CA: North Atlantic Books.

Evans, Stephan A. 2007. 'Doubting the Kālāma-sutta: Epistemology, Ethics, and the "Sacred."' *Buddhist Studies Review* 24 (1): 91–107.

Faure, Bernard. 1991. *The Rhetoric of Immediacy: A Cultural Critique of Chan/Zen Buddhism*. Princeton: Princeton University Press.

Faure, Bernard. 1998. *The Red Thread: Buddhist Approaches to Sexuality*. Princeton: Princeton University Press.

Faure, Bernard. 2003. *The Power of Denial: Buddhism, Purity and Gender*. Princeton: Princeton University Press.

Fenstermaker, Sarah and Candace West, ed. 2002. *Doing Gender Doing Difference*. Hoboken: Taylor and Francis.

Fields, Rick. 1992. *How the Swans Came to the Lake: A Narrative History of Buddhism in America* 3rd edn. Boston: Shambhala Publications.

Finnigan, Mary and Rob Hogendoorn. 2019. *Sex and Violence in Tibetan Buddhism: The Rise and Fall of Sogyal Rinpoche*. Portland: Jorvic Press.

Fogelin, Lars. 2015. *An Archaeological History of Indian Buddhism*. New York: Oxford University Press.

Foxeus, Niklas. 2019. 'The Buddha was a Devoted Nationalist: Buddhist Nationalism, *Ressentiment*, and Defending Buddhism in Myanmar'. *Religion* 49 (4): 661–90.

Frazier, Allie M. 1975. 'A European Buddhism'. *Philosophy East & West* 25 (2): 145–60.

Friedlander, Peter. 2009. 'Buddhism and Politics'. In *Routledge Handbook of Religion and Politics*, ed. Jeffrey Haynes, 11–25. New York: Routledge.

Frydenlund, Iselin. 2013. 'The Protection of Dharma and Dharma as Protection: Buddhism and Security across Asia'. In *The Routledge Handbook of Religion and Security*, ed. Chris Seiple, Dennis R. Hoover and Pauletta Otis, 102–12. New York: Routledge.

Frydenlund, Iselin. 2018. 'The Birth of Buddhist Politics of Religious Freedom in Myanmar'. *Journal of Religious and Political Practice* 4 (1): 107–21.

Frydenlund, Iselin. 2019. 'The Rise of Religious Offence in Transitional Myanmar'. In *Outrage: The Rise of Religious Offence in Contemporary South Asia*, ed. Paul Rollier, Kathinka Frøystad, and Arild Engelsen Ruud, 77–102. London: UCL Press.

Fuller, Paul. 2004. *The Notion of Ditthi in Theravada Buddhism: The Point of View*. Abingdon, Oxon: RoutledgeCurzon.

Fuller, Paul and David Webster. 2008. 'A View from the Crossroads: A Dialogue'. *Buddhist Studies Review* 25 (1): 106–12.

Fuller, Paul. 2013. 'The Dog-Duty Ascetic: Action in the Pali Canon with Reference to the Politics of Action in Modern Burma'. *Thai International Journal of Buddhist Studies* IV: 97–116.

Fuller, Paul. 2016. 'The Idea of "Blasphemy" in the Pāli Canon and Modern Myanmar'. *Journal of Religion and Violence* 4 (2): 159–81.

Fuller, Paul. 2017. 'Sitagu Sayadaw and Justifiable Evils in Buddhism'. *New Mandala*. 13 November.

Fuller, Paul. 2018. 'The Narratives of Ethnocentric Buddhist identity'. *The Journal of the British Association of Religious Studies* 20: 19–44.

Gard, Richard A. 1962. 'Buddhism and Political Authority.' In *The Ethic of Power: The Interplay of Religion, Philosophy, and Politics*, ed. Harold D. Lasswell and Harlan Cleveland, 39–70. New York: Harper & Brothers.

Garfield, Jay. 1995. *The Fundamental Wisdom of the Middle Way: Nāgārjuna's Mūlamadhyamakakārikā*. New York: Oxford University Press.

Gellner, David. 2009. 'The Uses of Max Weber: Legitimation and Amnesia in Buddhology, South Asian History, and Anthropological Practice Theory'. In *The Oxford Handbook of the Sociology of Religion*, ed. Peter B. Clarke, 48–63. New York: Oxford University Press.

Gethin, Rupert. 1997. 'Wrong View (miccha-ditthi) and Right View (samma-ditthi) in the Theravada Abhidhamma'. In *Recent Researches in Buddhist Studies: Essays in Honour of Professor Y. Karunadasa*, ed. Bhikkhu Kuala Lumpur Dhammajoti, Asanga Tilakaratne and Kapila Abhayawansa, 211–29. Hong Kong: Y. Karunadasa Felicitation Committee, Colombo, Chi Ying Foundation.

Gethin, Rupert. 1998. *The Foundations of Buddhism*. New York: Oxford University Press.

Gleig, Ann. 2012. 'Queering Buddhism or Buddhist De-Queering?'. *Theology & Sexuality* 18 (3): 198–214.

Gleig, Ann. 2019. *American Dharma: Buddhism Beyond Modernity*. New Haven: Yale University Press.

Gleig, Ann. 2021. 'Engaged Buddhism'. In *Oxford Research Encyclopedia of Religion*. New York: Oxford University Press. Full details unavailable at the time of publication.

Goldberg, Kory. 2013. 'Pilgrimage Re-Oriented: Buddhist Discipline, Virtue and Engagement in Bodhgayā'. *The Eastern Buddhist* 44 (2): 95–120.

Gombrich, Richard. 1975. 'Buddhist Karma and Social Control'. *Comparative Studies in Society and History* 17 (2): 212–20.

Gombrich, Richard. 2006. *Theravāda Buddhism: A Social History from Ancient Benares to Modern Colombo*, 2nd edn. London: Routledge.

Grant, Patrick. 2009. *Buddhism and Ethnic Conflict in Sri Lanka*. Albany: State University of New York Press.

Gravers, Mikael. 2012. 'Monks, Morality and Military: The Struggle for Moral Power in Burma—And Buddhism's Uneasy Relation with Lay Power'. *Contemporary Buddhism* 13 (1): 1–33.

Gravers, Mikael. 2013. 'Spiritual Politics, Political Religion, and Religious Freedom in Burma'. *The Review of Faith & International Affairs* 11 (2): 46–54.

Gravers, Mikael. 2015. 'Anti-Muslim Buddhist Nationalism in Burma and Sri Lanka: Religious Violence and Globalized Imaginaries of Endangered Identities'. *Contemporary Buddhism* 16 (1): 1–27.

Gross, Rita. 1993. *Buddhism After Patriarchy: A Feminist History, Analysis, and Reconstruction of Buddhism*. Albany: State University of New York Press.

Gross, Rita. 1997. 'Buddhist Resources for Issues of Population, Consumption, and the Environment'. In *Buddhism and Ecology: The Interconnection of Dharma and Deed*, ed. Mary Evelyn Tucker and Duncan Ryūken Williams, 291–311. Cambridge, MA: Harvard University Press.

Gross, Rita M. 2000a. 'Population, Consumption, and the Environment'. In *Dharma Rain: Sources of Buddhist Environmentalism*, ed. Stephanie Kaza and Kenneth Kraft, 409–22. Boston: Shambhala.

Gross, Rita M. 2000b. 'Toward a Buddhist Environmental Ethic'. In *Visions of a New Earth: Religious Perspectives on Population, Consumption and Ecology*, ed. Harold Coward and Daniel C. Maguire, 147–60. Albany: State University of New York Press.

Gross, Rita M. 2003. 'Toward a Buddhist Environmental Ethic'. In *Worldviews, Religion, and the Environment: A Global Anthology*, ed. Richard S. Foltz, 163–71. Belmont, CA: Wadsworth.

Gross, Rita. 2014. 'Buddhism'. In *The Oxford Handbook of Theology, Sexuality, and Gender*, ed. Adrian Thatcher, 467–84. New York: Oxford University Press

Gross, Rita. 2015. 'The Real Problem Regarding Buddhist Women and Gender Justice: Androcentric Models of Humanity'. In *Compassion and Social Justice*, ed. Karma Lekshe Tsomo, 242–46. Yogyakarta, Indonesia: Sakyadhita.

GutiérrezBaldoquín, Hilda, ed. 2004. *Dharma, Color, and Culture: New Voices in Western Buddhism*. Berkeley: Parallax Press.

Gyatso, Janet. 2005. 'Sex'. In *Critical Terms for the Study of Buddhism*, ed. Donald S. Lopez, 271–90. Chicago: The University of Chicago Press.

Gyatso, Janet. 2003. 'One Plus One Makes Three: Buddhist Gender, Monasticism, and the Law of the Non-excluded Middle'. *History of Religions* 43 (2): 89–115.

Habito, Ruben L. F. 2007. 'Environment or Earth Sangha: Buddhist Perspectives on Our Global Ecological Well-Being'. *Contemporary Buddhism* 8 (2): 131–47.

Harris, Elizabeth J. 2013. 'Buddhism and International Aid: A Case Study from Post-tsunami Sri Lanka'. In *Buddhism, International Relief Work, and Civil Society*, ed. Hiroko Kawanami and Geoffrey Samuel, 1–26. New York: Palgrave Macmillan.

Harris, Ian Charles. 1991. 'How Environmentalist Is Buddhism?' *Religion* 21 (2): 101–14.

Harris, Ian Charles. 1994a. 'Buddhism'. In *Attitudes to Nature*, ed. Jean Holm and John Bowker, 8–27. New York: Pinter Publishers.

Harris, Ian Charles. 1994b. 'Causation and "Telos": The Problem of Buddhist Environmental Ethics'. *Journal of Buddhist Ethics* 1: 45–56.

Harris, Ian Charles. 1995a. 'Buddhist Environmental Ethics and Detraditionalization: The Case of EcoBuddhism'. *Religion* 25: 199–211.

Harris, Ian Charles. 1995b. 'Getting to Grips with Buddhist Environmentalism: A Provisional Typology'. *Journal of Buddhist Ethics* 2: 173–90.

Harris, Ian Charles. 1997. 'Buddhism and the Discourse of Environmental Concern: Some Methodological Problems Considered'. In *Buddhism and Ecology: The Interconnection of Dharma and Deeds*, ed. Mary Evelyn Tucker and Duncan Ryūken Williams, 377–402. Cambridge, MA: Harvard University Press.

Harris, Ian Charles. 1999a. *Buddhism and Politics in Twentieth Century Asia*. London: Continuum.

Harris, Ian Charles. 1999b. 'Buddhism in Extremis: The Case of Cambodia'. In *Buddhism and Politics in Twentieth Century Asia*, ed. Ian Charles Harris, 24–78. London: Continuum.

Harris, Ian Charles. 2007. *Buddhism, Power and Political Order*. London: Routledge.

Harris, Ian Charles. 2009. 'Something Rotten in the State of Buddhaland: Good Governance in Theravāda Buddhism'. In *Destroying Mara Forever: Buddhist Ethics Essays in Honor of Damien Keown*, ed. John Powers and Charles S. Prebish, 221–36. Ithaca, NY: Snow Lion Publications.

Harris, Ian Charles. 2016. 'Introduction to Buddhism and the Political Process: Patterns of Interaction'. In *Buddhism and the Political Process*, ed. Hiroko Kawanami, 1–10. New York: Palgrave Macmillan.

Harris, Stephen. 2011. 'Does Anātman Rationally Entail Altruism? On Bodhicaryāvatāra 8:101-103'. *Journal of Buddhist Ethics* 18: 93–123.

Harrold, Richard. 2019. *My Buddha Is Pink: Buddhism for the Modern Homosexual*. Ontario: Sumeru Press.

Harvey, Peter. 1990. *An Introduction to Buddhism*. Cambridge: Cambridge University Press.

Harvey, Peter. 2000. *An Introduction to Buddhist Ethics: Foundations, Values and Issues*. Cambridge: Cambridge University Press.

Harvey, Peter. 2007. 'Avoiding Unintended Harm to the Environment and the Buddhist Ethic of Intention'. *Journal of Buddhist Ethics* 14: 1–34.

Hassan, Riaz. 2007. 'Expressions of Religiosity and Blasphemy in Modern Societies'. *Asian Journal of Social Science* 35: 111–25.

Hassner, Ron E. 2011. 'Blasphemy and Violence'. *International Studies Quarterly* 55 (1): 23–45.

Hayward, Susan. 2015. 'The Double-Edged Sword of "Buddhist Democracy" in Myanmar'. *The Review of Faith & International Affairs* 13 (4): 25–35.

Hayward, Susan and Matthew J. Walton. 2016. 'Advancing Religious Freedom and Coexistence in Myanmar: Recommendations for the Next U.S. Administration'. *The Review of Faith & International Affairs* 14 (2): 67–75.

Heikkilä-Horn, Marja-Leena. 1997. *Buddhism with Open Eyes: Belief and Practice of Santi Asoke*. Bangkok: Fah Apai.

Helbardt, Sascha, Dagmar Hellmann-Rajanayagam and Rüdiger Korff. 2013. 'Religionisation of Politics in Sri Lanka, Thailand and Myanmar'. *Politics, Religion and Ideology* 14 (1): 36–58.

Henning, Daniel H. 2002. *Buddhism and Deep Ecology*. Bloomington: AuthorHouse.

Henry, Phil. 2006. 'The Sociological Implications for Contemporary Buddhism in the United Kingdom: Socially Engaged Buddhism, a Case Study'. *Journal of Buddhist Ethics* 13: 1–43.

Henry, Phil. 2013. *Adaptation and Developments in Western Buddhism: Socially Engaged Buddhism in the UK*. London: Bloomsbury.

Heywood, Andrew. 2013. *Politics*. 4th edn. Basingstoke and Hampshire: Palgrave Macmillan.

Hickey, Wakoh Shannon. 2010. 'Two Buddhisms, Three Buddhisms and Racism'. *Journal of Global Buddhism* 11: 1–25.

Holder, John. J. 2007. 'A Suffering (But Not Irreparable) Nature: Environmental Ethics from the Perspective of Early Buddhism'. *Contemporary Buddhism* 8 (2): 113–30.

Hopkins, Jeffrey. 1997. 'The Compatibility of Reason and Orgasm in Tibetan Buddhism: Reflections on Sexual Violence and Homophobia'. In *Que(e) rying Religion: A Critical Anthology*, ed. Gary David Comstock and Susan E. Henking, 372–83. New York: Continuum.

Horner, Isaline B. 1930. *Women Under Primitive Buddhism: Laywomen and Almswomen*. London: G. Routledge & Son.

Horner, Isaline B. 1982. *The Book of the Discipline*, Part 2. London: Pāli Text Society.

Houtart, Francois. 1976. 'Buddhism and Politics in South-East Asia: Part One'. *Social Scientist* 5 (3): 3–23.

Houtart, Francois. 1976. 'Buddhism and Politics in South-East Asia: Part Two'. *Social Scientist* 5 (4): 30–45.

Houtman, Gustaaf. 1999. *Mental Culture in Burmese Crisis Politics: Aung San Suu Kyi and the National League for Democracy*. Tokyo: Institute for the Study of Languages and Cultures of Asia and Africa, Tokyo University of Foreign Studies.

Hsin Yun, Venerable. 2016. *Humanistic Buddhism: Holding True to the Original Intents of Buddha*. Trans. Mio Guang. Taiwan: Fo Guang Shan Cultural Enterprise Co. Ltd.

Hu, Hsiao-Lan. 2011. *This-Worldly Nibbana: A Buddhist-Feminist Social Ethic for Peacemaking in the Global Community*. Albany: State University of New York Press.

Hu, Hsiao-Lan. 2016. 'Buddhism and Sexual Orientation'. In *The Oxford Handbook of Contemporary Buddhism*, ed. Michael Jerryson, 662–77. New York: Oxford University Press.

Hunt-Badiner, Allan. ed. 1990. *Dharma Gaia: A Harvest of Essays in Buddhism and Ecology*. Berkeley: Parallax Press.

Hunt-Perry, Patricia and Lyne Fine, 2000. 'All Buddhism Is Engaged: Thich Nhat Hanh and the Order of Interbeing'. In *Engaged Buddhism in the West*, ed. Christopher S. Queen and Sallie B. King, 35–66. Somerville, MA: Wisdom Publications.

Hutchinson, John and Anthony D. Smith, eds 1996. *Ethnicity*. New York: Oxford University Press.

Huxley, Andrew. 1995. 'Buddhism and Law—The View from Mandalay'. *Journal of the International Association of Buddhist Studies* 18 (1): 47–95.

Ingram, Paul O. 1997. 'The Jeweled Net of Nature'. In *Buddhism and Ecology: The Interconnection of Dharma and Deeds*, ed. Mary Evelyn Tucker and Duncan Ryūken Williams, 71–88. Cambridge, MA: Harvard University Press.

International Network of Engaged Buddhists. 2012. 'Lesbian Couple to Take Vows in Nation's First Public Buddhist Same-Sex Union'. *Seeds of Peace* 28 (3): 31.

Ip, Hung-yok. 2009. 'Buddhist Activism and Chinese Modernity'. *Journal of Global Buddhism* 10: 145–92.

Ives, Christopher. 2001. 'Protect the Dharma, Protect the Country: The Continuing Question of Buddhist War Responsibility'. *The Eastern Buddhist* XXXIII (2): 37–45.

Ives, Christopher. 2008. 'Deploying the Dharma: Reflections on the Methodology of Constructive Buddhist Ethics'. *Journal of Buddhist Ethics* 15: 23–44.

Ives, Christopher. 2009a. 'In Search of a Green Dharma: Philosophical Issues in Buddhist Environmental Ethics'. In *Destroying Mara Forever: Buddhist Ethics*

Essays in Honor of Damien Keown, ed. Charles Prebish and John Powers, 165–86. Ithaca, NY: Snow Lion Publications.

Ives, Christopher. 2009b. 'Buddhism and Sustainability'. In *The Spirit of Sustainability*, ed. Willis Jenkins and Whitney A. Bauman, 38–50. Great Barrington, MA: Berkshire Publishing.

Ives, Christopher. 2013. 'Resources for Buddhist Environmental Ethics'. *Journal of Buddhist Ethics* 20: 541–71.

Ives, Christopher. 2019. 'Buddhist Responses to the Ecological Crisis: Recent Publications on Buddhism and Ecology'. *Journal of Buddhist Ethics* 26: 291–306.

Jackson, Peter A. 1998. 'Male Homosexuality and Transgenderism in the Thai Buddhist Tradition'. In *Queer Dharma: Voices of Gay Buddhists* (vol. 1), ed. Winston Leyland, 55–89. San Francisco: Gay Sunshine Press.

Jackson, Peter A. 2003. *Buddhadāsa: Theravada Buddhism and Modernist Reform in Thailand*. Chiang Mai: Silkworm.

Jacoby, Sarah. H. 2018. Response to Ann Gleig and Amy Langenberg's AAR panel, 'From Rape Texts to Bro Buddhism: Critical Canonical and Contemporary Perspectives on the Sex Abuse Scandals In Western Buddhism'. *Sakyadhita* 27: 5–9.

James, Simon P. 2013. 'Buddhism and Environmental Ethics'. In *A Companion to Buddhist Philosophy*, ed. Steven M. Emmanuel, 601–12. Chichester: Wiley-Blackwell.

Jaquet, Carine and Matthew J. Walton. 2013. 'Buddhism and Relief in Myanmar: Reflections on Relief as a Practice of *Dāna*'. In *Buddhism, International Relief Work, and Civil Society*, ed. Hiroko Kawanami and Geoffrey Samuel, 51–74. New York: Palgrave Macmillan,

Jayasuriya, Laksiri. 2008. 'Buddhism, Politics, and Statecraft'. *International Journal of Buddhist Thought & Culture* 11: 41–74.

Jenkins, Richard. 1997. *Rethinking Ethnicity: Arguments and Explorations*. London: SAGE Publications.

Jenkins, Stephen. 2003. 'Do Bodhisattvas Relieve Poverty?' In *Action Dharma: New Studies in Engaged Buddhism*, ed. Christopher Queen, Charles Prebish and Damien Keown, 38–49. London: RoutledgeCurzon.

Jerryson, Michael. 2015. 'Buddhists and Violence: Historical Continuity/Academic Incongruities'. *Religion Compass* 9: 141–50.

Jerryson, Michael. 2016a. *The Oxford Handbook of Contemporary Buddhism*. New York: Oxford University Press.

Jerryson, Michael. 2016b. 'Introduction: Buddhism, Blasphemy, and Violence'. *Journal of Religion and Violence* 4 (2): 119–28.

Jerryson, Michael. 2018. *If You Meet the Buddha on the Road: Buddhism, Politics, and Violence*. New York: Oxford University Press.

Johnson, Ronald Lee Lloyd. 2019. 'A Brief History of Mindfulness in Addictions Treatment'. *International Journal for the Advancement of Counselling* 41 (2): 284–95.

Johnston, Lucas. 2006. 'The "Nature" of Buddhism: A Survey of Relevant Literature and Themes'. *Worldviews: Environment, Culture, Religion* 10 (1): 69–99.

Jones, Charles B. 2009. 'Modernization and Traditionalism in Buddhist Almsgiving: The Case of the Buddhist Compassion Relief Tzu-chi Association in Taiwan'. *Journal of Global Buddhism* 10: 291–319.

Jones, Ken. 2003. *The New Social Face of Buddhism: An Alternative Sociopolitical Perspective*. Boston: Wisdom Publications.

Kabat-Zinn, Jon. 2004. *Wherever You Go, There You Are: Mindfulness Meditation for Everyday Life*. London: Piatkus.

Kabat-Zinn, Jon. 2005. *Coming to Our Senses: Healing Ourselves and the World Through Mindfulness*. New York: Hyperion.

Kabilsingh, Chatsumarn. 1987. *A Cry from the Forest: Buddhist Perception of Nature. A New Perspective for Conservation Education*. Bangkok: Wildlife Fund Thailand.

Kakuyo, Alex. 2020. *Perfectly Ordinary: Buddhist Teachings for Everyday Life*. Independently Published.

Karunaratne, T. B. 1969. 'The Buddhist Wheel Symbol'. *The Wheel Publication* (137/138). Kandy, Sri Lanka: Buddhist Publication Society.

Kawanami, Hiroko. 1999. 'Japanese Nationalism and the Universal *Dharma*'. In *Buddhism and Politics in Twentieth-Century Asia*, ed. Ian Charles Harris, 105–26. London: Continuum.

Kawanami, Hiroko, ed. 2016a. *Buddhism and the Political Process*. Basingstoke: Palgrave Macmillan.

Kawanami, Hiroko. 2016b. 'U Nu's Liberal Democracy and Buddhist Communalism in Modern Burma'. In *Buddhism and the Political Process*, ed. Hiroko Kawanami, 31–55. Basingstoke: Palgrave Macmillan.

Kawanami, Hiroko. 2020. *The Culture of Giving in Myanmar: Buddhist Offerings, Reciprocity and Interdependence*. London: Bloomsbury.

Kawanami, Hiroko and Geoffrey Samuel, eds 2013. *Buddhism, International Relief Work, and Civil Society*. New York: Palgrave Macmillan.

Kaza, Stephanie. 2006. 'Agents in Indra's Net'. In *Mindful Politics: A Buddhist Guide to Making the World a Better Place*, ed. Melvin McLeod, 201–12. Boston: Wisdom Publications.

Kaza, Stephanie. 2019. *Green Buddhism: Practice and Compassionate Action in Uncertain Times*. Boulder, CO: Shambhala.

Kaza, Stephanie and Kenneth Kraft, eds 2000. *Dharma Rain: Sources of Buddhist Environmentalism*. Boston: Shambhala.

Keller, David R. 2009. 'Deep Ecology'. In *Encyclopedia of Environmental Ethics and Philosophy*, ed. J Baird Callicott and Robert Frodeman, 206–11. Farmington Hills, MI: Gale, Cengage Learning.

Kent, Daniel. W. 2015. 'Preaching in a Time of Declining Dharma: History, Ethics and Protection in Sermons to the Sri Lankan Army'. *Contemporary Buddhism* 16 (1): 188–223.

Keown, Damien. 2003. *A Dictionary of Buddhism*. New York: Oxford University Press.

Keown, Damien, Charles S Prebish and Wayne R. Husted, eds 2012. *Buddhism and Human Rights*. London: Routledge.

Keyes, Charles F. 1989. 'Buddhist Politics and Their Revolutionary Origins in Thailand'. *International Political Science Review* 10 (2): 121–42.

Keyes, Charles F. 2013. 'Buddhists Confront the State'. In *Buddhism, Modernity, and the State in Asia*, ed. John Whalen-Bridge and Pattana Kitiarsa, 17–39. New York: Palgrave Macmillan.

Keyes, Charles F.. 2016. 'Theravāda Buddhism and Buddhist Nationalism: Sri Lanka, Myanmar, Cambodia, and Thailand'. *The Review of Faith & International Affairs* 14 (4): 41–52.

Khuankaew, Ouyporn. 2009. 'Buddhism and Domestic Violence: Using the Four Noble Truths to Deconstruct and Liberate Women's Karma'. In *Rethinking Karma: The Dharma of Social Justice*, ed Jonathan S. Watts, 199–226. Chiang Mai: Silkworm Books.

King, Richard. 1999. *Orientalism and Religion: Post-colonial Theory, India and the Mystic East*. London: Routledge.

King, Sallie B. 1996. 'Thich Nhat Hanh and the Unified Buddhist Church'. In *Engaged Buddhism: Buddhist Liberation Movements in Asia*, ed. Christopher S. Queen and Sallie B. King, 321–63. Albany: State University of New York Press.

King, Sallie B. 2006. *Being Benevolence: The Social Ethics of Engaged Buddhism*. Honolulu: University of Hawaiï Press.

King, Sallie B. 2009. *Socially Engaged Buddhism*. Honolulu: University of Hawai'i Press.

King, Sallie B. 2012. 'Socially Engaged Buddhism'. In *Buddhism in the Modern World*, ed. David L. McMahan, 195–214. New York: Routledge.

King, Sallie B. 2017. 'Right Speech Is Not Always Gentle: The Buddha's Authorization of Sharp Criticism, Its Rationale, Limits, and Possible Applications'. *Journal of Buddhist Ethics* 24: 347–67.

King, Sallie B. 2018. 'The Ethics of Engaged Buddhism in Asia'. In *The Oxford Handbook of Buddhist Ethics*, ed. Daniel Cozort and James Mark Shield, 479–500. New York: Oxford University Press.

Kitagawa, Joseph M. 1980. 'Buddhism and Social Change: An Historical Perspective'. In *Buddhist Studies in Honour of Walpola Rahula*, ed. Somaratna Balasooriya, 84–102. London: Gordon Fraser.

Kittel, Laura. 2011. 'Healing Heart and Mind: The Pursuit of Human Rights in Engaged Buddhism as Exemplified by Aung San Suu Kyi and the Dalai Lama'. *The International Journal of Human Rights* 15 (6): 905–25.

Klinken, Gerry van and Su Mon Thazin Aung. 2017. 'The Contentious Politics of Anti-Muslim Scapegoating in Myanmar'. *Journal of Contemporary Asia* 47 (3): 353–75.

Kraft, Kenneth, ed. 1992. *Inner Peace, World Peace: Essays on Buddhism and Nonviolence*. Albany: State University of New York Press.

Kraft, Kenneth. 1997. 'Nuclear Ecology and Engaged Buddhism'. In *Buddhism and Ecology: The Interconnection of Dharma and Deeds*, ed. Mary Evelyn Tucker and Duncan Ryūken Williams, 269–90. Cambridge, MA: Harvard University Press.

Kraft, Kenneth. 1999. *The Wheel of Engaged Buddhism: A New Map of the Path*. Boston: Weatherhill.

Kraft, Kenneth. 2000. 'New Voices in Engaged Buddhist Studies'. In *Engaged Buddhism in the West*, ed. Christopher S. Queen, 485–512. Boston: Wisdom Publications.

Lachs, Stuart. n.d. *Tibetan Buddhism Enters the 21st Century: Trouble in Shangri-la*. Available online at: https://info-buddhism.com/Tibetan_Buddhism_21st_Century-Stuart_Lachs.html. Accessed 9 October 2019.

Ladwig, Patrice. 2006. 'Applying Dhamma to Contemporary Society: Socially-Engaged Buddhism and Development Work in the Lao PDR'. *Juth Pakai* 7: 16–26.

Ladwig, Patrice. 2014. 'Millennialism, Charisma and Utopia: Revolutionary Potentialities in Pre-modern Lao and Thai Theravāda Buddhism'. *Politics, Religion & Ideology* 15: 308–29.

Langenberg, Amy. 2015. 'Sex and Sexuality in Buddhism: A Tetralemma: Sex and Sexuality in Buddhism'. *Religion Compass* 9 (9): 277–86.

Langenburg, Amy P. 2018. 'Buddhism and Sexuality'. In *The Oxford Handbook of Buddhist Ethics*, eds Daniel Cozort and James Mark Shield, 567–91. New York: Oxford University Press.

Langenberg, Amy P. 2019. 'Reading Against the Grain: Female Sexuality in Classical South Asian Buddhism'. *Religion* 49 (4): 728–34.

Langenberg, Amy P. 2020. 'Love, Unknowing, and Female Filth: The Buddhist Discourse of Birth as a Vector of Social Change for Monastic Women in Premodern South Asia'. In *Primary Sources and Asian Pasts*. Berlin and Boston: De Gruyte.

Larsson, Tomas. 2015. 'Monkish Politics in Southeast Asia: Religious Disenfranchisement in Comparative and Theoretical Perspective'. *Modern Asian Studies* 49 (46): 40–82.

Larsson, Tomas. 2016. 'Buddha or the Ballot: The Buddhist Exception to Universal Suffrage in Contemporary Asia'. In *Buddhism and the Political Process*, ed. Hiroko Kawanami, 78–96. Basingstoke: Palgrave Macmillan.

Lele, Amod. 2019. 'Disengaged Buddhism'. *Journal of Buddhist Ethics* 26: 239–89.

Levine, Noah. 2004. *Dharma Punx*. New York: HarperCollins.

Leyland, Winston, ed. 1998. *Queer Dharma: Voices of Gay Buddhists*. San Francisco: Gay Sunshine Press.

Leyland, Winston, ed. 2000. *Queer Dharma: Voices of Gay Buddhists Volume 2*. San Francisco: Gay Sunshine Press.

Ling, Trevor. 1983. 'Kingship and Nationalism in Pali Buddhism'. In *Buddhist Studies: Ancient and Modern*, ed Philip Denwood and Alexander Piatgorsky, 60–73. London: Curzon Press.

Linehan, Thomas. 2012. 'Comparing Antisemitism, Islamophobia, and Asylophobia: The British Case.' *Studies in Ethnicity and Nationalism*: 366–86.

Liow, Joseph C. 2016. *Religion and Nationalism in Southeast Asia*. Cambridge: Cambridge University Press.

Long, William J. 2019. *Tantric State: A Buddhist Approach to Democracy and Development in Bhutan*. New York: Oxford University Press.

Lopez, Donald S. 1995. *Curators of the Buddha: The Study of Buddhism Under Colonialism*. Chicago: University of Chicago Press.

Lopez, Donald S. 1998a. *Prisoners of Shangri-la: Tibetan Buddhism and the West*. Chicago: University of Chicago Press.

Lopez, Donald S. Jr. 1998b. 'Belief'. In *Critical Terms for Religious Studies*, ed. Mark C. Taylor, 21–35. Chicago: University of Chicago Press.

Lopez, Donald S. 2002. *A Modern Buddhist Bible: Essential Readings from East and West*. Boston: Beacon Press.

Lopez, Donald S. 2008. *Buddhism and Science: A Guide for the Perplexed*. Chicago: University of Chicago Press.

Lopez, Donald S. 2012. *The Scientific Buddha: His Short and Happy Life*. New Haven: Yale University Press.

Lopez, Donald S. 2013. *From Stone to Flesh: A Short History of the Buddha*. Chicago: University of Chicago Press.

Loy, David R. 1993. 'Indra's Postmodern Net'. *Philosophy East and West* 43 (3): 481–510.

Loy, David R. 2003. *The Great Awakening: A Buddhist Social Theory*. Boston: Wisdom Publications.

Loy, David R. 2008. *Money, Sex, War, Karma: Notes for a Buddhist Revolution*. Boston: Wisdom Publications.

Loy, David R. 2019. *Ecodharma: Buddhist Teachings for Ecological Crisis*. Boston: Wisdom Publications.

MacKenzie, Rory. 2007. *New Buddhist Movements in Thailand: Towards an understanding of Wat Phra Dhammakāya and Santi Asoke*. Abingdon: Routledge.

Macy, Joanna. 1979. 'Dependent Co-Arising: The Distinctiveness of Buddhist Ethics'. *Journal of Religious Ethics* 7 (1): 38–52.

Macy, Joanna. 1983. *Dharma and Development: Religion as a Resource in the Sarvodaya Self-Help Movement*. Hartford: Kumarian Press.

Macy, Joanna. 1990. 'The Greening of the Self'. In *Dharma Gaia: A Harvest of Essays in Buddhism and Ecology*, ed. Allan Hunt-Badiner, 53–63. Berkeley: Parallax Press.

Macy, Joanna. 1991. *Mutual Causality in Buddhism and General Systems Theory: The Dharma of Natural Systems*. Albany: State University of New York.

Macy, Joanna. 2000. 'Guarding the Earth'. In *Dharma Rain: Sources of Buddhist Environmentalism*, ed. Stephanie Kaza and Kenneth Kraft, 293–302. Boston: Shambhala.

Magee, Ronda V. 2016. 'Community-Engaged Mindfulness and Social Justice: An Inquiry and Call to Action'. In *Handbook of Mindfulness: Culture, Context, and Social Engagement*, ed. Ronald E Purser, David Forbes and Adam Burke, 425–40. Switzerland: Springer.

Main, Jessica L. and Rongdao Lai. 2013. 'Introduction: Reformulating "Socially Engaged Buddhism" as an Analytical Category'. *The Eastern Buddhist* 44 (2): 1–34.

Manders, K., and Elizabeth Marston, eds 2019. *Transcending: Trans Buddhist Voices*. Berkeley, CA: North Atlantic Books.

Matthews, Bruce. 1999. 'The Legacy of Tradition and Authority: Buddhism and the Nation in Myanmar'. In *Buddhism and Politics in Twentieth-Century Asia*, ed. Ian Charles Harris, 26–53. London: Continuum.

McCarthy, Gerard and Jacqueline Menager. 2017. 'Gendered Rumours and the Muslim Scapegoat in Myanmar's Transition'. *Journal of Contemporary Asia* 47 (3): 396–412.

McCarthy, Stephen. 2008. 'Overturning the Alms Bowl: The Price of Survival and the Consequences for Political Legitimacy in Burma'. *Australian Journal of International Affairs* 62 (3): 298–314.

McGuire, Robert. 2018. 'An All-New Timeless Truth: A Madhyamaka Analysis of Conflict and Compromise in Buddhist Modernism'. *Contemporary Buddhism* 18 (2): 385–401.

McLeod, Melvin. 2006. *Mindful Politics: A Buddhist Guide for Making the World a Better Place*. Boston: Wisdom Publications.

McMahan, David L. 2008. *The Making of Buddhist Modernism*. New York: Oxford University Press.

McMahan, David L., ed. 2012. *Buddhism in the Modern World*. London: Routledge.

McMahan, David and Erik Braun, eds 2017. *Meditation, Buddhism, and Science*. New York: Oxford University Press.

Mellor, Philip A. 1991. 'Protestant Buddhism? The Cultural Translation of Buddhism in England'. *Religion* 21 (2): 73–92.

Metraux, Daniel A. 1996. 'The Soka Gakkai: Buddhism and the Creation of a Harmonious and Peaceful Society'. In *Engaged Buddhism: Buddhist Liberation Movements in Asia*, ed. Christopher S. Queen and Sallie B. King, 365–400. Albany: State University of New York Press.

Miller, Lama Willa B. 2018. 'Breaking the Silence on Sexual Misconduct'. *Lion's Roar*, 19 May.

Mitchell, Scott A. 2016. *Buddhism in America: Global Religion, Local Contexts*. London: Bloomsbury.

Monson, Elizabeth. 2018. 'Ahimsa: Envisioning a New Buddhism in the West', in *Buddhist Project Sunshine, Phase 2 Final Report*. Available online: http://andreamwinn.com/project_sunshine/Buddhist_Project_Sunshine_Phase_2_Final_Report.pdf. Accessed 8 October 19.

Moore, Matthew J. 2015. 'Political Theory in Canonical Buddhism'. *Philosophy East and West* 65 (1): 36–64.

Moore, Matthew J. 2016a. *Buddhism and Political Theory*. New York: Oxford University Press.

Moore, Matthew J. 2016b. 'Buddhism, Mindfulness, and Transformative Politics'. *New Political Science* 38 (2): 272–82.

Mrozik, Susanne. 2002. 'The Value of Human Differences: South Asian Buddhist Contributions Toward an Embodied Virtue Theory'. *Journal of Buddhist Ethics* 9: 1–33.

Muller, Charles A. 2018. 'An Inquiry into Views, Beliefs and Faith: Lessons from Buddhism, Behavioural Psychology and Constructivist Epistemology'. *Contemporary Buddhism* 19 (2): 362–81.

Myint, Tun. 2015. 'Buddhist Political Thought'. In *The Encyclopedia of Political Thought*, ed. Michael T. Gibbons, 390–6. New York: John Wiley.

Naess, Arne. 1973. 'The Shallow and the Deep, Long-Range Ecology Movement. A Summary'. *Inquiry* 16: 95–100.

Naess, Arne. 1986. 'The Deep Ecology Movement: Some Philosophical Aspects'. *Philosophical Inquiry* 8: 10–31.

Ñāṇamoli, Bhikkhu. 1962. *The Guide*. London: PTS.

Nash, David. 2007. *Blasphemy in the Christian World: A History*. New York: Oxford University Press.

Nash, David. 2008. 'Introduction: Blasphemy'. *Journal of Religious History* 32: 393–7.

Nattier, Jan. 1991. *Once Upon a Future Time: Studies in a Buddhist Prophecy of Decline*. Berkeley: Asian Humanities Press.

Naw, Noreen. 2015. *Democratic Voice of Burma*, 2 June.

New York Post. 2018. '#MeToo Claims High-Ranking Chinese Buddhist Monk'. 3 August.

Newland, Tahlia. 2019. *Fallout: Recovering from Abuse in Tibetan Buddhism*. New South Wales, Australia: Escarpment Publishing.

Newman, Andy. 2018. 'The "King" of Shambhala Buddhism Is Undone by Abuse Report'. *The New York Times*, 11 July.

Ng, Zhiru. 2006. 'Purifying the Mind, Sanctifying the Earth: Visualizing Environmental Protection in Humanistic Buddhism in Taiwan'. Center for the Study of World Religions, Harvard University.

Nhat Hanh, Thich. 1964. *Dao phat di vao cuoc doi* (Engaged Buddhism/Buddhism Entering into Life). Saigon: Lá Bối.

Nhat Hanh, Thich. 1965a. *Engaged Buddhism (With Other Essays)*. trans. Trinh Van Du. Saigon: Lá Bối: Typewritten manuscript.

Nhat Hanh, Thich. 1965b. *Dao phat ngay nay* (Buddhism Today). Saigon: La Boi.

Nhat Hanh, Thich. 1965c. *Dao Phat hien dai hoa* (Modernization of Buddhism). Saigon: La Boi.

Nhat Hanh, Thich. 1967. *Vietnam: Lotus in the Sea of Fire*. New York: Hill and Wang.

Nhat Hanh, Thich. 1988a. 'The Individual Society and Nature'. In *The Path of Compassion: Writings on Socially Engaged Buddhism*, ed. Fred Eppsteiner, 40–6. Berkeley: Parallax Press.

Nhat Hanh, Thich. 1988b. *The Heart of Understanding: Commentaries on the Prajñaparamita Heart Sutra*. Berkeley: Parallax Press.

Nhat Hanh, Thich. 1993a. *Interbeing: The Fourteen Guidelines for Engaged Buddhism*. Berkeley: Parallax Press.

Nhat Hanh, Thich. 1993b. *Love in Action: Writings on Nonviolent Social Change*. Berkeley: Parallax Press.

Nhat Hanh, Thich. 1998. *Interbeing: Fourteen Guidelines for Engaged Buddhism*, 3rd edn, ed. Fred Eppsteiner. Berkeley: Parallax Press.

Nhat Hanh, Thich. 2008a. 'History of Engaged Buddhism: A Dharma Talk by Thich Nhat Hanh, Hanoi, Vietnam, May 6–7, 2008'. *Human Architecture: Journal of the Sociology of Self-knowledge* 6 (3): 29–36.

Nhat Hanh, Thich. 2008b. 'Spiritual Reflections on War and Peace: A Talk by Thich Nhat Hanh, Peace Forum, March 19, 2003'. *Human Architecture: Journal of the Sociology of Self-knowledge* 6 (3): 7–13.

Nhat Hanh, Thich. 2009. *Happiness: Essential Mindfulness Practices*. Berkeley: Parallax Press.

Nhat Hanh, Thich. 2010. Unpublished lecture given at the European Institute of Applied Buddhism, Germany, 11 June.

Nhat Hanh, Thich. 2014. *Mindfulness Survival Kit: Five Essential Practices*. Berkeley: Parallax Press.

Nichtern, Ethan. 2007. *One City: A Declaration of Interdependence*. Boston: Wisdom Publications

Norman, Kenneth R. trans. 2001. *The Group of Discourses (Sutta-Nipāta)*. Oxford: PTS.

Numrich, Paul David. 2009. 'The Problem with Sex According to Buddhism'. *Dialog* 48 (1): 62–73.

Obeyesekere, Gananath. 2003. 'Buddhism, Ethnicity and Identity: A Problem of Buddhist History'. *Journal of Buddhist Ethics* 10: 192–242.

Obeyesekere, Gananath and Richard Gombrich. 1988. *Buddhism Transformed: Religious Change in Sri Lanka*. Princeton, NJ: Princeton University Press.

Obeyesekere, Gananath, Frank Reynolds and Bardwell L. Smith, eds 1972. *The Two Wheels of Dharma: Essays on the Theravada Tradition in India and Ceylon*. Chambersburg, PA: American Academy of Religion.

Ohnuma, Reiko. 2000. 'The Story of Rūpāvatī: A Female Past Birth of the Buddha'. *Journal of the International Association of Buddhist Studies* 23 (1): 103–45.

Ohnuma, Reiko. 2006. 'Debt to the Mother: A Neglected Aspect of the Founding of the Buddhist Nuns' Order'. *Journal of the American Academy of Religion* 74 (4): 861–901.

Ohnuma, Reiko. 2017. *Unfortunate Destiny: Animals in the Indian Buddhist Imagination*. New York: Oxford University Press.

Pandita, Ven. 2019. 'Sexual Misconduct in Early Buddhist Ethics: A New Approach'. *Journal of Buddhist Ethics* 26: 151–87.

Parallax Press, ed. 2019. *True Peace Work: Essential Writings on Engaged Buddhism*. Berkeley: Parallax Press.

Parkum, Virginia Cohn and Stultz J. Anthony. 2000. 'The Angulimala Lineage: Buddhist Prison Ministries'. In *Engaged Buddhism in the West*, ed. Christopher Queen, 347–71. Boston: Wisdom Publications.

Paul, Diana Y. 1985. *Women in Buddhism: Images of the Feminine in the Mahāyāna Tradition*. Berkeley: University of California Press.

Peach, Lucinda Joy. 2002. 'Social Responsibility, Sex Change, and Salvation: Gender Justice in the Lotus Sutra'. *Philosophy East and West* 52 (1): 50–74.

Pellegrini, Ann. 2018. '#MeToo: Before and After'. *Studies in Gender and Sexuality* 19 (4): 262–4.

Pistono, Matteo. 2019. *Roar: Sulak Sivaraksa and the Path of Socially Engaged Buddhism*. Berkeley: North Atlantic Books.

Pitt, Martin. 1990. 'The Pebble and the Tide'. In *Dharma Gaia: A Harvest of Essays in Buddhism and Ecology*, ed. Allan Hunt-Badiner, 102–5. Berkeley: Parallax Press.

Pittman, Don A. 1993. 'The Modern Buddhist Reformer T'ai-hsü on Christianity'. *Buddhist-Christian Studies* 13: 71–83.

Poethig, Kathryn. 2002. 'Movable Peace: Engaging the Transnational in Cambodia's Dhammayietra'. *Journal for the Scientific Study of Religion* 41 (1): 19–28.

Powers, John. 2009. *A Bull of a Man: Images of Masculinity, Sex, and the Body in Indian Buddhism*. Cambridge, MA: Harvard University Press.

Powers, John. 2018. 'Compassion and Rebirth: Some Ethical Implications'. In *Buddhist Philosophy: A Comparative Approach*, ed. Steven Emmanuel, 221–37. Hoboken, NJ: John Wiley & Sons.

Powers, John. 2019. 'Indian Buddhist Concepts of Normative and Deviant Bodies: Can Ancient Sexual Mores Be Reconciled with Modern Sensibilities?' *Religion* 49 (4): 735–44.

Prebish, Charles and Martin Baumann, eds 2002. *Westward Dharma: Buddhism Beyond Asia*. Berkeley: University of California Press.

Purser, Ronald E., Forbes, David and Burke, Adam, eds 2016. *Handbook of Mindfulness: Culture, Context, and Social Engagement*. Switzerland: Springer.

Queen, Christopher S. 2013. 'Socially Engaged Buddhism: Emerging Patterns of
    Theory and Practice'. In *A Companion to Buddhist Philosophy*, ed. Steven M.
    Emmanuel, 524–35. Chichester: Wiley-Blackwell.

Queen, Christopher S. 1996a. 'Introduction: The Shapes and Sources of Engaged
    Buddhism'. In *Engaged Buddhism: Buddhist Liberation Movements in Asia*,
    ed. Christopher S. Queen and Sallie B. King, 1–44. Albany: State University of
    New York Press.

Queen, Christopher S. 1996b. 'Dr. Ambedkar and the Hermeneutics of Buddhist
    Liberation'. In *Engaged Buddhism: Buddhist Liberation Movements in Asia*,
    ed. Christopher Queen and Sallie B. King, 45–72. Albany: State University of
    New York Press.

Queen, Christopher S. ed. 2000. *Engaged Buddhism in the West*. Boston:
    Wisdom Publications.

Queen, Christopher S. 2002. 'Engaged Buddhism: Agnosticism,
    Interdependence, Globalization'. In *Westward Dharma: Buddhism beyond
    Asia*, ed. Charles S. Prebish and Martin Baumann, 324–47. Berkeley: University
    of California Press.

Queen, Christopher S. 2003. 'Gentle or Harsh? The Practice of Right Speech
    in Engaged Buddhism'. In *Socially Engaged Spirituality: Essays in Honor of
    Sulak Sivaraksa on His 70th Birthday*, ed. David W. Chappell, 2–19. Bangkok:
    Sathirakoses-Nagapradipa Foundation.

Queen, Christopher S. 2004. 'Ambedkar's Dhamma: Source and Method in
    the Construction of Engaged Buddhism'. In *Reconstructing the World: B. R.
    Ambedkar and Buddhism in India*, ed. Surendra Jondhale and Johannes Beltz,
    132–50. New York: Oxford University Press.

Queen, Christopher S. 2018. 'The Ethics of Engaged Buddhism in the West'. In
    The Oxford Handbook of Buddhist Ethics, ed. Daniel Cozort and James Mark
    Shield, 501–27. New York: Oxford University Press.

Queen, Christopher S. and Sallie B. King, eds 1996. *Engaged Buddhism: Buddhist
    Liberation Movements in Asia*. Albany: State University of New York Press.

Queen, Christopher S., Charles Prebish and Damien Keown, eds 2003. *Action
    Dharma: New Studies in Engaged Buddhism*. London: RoutledgeCurzon.

Quli, Natalie E. 2009. 'Western Self, Asian Other: Modernity, Authenticity, and
    Nostalgia for "Tradition" in Buddhist Studies'. *Journal of Buddhist Ethics* 16:
    1–38.

Rahula, Walpola. 1974. *The Heritage of the Bhikkhu: A Short History of the
    Bhikkhu in the Educational, Cultural, Social and Political Life*. New York: Grove
    Press.

Rathore, Aakash Singh and Ajay Verma, eds 2011. *The Buddha and His Dhamma:
    A Critical Edition*. New York: Oxford University Press.

Remski, Matthew. 2019. *Practice and All Is Coming: Abuse, Cult Dynamics, and
    Healing in Yoga and Beyond*. Rangiora, New Zealand: Embodied Wisdom
    Publishing.

Renson, Audrey, Chance Krempasky and Finn Schubert. 2016. *Developing
    Trans Competence: A Short Guide to Improving Transgender Experiences at
    Meditation and Retreat Centers*. transbuddhists.org.

Rinker, Jeremy A. 2018. *Identity, Rights, and Awareness: Anticaste Activism in
    India and the Awakening of Justice Through Discursive Practices*. Lanham,
    MD: Lexington Books.

Ritzinger, Justin. 2017. *Anarchy in the Pure Land: Reinventing the Cult of Maitreya in Modern Chinese Buddhism*. New York: Oxford University Press.

Robinne, François. 2019. 'Thinking through Heterogeneity: An Anthropological Look at Contemporary Myanmar'. *Journal of Burma Studies* 23 (2): 285–322.

Rolling, James Haywood. 2008. 'Secular Blasphemy: Uttere(d) Transgressions Against Names and Fathers in the Postmodern Era'. *Qualitative Inquiry* 14: 926–48.

Romberg, Claudia. 2002. 'Women in Engaged Buddhism'. *Contemporary Buddhism* 3 (2): 161–70.

Rorty, Richard. 1989. 'Solidarity or Objectivity?' In *Relativism: Interpretation and Confrontation*, ed. Michael Krausz, 35–50. Notre Dame: University of Notre Dame Press.

Ross, Rebecca. 2012. 'Blasphemy and the Modern, "Secular" State'. *Appeal* 17: 3–19.

Rothberg, Donald. 1998. 'Responding to the Cries of the World: Socially Engaged Buddhism in North America'. In *The Faces of Buddhism in America*, ed. Charles S. Prebish and Kenneth K. Tanaka. Berkeley: University of California Press.

Rylance, Valerie J. J. 2011. 'Lesbian Buddhism?' Mphil thesis. SOAS, University of London. http://eprints.soas.ac.uk/18468. Accessed 15 April 2019.

Said, Edward. 1978. *Orientalism: Western Conceptions of the Orient*. London: Routledge and Kegan Paul.

Sakyadhita. 2019. *New Horizons in Buddhism: The Proceedings of the 16th Sakyadhita International Conference on Buddhist Women*. The Planning Committee of the 16th Sakyadhita Conference in Australia.

Santikaro, Bhikkhu. 1996. 'Buddhadasa Bhikkhu: Life and Society through the Natural Eyes of Voidness'. In *Engaged Buddhism: Buddhist Liberation Movements in Asia*, ed. Christopher S. Queen and Sallie B. King, 147–93. Albany: State University of New York Press.

Schak, David and Michael Hsiao Hsin-Huang. 2005. 'Taiwan's Socially Engaged Buddhist Groups'. *China Perspectives* 59: 43–55.

Scherer, Burkhard. 2006. 'Gender Transformed and Meta-Gendered Enlightenment: Reading Buddhist Narratives as Paradigms of Inclusiveness'. *Revista de Estudos da Religião* 3: 65–76.

Schissler, Matt, Matthew J. Walton and Phyu Phyu Thi. 2017. 'Reconciling Contradictions: Buddhist-Muslim Violence, Narrative Making and Memory in Myanmar'. *Journal of Contemporary Asia* 47 (3): 376–95.

Schmithausen, Lambert. 1991. 'Buddhism and Nature'. The Lecture delivered on the Occasion of the EXPO 1990 - An Enlarged Version with Notes. Studia Philologica Buddhica Occasional Paper Series: Nr. VII. Tokyo: International Institute for Buddhist Studies.

Schmithausen, Lambert. 1997. 'The Early Buddhist Tradition and Ecological Ethics'. *Journal of Buddhist Ethics* 4: 1–74.

Schmithausen, Lambert. 1999. 'Aspects of the Buddhist Attitude Towards War'. In *Violence Denied: Violence, Non-Violence and the Rationalization of Violence in South Asian Cultural History*, ed. Jan E. M. Houben and Karel Rijk Van Kooij, 45–67. Leiden: Brill.

Schober, Juliane. 2017. 'Belonging in a New Myanmar: Identity, Law, and Gender in the Anthropology of Contemporary Buddhism'. *Religion and Society: Advances in Research* 8: 158–72.

Schonthal, Benjamin and Matthew J. Walton. 2016. 'The (New) Buddhist Nationalisms? Symmetries and Specificities in Sri Lanka and Myanmar'. *Contemporary Buddhism* 17 (1): 81–115.

Schopen, Gregory. 1997. *Bones, Stones, and Buddhist Monks: Collected Papers on the Archaeology, Epigraphy, and Texts of Monastic Buddhism in India.* Honolulu: University of Hawai'i Press.

Schuster, Nancy. 2005. 'Changing the Female Body: Wise Women and the Bodhisattva Career in Some Maharatnakūtasūtras'. *Journal of the International Association of Buddhist Studies* 4 (1981): 24–69; reprinted in *Buddhism: Critical Concepts in Religious Studies*, ed. Paul Williams, 329–67. London: Routledge.

Scott, Rachelle M. 2009. *Nirvana for Sale? Buddhism, Wealth, and the Dhammakāya Temple in Contemporary Thailand.* Albany: State University of New York Press.

Seneviratna, Anuradha. 1994. *King Aśoka and Buddhism: Historical and Literary Studies.* Kandy: Buddhist Publication Society.

Shaw, Sarah. 2006. *The Jātakas: Birth Stories of the Bodhisatta.* London: Penguin Books.

Shields, James Mark. 2010. 'Sexuality, Exoticism and Iconoclasm in the Media Age: The Strange Case of the Buddha Bikini'. In *God in the Details: American Religion in Popular Culture*, revised 2nd edn, ed. Eric M. Mazur and Kate McCarthy, 80–101. London: Routledge.

Shields, James Mark. 2016. 'Opium Eaters: Buddhism as Revolutionary Politics'. In *Buddhism and the Political Process*, ed. Hiroko Kawanami, 213–34. Basingstoke and Hampshire: Palgrave Macmillan.

Shiu, Henry and Leah Stokes. 2008. 'Buddhist Animal Release Practices: Historic, Environmental, Public Health and Economic Concerns'. *Contemporary Buddhism* 9 (2): 181–96.

Shun'ei, Hakamata Toshihide, and Jonathan S. Watts. 2013. 'From a Disconnected Society to an Interconnected Society'. *The Eastern Buddhist* 44 (2): 77–94.

Silk, Jonathan A. 1994. 'The Victorian Creation of Buddhism'. *Journal of Indian Philosophy* 22 (2): 171–96.

Silverstein, Josef. 1996. 'The Idea of Freedom in Burma and the Political Thought of Daw Aung San Suu Kyi'. *Pacific Affairs* 69 (2): 211–28.

Sirimanne, Chand R. 2016. 'Buddhism and Women—The Dhamma Has No Gender'. *Journal of International Women's Studies* 18 (1): 273–92.

Sivaraksa, Sulak. 1992. *Seeds of Peace: A Buddhist Vision for Renewing Society.* Berkeley: Parallax Press.

Sivaraksa, Sulak. 1998. *Loyalty Demands Dissent: Autobiography of an Engaged Buddhist.* Berkeley: Parallax Press.

Sivaraksa, Sulak. 2002. 'Economic Aspects of Social and Environmental Violence from a Buddhist Perspective'. *Buddhist-Christian Studies* 22: 47–60.

Sivaraksa, Sulak. 2005. *Conflict, Culture, and Change: Engaged Buddhism in a Globalizing World.* Boston: WisdomPublications.

Skidmore, Monique. 1996. 'In the Shade of the Bodhi Tree: Dhammayietra and the Reawakening of Community in Cambodia'. *Crossroads: An Interdisciplinary Journal of Southeast Asian Studies* 10 (1): 1–32.

Slott, Michael. 2015. 'Secular, Radically Engaged Buddhism: At the Crossroads of Individual and Social Transformation'. *Contemporary Buddhism* 16 (2): 278–98.

Smith, David R., Graeme Nixon and Jo Pearce. 2018. 'Bad Religion as False Religion: An Empirical Study of UK Religious Education Teachers' Essentialist Religious Discourse'. *Religions* 9 (11): 361.

Smith, Sharon E., Sally R. Munt and Andrew Kam-Tuck Yip. 2016. *Cosmopolitan Dharma: Race, Sexuality, and Gender in British Buddhism*. Leiden: Brill.

Snyder, Gary. 1985. 'Buddhism and the Possibilities of a Planetary Culture'. Reprinted in *Deep Ecology: Living as If Nature Mattered*, ed. Bill Devall and George Sessions, 251–3. Utah: Gibbs Smith Publisher.

South, Ashley. 2018. 'Buddhism, Politics and Political Thought in Myanmar'. *Journal of Contemporary Asia* 48 (5): 855–6.

Spiro, Melford E. 1982. *Buddhism and Society: A Great Tradition and Its Burmese Vicissitudes*. 2nd edn. Berkeley: University of California Press.

Sponberg, Alan.1992. 'Attitudes toward Women and the Feminine in Early Buddhism'. In *Buddhism, Sexuality and Gender* ed. José Cabezón, 3–36. Albany: State University of New York Press.

Steinberg, David I. 2014. 'Myanmar's Militant Monks Smash Stereotypes'. *East Asia Forum* 13.

Stone, Jacqueline. 2003. 'Nichiren's Activist Heirs: Soka Gakkai, Rissho Kosekai, Nipponzan Myohoji'. In *Action Dharma: New Studies in Engaged Buddhism*, ed. Christopher S. Queen, Charles Prebish, and Damien Keown, 63–94. London: RoutledgeCurzon.

Strong, John S. 1983. *The Legend of King Aśoka: A Study and Translation of the Aśokāvadāna*. Princeton: Princeton University Press.

Strong, John S. 1989. *The Legend of King Aśoka: A Study and Translation of the Aśokāvadāna*. Princeton: Princeton University Press.

Strong, John S. 2004. *Relics of the Buddha*. Princeton: Princeton University Press.

Stuart-Fox, Martin. 1999. 'Laos: From Buddhist Kingdom to Marxist State'. In *Buddhism and Politics in Twentieth-Century Asia*, ed. Ian Charles Harris, 153–72. London: Continuum.

Sturges, Paul. 2015. 'Limits to Freedom of Expression? The Problem of Blasphemy'. *Federation of Library Associations and Institutions* 4: 112–19.

Suksamran, Somboon. 1988. 'A Buddhist Approach to Development: The Case of "Development Monks" in Thailand'. In *Reflections on Development in Southeast Asia*, ed. Lim Tack Ghee, 26–48. Singapore: ASEAN Economic Research Unit, Institute of Southeast Asian Studies.

Suksamran, Somboon. 1993. *Buddhism and Political Legitimacy*. Bangkok: Research Dissemination Project, Chulalongkorn University.

Sujato, Venerable. 2012. 'Why Buddhists Should Support Marriage Equality'. *Sujato's Blog*, 21 March. https://sujato.wordpress.com/2012/03/21/1430/. Accessed 30 September 2019.

Sunim, Hae-ju. 1999. 'Can Women Achieve Enlightenment? A Critique of Sexual Transformation for Enlightenment'. In *Buddhist Women Across Cultures: Realizations*, ed. Karma Lekshe Tsomo, 123–41. Albany: State University of New York Press.

Swearer, Donald K. 1996. 'Sulak Sivaraksa's Buddhist Vision for Renewing Society'. In *Engaged Buddhism: Buddhist Liberation Movements in Asia*, ed.

Christopher S. Queen and Sallie B. King, 195–238. Albany: State University of New York Press.

Swearer, Donald K. 1997. 'The Hermeneutics of Buddhist Ecology in Contemporary Thailand: Buddhadasa and Dhammapitaka'. In *Buddhism and Ecology: The Interconnection of Dharma and Deeds*, ed. Mary Evelyn Tucker and Duncan Ryūken Williams, 21–44. Cambridge, MA: Harvard University Press.

Swearer, Donald K. 1999. 'Centre and Periphery: Buddhism and Politics in Modern Thailand'. In *Buddhism and Politics in Twentieth Century Asia*, ed. Ian Charles Harris, 194–228. London: Continuum.

Swearer, Donald K. 2004. *Becoming the Buddha: The Ritual of Image Consecration in Thailand*. Princeton: Princeton University Press.

Sweet, Michael J. and Leonard Zwilling. 1993. 'The First Medicalization: The Taxonomy and Etiology of Queerness in Classical Indian Medicine'. *Journal of the History of Sexuality* 3 (4): 590–607.

Swidler, Arlene, ed. 1993. *Homosexuality in World Religions*. Harrisburg: Trinity Press.

Tambiah, Stanley J. 1973. 'Buddhism and This-Worldly Activity'. *Modern Asian Studies* 7 (1): 1–20.

Tambiah, Stanley J. 1976. *World Conqueror and World Renouncer: A Study of Buddhism and Polity in Thailand Against a Historical Background*. Cambridge: Cambridge University Press.

Tambiah, Stanley J. 1984. *The Buddhist Saints of the Forest and the Cult of Amulets: A Study in Charisma, Hagiography, Sectarianism, and Millennial Buddhism*. Cambridge: Cambridge University Press.

Tambiah, Stanley J. 1987. *The Buddhist Conception of Universal King and Its Manifestations in South and Southeast Asia*. Kuala Lumpur: University of Malaya.

Tambiah, Stanley J. 1989. 'King Mahāsammata: The First King in the Buddhist Story of Creation, and His Continuing Relevance'. *Journal of the Anthropological Society of Oxford* 20 (2): 101–22.

Tambiah, Stanley J. 1992. *Buddhism Betrayed? Religion, Politics, and Violence in Sri Lanka*. Chicago: University of Chicago Press.

Tannenbaum, Nicola. 2000. 'Protest, Tree Ordination, and the Changing Context of Political Ritual'. *Ethnology* 39 (2): 109–27.

Tegbaru, Amare. 1998. 'Local Environmetalism in Northeast Thailand'. In *Environmental Movements in Asia*, ed. Arne Kalland and Gerard Persoon, 151–78. Richmond: Curzon Press.

Temprano, Victor Gerard. 2013. 'Defining Engaged Buddhism: Traditionists, Modernists, and Scholastic Power'. *Buddhist Studies Review* 30 (2): 261–74.

Thanissara. 2015. *Time to Stand Up: An Engaged Buddhist Manifesto for Our Earth*. Berkeley: North Atlantic Books.

The Guardian. 2018. 'Senior Chinese Monk Resigns Amid Sexual Misconduct Claims', 15 August.

Thepwisutthimethi, Phra and Donald Swearer. 1989. *Me and Mine: Selected Essays of Bhikkhu Buddhadāsa*. Albany: State University of New York Press.

Thompson, Evan. 2020. *Why I Am Not a Buddhist*. New Haven, CT: Yale University Press.

Tiyavanich, Kamala. 1997. *Forest Recollections: Wandering Monks in Twentieth-Century Thailand*. Honolulu: University of Hawaii Press.

Tsomo, Karma Lekshe, ed. 2004. *Buddhist Women and Social Justice Ideals, Challenges, and Achievements*. Albany: State University of New York Press.

Tsomo, Karma Lekshe. 2009. 'Socially Engaged Buddhist Nuns: Activism in Taiwan and North America'. *Journal of Global Buddhism* 10: 459–85.

Tsomo, Karma Lekshe, ed. 2012. *Out of the Shadows: Socially Engaged Buddhist Women*. New Delhi: Sri Satguru Publications.

Tsomo, Karma Lekshe. 2014. 'Karma, Monastic Law, and Gender Justice'. In *Buddhism and Law: An Introduction*, ed. Rebecca Redwood French and Mark A. Nathan, 334–49. Cambridge: Cambridge University Press.

Tucker, Mary Evelyn and Duncan Ryūken Williams, eds 1997. *Buddhism and Ecology: The Interconnection of Dharma and Deeds*. Cambridge, MA: Harvard University Press.

Turner, Alicia. 2014. *Saving Buddhism: The Impermanence of Religion in Colonial Burma*. Honolulu: University of Hawai'i Press.

Vanh, Thuy. 2019. 'Barriers Faced by Trans People of Color in Buddhist Communities'. In *Transcending: Trans Buddhist Voices*, ed. Kevin Manders and Elizabeth Marston, 229–34. Berkeley: North Atlantic Books.

Vasubandhu. 1988. *Abhidharmakośabhāṣyam*. Trans. Louis de La Vallée Poussin (French) and Leo M. Pruden (English). Berkeley: Asian Humanities Press.

Vehaba, Alana. 2019. 'Buddhism, Death, and Resistance: What Self-Immolation in Tibet has Borne'. *Politics, Religion & Ideology* 20 (2): 215–43.

Vella, Santino. 2019. 'Uppity Apostate Transgender Monk Questions Transphobia and Sexism in Buddhist Monasticism'. In *Transcending: Trans Buddhist Voices*, ed. Kevin Manders and Elizabeth Marston, 57–64. Berkeley: North Atlantic Books:

Vesely-Flad, Rima. 2017. 'Black Buddhists and the Body: New Approaches to Socially Engaged Buddhism'. *Religions* 8: 1–9.

Victoria, Brian Daizen. 2001. 'Engaged Buddhism: A Skeleton in the Closet?' *Journal of Global Buddhism* 2: 72–91.

Victoria, Brian Daizen. 2004. *Zen War Stories*. London: Routledge.

Vroom, Henk. 2011. 'On Blasphemy: An Analysis'. *Ars Disputandi Supplement* 5: 75–94.

Wallace, B. Alan, ed. *Buddhism and Science: Breaking New Ground*. New York: Columbia University Press.

Walshe, Maurice. 1995. *The Long Discourses of the Buddha: A Translation of the Dīgha Nikāya*. Boston: Wisdom Publications.

Walton, Matthew J. 2013. 'The "Wages of Burman-ness:" Ethnicity and Burman Privilege in Contemporary Myanmar'. *Journal of Contemporary Asia* 43 (1): 1–27.

Walton, Matthew J. 2015. 'Monks in Politics, Monks in the World: Buddhist Activism in Contemporary Myanmar'. *Social Research: An International Quarterly* 82 (2): 507–30.

Walton, Matthew J. 2016. 'Buddhist Monks and Democratic Politics in Contemporary Myanmar'. In *Buddhism and the Political Process*, ed. Hiroko Kawanami, 56–77. Basingstoke: Palgrave Macmillan.

Walton, Matthew J. 2017a. *Buddhism, Politics and Political Thought in Myanmar*. Cambridge: Cambridge University Press.

Walton, Matthew J. 2017b. 'Buddhism, Nationalism, and Governance'. In *The Oxford Handbook of Contemporary Buddhism*, ed. Michael Jerryson, 532–45. New York: Oxford University Press.

Walton, Matthew J. and Michael Jerryson. 2016. 'The Authorization of Religio-Political Discourse: Monks and Buddhist Activism in Contemporary Myanmar and Beyond'. *Politics & Religion* 9 (4): 794–814.

Walton, Matthew J. and Susan Hayward. 2014. 'Contesting Buddhist Narratives: Democratization, Nationalism, and Communal Violence in Myanmar'. *Policy Studies*, 71. Honolulu: East-West Center.

Walton, Matthew J. and Melyn McKay and Khin Mar Mar Kyi. 2015. 'Women and Myanmar's "Religious Protection Laws"'. *The Review of Faith & International Affairs* 13 (4): 36–49.

Warder, Anthony K. 1970. *Indian Buddhism*. Delhi: Motilal Banarsidass.

Watts, Jonathan S., ed. 2009. *Rethinking Karma: The Dharma of Social Justice*. Chiang Mai: Silkworm Books.

Weber, Max. 1958. *The Religion of India: The Sociology of Hinduism and Buddhism*. Trans. and ed. Hans Gerth and Don Martindale. Glencoe, IL: The Free Press.

Weiner, Matthew. 2003. 'Maha Ghosananda as a Contemplative Social Activist'. In *Action Dharma: New Studies in Engaged Buddhism*, ed. Christopher S. Queen, Charles Prebish and Damien Keown, 110–25. London: RoutledgeCurzon.

Welbon, Guy. 1968. *The Buddhist Nirvāna and Its Western Interpreters*. Chicago: University of Chicago Press.

West, Candace and Don H. Zimmerman. 1987. 'Doing Gender'. *Gender and Society* 1 (2): 125–51.

Westerhoff, Jan. 2017. 'Buddhism without Reincarnation? Examining the Prospects of a "Naturalized" Buddhism'. In *A Mirror Is for Reflection: Understanding Buddhist Ethics*, ed. Jake H Davis, 146–65. New York: Oxford University Press.

Whalen-Bridge, John and Kitiarsa, Pattana, eds 2013. *Buddhism, Modernity, and the State in Asia*. New York: Palgrave Macmillan.

Whalen-Bridge, John. 2014. *Tibet on Fire: Buddhism, Protest, and the Rhetoric of Self-Immolation*. London: Palgrave Macmillan.

White, Cecile Holmes. 1989. 'Engaged Buddhism: Monk Tells How to Put Feet onto Faith'. *Houston Chronicle*, 25 March.

Williams, Angel Kyodo, Lama Rod Owens and Jasmine Syedullah. 2016. *Radical Dharma: Talking Race, Love, and Liberation*. Berkeley: North Atlantic Books.

Williams, Paul. 2009. *Mahāyāna Buddhism: The Doctrinal Foundations*, 2nd edn. London: Routledge.

Willis, Jan. 2020. *Dharma Matters: Women, Race, and Tantra*. Boston: Wisdom Publications.

Willis, Janice D. 1985. 'Nuns and Benefactresses: The Roles of Women in the Development of Buddhism'. In *Women, Religion and Social Change*, ed. Yvonne Yazbeck Haddad and Ellison Banks Findly, 59–86. Albany: State University of New York Press.

Wilson, Jeff. 2012. 'All Beings Are Equally Embraced by Amida Buddha: Jodo Shinshu Buddhism and Same-Sex Marriage in the United States'. *Journal of Global Buddhism* 13: 31–59.

Wilson, Jeff. 2019. 'Blasphemy as Bhāvana: Anti-Christianity in a New Buddhist Movement'. *Nova Religio* 22 (3): 8–35.

Wright, Dale S. 2004. 'Critical Questions Towards a Naturalized Concept of Karma in Buddhism'. *Journal of Buddhist Ethics* 11: 78–93.

Wright, Robert. 2017. *Why Buddhism is True: The Science and Philosophy of Meditation and Enlightenment*. New York: Simon & Schuster Press.

Wynne, Alexander. 2015. *Buddhism: An Introduction*. New York: I.B. Tauris.

Yancy, Georg. and Emily McRae, eds 2019. *Buddhism and Whiteness: Critical Reflections*. London: Lexington Books.

Yao, Yu Shuang. 2012. *Taiwan's Tzu Chi as Engaged Buddhism: Origins, Organization, Appeal and Social Impact*. Leiden: Brill.

Yarnall, Thomas Freeman. 2000. 'Engaged Buddhism: New and Improved!(?) Made in the U.S.A. of Asian Materials'. *Journal of Buddhist Ethics*, 1–88.

Yarnall, Thomas Freeman. 2003. 'Engaged Buddhism: New and Improved!(?) Made in the U. S. A: of Asian Materials'. In *Action Dharma: New Studies in Engaged Buddhism*, ed. Christopher S. Queen, Charles Prebish and Damien Keown, 286–344. London: Routledge Curzon.

Yip, Andrew K. T. and Sharon Smith. 2010. 'Queerness and Sangha Exploring Buddhist Lives'. In *Queer Spiritual Spaces: Sexuality and Sacred Places*, ed. Kath Browne, Sally R. Munt and Andrew Kam-Tuck Yip, 111–38. Burlington, VT: Ashgate.

Yoon, Young-Hae and Sherwin Jones. 2014. 'Ecology, Dharma and Direct Action: A Brief Survey of Contemporary Eco-Buddhist Activism in Korea'. *Buddhist Studies Review* 31 (2): 293–311.

Zarni, Mann. 2015. *The Irrawaddy*, 2 June.

Zimmerman, Michael. 2006. 'Only a Fool Becomes a King: Buddhist Stances on Punishment'. In *Buddhism and Violence*, ed. Michael Zimmermann, 213–42. Lumbini: International Research Institute.

Zwilling, Leonard. 1992. 'Homosexuality as Seen in Indian Buddhist Texts'. In *Buddhism, Sexuality and Gender*, ed. José Cabezón, 203–14. Albany: State University of New York Press.

Zwilling, Leonard. 1998. 'Avoidance and Exclusion: Same-Sex Sexuality in Indian Buddhism'. In *Queer Dharma: Voices of Gay Buddhists* (vol. 1), ed. Winston Leyland, 45–54. San Francisco, CA: Gay Sunshine Press.

Index

NOTE: Page references in *italics* refer to figures.